HOW, WHEN, AND WHY
MODERN ART CAME TO NEW YORK

HOW, WHEN, AND WHY
MODERN ART CAME TO NEW YORK

Marius de Zayas

edited by
Francis M. Naumann

The MIT Press
Cambridge, Massachusetts
London, England

This book was set in Geometric, Perpetua, and Bembo by Graphic Composition, Inc., and was printed and bound in the United States of America.

Library of Congress Cataloging-in-Publication Data

Zayas, Marius de.

   How, when, and why modern art came to New York / Marius de Zayas ; edited by Francis M. Naumann.

      p.   cm.

   Includes bibliographical references.

   ISBN 0-262-04153-7 (hc : alk. paper)

   1. Art, Modern—20th century—Marketing.   2. Art patronage—New York (N.Y.) 3. Art appreciation—New York (N.Y.)   I. Naumann, Francis M.   II. Title.

N6490.Z365   1996

709′.747′.109041—dc20   95-49910

                                                                            CIP

CONTENTS

1 *Marius de Zayas at "291,"* 1913. Photograph by Alfred Stieglitz.

INTRODUCTION

In April 1916, Marius de Zayas began an article in defense of modern art with the simple statement "All art is composed of two elements, the fact and the idea."[1] During the second decade of the twentieth century, de Zayas and his good friend and associate Alfred Stieglitz did more to bring these two elements of art to the public's attention—the fact and the idea—than any other men of their generation. The numerous exhibitions they organized, either jointly or in their separate galleries, exposed the New York art world to the highest quality of modern works available on their side of the Atlantic. While Stieglitz's inspiring talks stimulated the many visitors to his gallery, de Zayas's writings were among the first publications in the United States to offer the bewildered American public an intellectual basis for understanding the new art.

Subsequent histories of this period have widely acknowledged Stieglitz's pioneering efforts in the promotion and acceptance of modern art in America. But, until recently, de Zayas's position has remained relatively obscure, partly because of his desire to maintain a low profile and partly because his modesty prevented him from extolling his own accomplishments.[2] He preferred letting the artworks he believed in speak for themselves, while the publication of his theories on the evolution of modern art quietly provided guidance for those who sought it.

Marius de Zayas Enriquez y Calmet was born to wealthy and aristocratic parents in Veracruz, Mexico, on March 13, 1880.[3] His father, Rafael de Zayas (1848–1932), was a noted historian, orator, and lawyer, named poet laureate of his country. He established two newspapers in Veracruz, and it was in providing illustrations for these publications that two of his sons, Marius and Rafael, received their first artistic training. In 1906, with the artist Carlo de Fornaro, they drew caricatures for Mexico City's leading newspaper, *El diario* (founded and edited by the American-born social critic Benjamin de Casseres). The de Zayas newspapers adopted an editorial policy strongly in support of democratic principles. But in 1907 their opposition to the dictatorial principles of Porfirio Díaz forced the family to flee their homeland and settle in New York.

Shortly after his arrival in the United States, Marius de Zayas accepted a position on the staff of the *New York Evening World,* where he quickly established a reputation for his witty caricatures of the city's leading celebrities in the theater, dance, and society. Typical of his work from this period is the illustration that accompanied

2 Marius de Zayas, *"Boulevardiers" of New York,* 1910.

an article on the Black Hand Fakirs' Annual Costume Ball, an event that reportedly attracted some eight hundred art students and teachers. De Zayas's quick but keenly perceptive line comically captures the most notable personalities who attended: William Merritt Chase, James Montgomery Flagg, John Nilson Laurvik, Ernest Lawson, Everett Shinn, and Alfred Stieglitz.

It was de Zayas's creative work that first brought him to the attention of Stieglitz and those who congregated at the Little Gallery of the Photo-Secession, or "291," as it had become known from its Fifth Avenue address.[4] In January 1909, Stieglitz gave de Zayas his first public showing, which included caricatures of New York's social set and of members of the Photo-Secession. Apart from the praise of de Zayas's friend Benjamin de Casseres,[5] the show failed to attract the attention of New York's generally conservative press. But de Zayas's next exhibition, which ran for more than six months—from April through November 1910—was, in terms of attendance and critical response, one of the most successful events ever held at "291." On a large wooden platform, de Zayas arranged some hundred free-standing cardboard caricatures of New York's most prominent inhabitants strolling up and down Fifth Avenue in front of the Plaza Hotel. This elaborate dioramic tableau attracted crowds to the cramped premises of "291," and one reviewer noted that lines of waiting spectators often reached far into the hallway of the building. This same reporter congratulated de Zayas for having created "the only spectacle of the season that escaped without a single unkind word from any critic."[6]

In October 1910, while this exhibition was still on view, de Zayas took his first extended trip to Paris, where he remained for almost a year, functioning in part as emissary and talent scout for Stieglitz. The city must have been familiar to the young artist from his student days, but the new art scene took him completely by surprise. On October 28, 1910, two weeks after his arrival, de Zayas informed Stieglitz that he had spent most of his time visiting museums and had already been to see the Salon d'Automne four times.[7] Although he claimed that the important work at "291" prepared him to view the exhibition with "open eyes," he was baffled by Cubism, which he referred to as a "deadly movement." What bothered him most was a painting by Metzinger, whose work, he told Stieglitz, "is absolutely consequent with his theory . . . he sees everything geometrically." In his published review of this exhibition, de Zayas admitted that at first he understood nothing: "I looked, but did not see," he informed his American readers. "It seemed to me as if I were in the Tower of Babel painting, in which all the languages of technique, color and subjects, were spoken in an incoherent and absurd manner, and I began to surmise that this Salon was nothing but a charge d'atelier, peculiar to the humorous artist."[8] He went on to say that he felt Cubism was "more reactionary than evolutionary" and wondered if anything would ever come of this new movement. In his letter to Stieglitz he also added that he had been informed that Metzinger was actually "an imitator," and that "the real article is a Spaniard," whose name he did not recall.

From such inauspicious beginnings, it is remarkable to realize that less than three months after he wrote these words, de Zayas would not only get to meet this Spaniard—who was, of course, Picasso—but would also become so familiar with his work that he would write the first significant article on Picasso to appear in the American press.[9] Because of their common language, de Zayas was able to conduct extensive, in-depth interviews with the Spanish painter, and his article became the first publication to record Picasso's views of his own work. From Paris, de Zayas also helped to arrange the first Picasso exhibition held in the United States, a show of watercolors and drawings at "291" in April 1911.

It was also during this sojourn in Paris, perhaps through his friendship with Picasso, that de Zayas fully recognized the importance of African art and its influence on the development of modern art. In another letter to Stieglitz, he even remarked that "some of the sculptors have merely copied it [African art], without taking the trouble to translate it into French."[10] He went on to propose an exhibition of African sculpture, a show that materialized several years later (in November 1914). His interests in the relation of primitive to modern art continued throughout his career, and in 1916 he published a book on the subject, entitled *African Negro Art: Its Influence on Modern Art*.[11]

Returning to New York in the fall of 1911, de Zayas renewed his friendship with the group at "291" and continued his work as a caricaturist for the New York papers. By this time, however, he had developed a new, noncommercial, more abstract style of caricature. Already in Paris he had informed Stieglitz of his dissatisfaction with the traditional methods of caricature and said that he was working on a new idea for what he called the "philosophical collection." This new approach culminated in the drawings exhibited in his last but most important showing at "291," in April–May 1913. Caricatures based on the subjects' physical appearance, which he called "relative" (see figures 4 and 98), were hung in the company of the more abstract, or "absolute," portraits (see figures 64 and 97), which, according to de Zayas, were based on a deeper analysis of the subjects' "intrinsic expression." Although a complete understanding of these caricatures can be realized only through the detailed examination of de Zayas's writings, they can be said to represent a highly personal formula for the assimilation of Cubist form with the most advanced theories of abstraction.[12] De Zayas's theories on the origins and evolution of modern art periodically appeared in the pages of *Camera Work,* and in 1913 he and Paul Haviland wrote one of the first books on modern art to appear in the United States, *A Study of the Modern Evolution of Plastic Expression*. Although de Zayas had once confided in Stieglitz that he wished someone with greater literary aptitude would undertake the job of writing about contemporary art,[13] his publications remain, as William Homer noted, among the "first serious attempts to deal with the central problems of modern art."[14]

3 "At the 'Black Hand Fakir's Eighteenth Annual Stab,'" *New York Evening World*, April 18, 1909. Caricatures by Marius de Zayas.

In the spring of 1914 de Zayas returned to France, where he renewed his friendship with Francis Picabia (whom he probably first met in New York at the time of the Armory Show), who immediately introduced him to the circle of artists and writers connected with the avant-garde magazine *Les soirées de Paris,* particularly its editor, Guillaume Apollinaire. Resuming his correspondence with Stieglitz, de Zayas reported also having met Gertrude Stein, Alice B. Toklas, and, on a trip to London, George Bernard Shaw, Roger Fry, and Alvin Langdon Coburn. In his letters to Stieglitz, he repeatedly stressed the importance in establishing a closer contact with the avant-garde ideas and activities of the French capital. He proposed new exhibitions of the most recent work of Picasso and Picabia, and suggested the first American showings of Rousseau, Braque, and Marie Laurencin.

When the war broke out in 1914, de Zayas was forced to make a hasty return to New York. He arrived at the piers not only with a cargo of works for exhibition at "291" but also with the anxious desire to incorporate in his own work the newest artistic theories to which he had been introduced by his Parisian friends. He was particularly impressed by Simultanism in literature, which, he had informed Stieglitz in the summer of 1914, was the "last word in art in Paris."[15] Simultanism stressed the interrelationship of all things, physical and emotional, and led to the development of Apollinaire's *idéogrammes* and de Zayas's most radical approach toward caricature, the "psychotype," where typographical characters merge with geometric shapes to form an abstract portrait (see figure 90).[16] These newest experiments were published in the avant-garde periodical he helped found and edit, *291*.

In an effort to make his activities and those of his associates known to a larger, more international audience, de Zayas sent numerous copies of this vanguard publication to friends in Europe. In the fall of 1916, he entered into correspondence with Tristan Tzara, one of the founders of the Dada movement in Zurich. They immediately began an exchange of their respective publications, and, thereby, de Zayas was singly responsible for bringing the first notices of Dada to American shores.[17] Because de Zayas had earlier written an article in *Camera Work* that began with the explosive words "Art is dead," by which he meant that traditional attitudes toward art were no longer viable, and because of his early correspondence with Tzara, historians have tended to include de Zayas as a member of the Dada group. But the avowed nihilism of this movement is something he surely would have rejected, both as an artist and as a theoretician. Adolf Wolff, the anarchist sculptor who exhibited his work at the Modern Gallery, probably expressed it best when he inscribed a copy of his published poems with the words "To Marius de Zayas, who said art is dead and proved that it isn't."[18]

De Zayas had long planned to write a book on the introduction of modern art to America. The October 1922 issue of *Littérature* advertised such a work in two volumes by de Zayas to be entitled "L'art moderne à New York." But in 1951 Bernard Karpel reported in the bibliography of Robert Motherwell's *Dada Painters and Poets* that de Zayas was apparently still working on this publication.[19] As de Zayas's introduction to "How, When, and Why Modern Art Came to New York" suggests, he prepared his manuscript (datable to the late 1940s) at the request of Alfred H. Barr, Jr., then director of the Museum of Modern Art in New York.[20] At the time de Zayas compiled this account, little had been written on this subject. As he explains, his work consists largely in the citation of numerous press reviews. And because most of the newspapers from this period were not indexed, in many cases these important documents resurface here for the first time since their publication. Moreover, the photographs de Zayas selected to illustrate this account specify which works were shown in the exhibitions he discusses; often the catalogues, if any appeared, listed the works shown only by vague titles. In addition, many of the photographs represent works that have been lost or destroyed since the time of their exhibition.[21]

De Zayas's work on *291* (the magazine), his further relations with Stieglitz, and his establishment of the Modern Gallery, are best told by de Zayas himself in the account that follows. (A summation of his activities after this period is included in the afterword, and a list of the exhibitions he organized at the Modern and De Zayas Galleries is provided in appendix A.)

4 Marius de Zayas, *Rodin and Steichen* (from *Camera Work* [October 1914]).

HOW, WHEN, AND WHY
MODERN ART CAME TO NEW YORK

Marius de Zayas

My Dear Mr. Barr,

Many years ago I promised you I would write an account of how, when and why modern art came to New York. I do not need to apologize for the delay because it is of no consequence, and undoubtedly you have forgotten my promise. I have gone to work with the documents I have to help my recollections. Unfortunately these documents are scanty and I cannot be accurate as to exact dates and other items. Just the same, the sequence of events is correct.

I have avoided, as much as possible, expressing personal opinions, being as I am, prejudiced in favor of modern art. I wanted to stick to facts, and to do it I have used freely the criticisms published in the press for each of the exhibitions I mention, with the exception of a few. They have the advantage, from the historical point of view, of giving the personal opinion of critics of different art creeds, reflecting in a general way the opinion of the public, and of quoting the ideas or theories of the artist whose work they reviewed.

Modern art, to become, let us say, popular in New York took eleven years of hard labor, from 1908 to 1918. These years can be divided into three periods: the first under the name of Photo-Secession; the middle period, when "291," instead of meaning only the number of a building, became a symbol, the symbol of something in which each individual person believed; and finally the period of the Modern Gallery.

In 1905, Alfred Stieglitz opened in New York a little gallery under the name of "Photo-Secession" with the purpose of exhibiting pictorial photography. The "photo" part of the name given to the gallery stands for photographers and not for light, and the "secession" part meant that a group of photographers had, led by Stieglitz, left the "Camera Club" which apparently did not stand for pictorial photography.

The Photo-Secession galleries were on the top floor, or rather in the attic, of an old and decrepit building at number 291 Fifth Avenue. The floor space was 15 feet by 15 feet, most of it occupied by a large box covered with burlap on which always stood a big bronze bowl full of dry branches and pussy willows, a decoration characteristic of the epoch.

Prominent among the Secessionists was Edward Steichen, already a famous photographer aspiring also to be a famous painter, an aspiration which took him to Paris shortly after the opening of the Little Galleries. While in Paris, Steichen cultivated the friendship of Rodin and Matisse, and as a result of this, the Photo-Secession began a series of exhibitions of the work of modern artists.

RODIN

In 1907, Stieglitz started his mission as a promoter of modern art with an exhibition of fifty-eight drawings by Rodin carefully selected by the sculptor himself and by Steichen. At that time, Rodin was still considered a modernist, an innovator, and a revolutionary. His sculptures were known all over the world, but not his drawings. Steichen must have seen in them all the elements needed to stir up things in New York. And they did. With this exhibition the Photo-Secession became the key which opened the doors of New York to modern art.

New York was under the spell of moral rectitude when the first art exhibition in the Photo-Secession gallery took place with drawings by Rodin (1908).

> The exhibition of drawings by Rodin . . . is of unusual artistic and human interest. It is also a challenge to the prurient prudery of our puritanism. As one looks at these amazing records of unabashed observations of an artist who is also a man, one marvels that this little gallery has not long since been raided by the blind folly that guards our morals.
>
> (J. N. Laurvik in the Times)

> Living in a community which insists that even babies must wear clothes, not for warmth and health, but in the interest of what we are pleased to call morality, Rodin for years has tried to supply the lack of nudity which was visible on every hand in Old Greece and Recent Japan, by keeping his studio at the temperature the Princess Pauline Bonaparte would have approved, and by causing a number of persons to loaf about in that balmy air without a stitch upon them.
>
> (Charles DeKay in the Evening Post)

5 Auguste Rodin, *Nude with Drapery.*

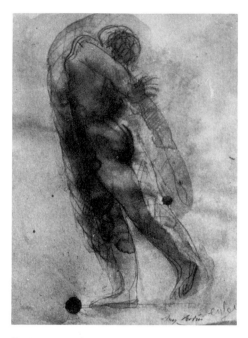

7 Auguste Rodin, *Standing Nude.*

6 Auguste Rodin, *Nude with Shawl.*

8 Auguste Rodin, *Horseman,* 1889.

9 Henri Matisse, *Reclining Male Nude.*

10 Henri Matisse, *Seated Nude Leaning on Her Arm,*
c. 1907.

11 Henri Matisse, *Decorative Figure*, 1906. Bronze.

12 Henri Matisse, *Reclining Nude: I*, 1907. Bronze.

So much for the moral atmosphere. As to the comments of the critics from the artistic viewpoints, here are some of them:

> *These jottings (Rodin's drawings)—for they are no more than that—are indeed the merest suggestions or impressions, working notes rather of movement than of form, full of character in a way, too, but most loosely indicated, with now and then a thin wash spread over them so carelessly indeed, that not even a contour has been adhered to . . .*
>
> *(Arthur Hoeber in the* Globe*)*

> *Strange are the things that are done in a great man's name under the beclouding influence of "art." This moral reflexion is induced by the opening of an exhibition of fifty-eight drawings by Auguste Rodin in the Photo-Secession gallery. . . . Stripped of all "art" atmosphere they stand as drawings of nude women in attitudes that may interest the artist who drew them but which are not for public exhibitions.*
>
> *(W. B. McCormick in the* Press*)*

> *Considered as a kind of studio driftwood they are of interest to students of the French sculptor. . . . This skill, however, is discounted for the connoisseur of draftmanship by the scrawling and sometimes meaningless touch of the artist. His sense of beauty rarely peeps forth. . . . They have not the beauty or the character for which the fragments of pure technique left by a master are cherished.*
>
> *(Royal Cortissoz in the* Tribune*)*

The comment on this exhibition written by the editor of *Camera Work* (possibly Stieglitz himself) gives information about how the public took it:

> *In art matters the month of January was very alive in New York; several important exhibitions took place simultaneously, but none attracted more or probably as much attention as that of the Rodin drawings at the little galleries of the Photo-Secession. During the three weeks these were shown connoisseurs, art-lovers of every type, and students from far and near flocked to the garret of "291." It was an unusual assemblage—even for that place—that gathered there to pay homage to one of the greatest artists of all time. It may be said to the credit of New York—provincial as it undoubtedly is in art matters generally—that in this instance a truer and more spontaneous appreciation could nowhere have been given to these remarkable drawings. In this exhibition an opportunity is, for the first time, given to the American public to study drawings by Rodin. The fifty-eight now showing were selected for this purpose by Rodin and Mr. Steichen.*
>
> *(Camera Work, April 1908)*

We take this as a true account of the success of the exhibition. It had all the elements to succeed. Rodin was at that time more advertised than a moving picture star is today. He was actually considered "one of the greatest artists of all time."

This exhibition which was advertised by a few critics as "immoral," was the first of Rodin drawings to take place in New York. It was an unknown phase of the popular artist. It was, indeed, very wise and clever of Steichen and Stieglitz to have started their art exhibition with such drawings—the Photo-Secession was put on the map as a progressive, radical, educational and immoral institution.

We must also remember that at that time the radicals, the rebels, the rejected ones by official art bodies, were artists like Robert Henri, Glackens, Sloan, Luks, etc., followers of the Impressionists.

The Rodin drawings exhibition started the ball rolling towards real modern art. Whether or not it was premeditated, this exhibition was a good beginning, an excellent "aperitif" for what New York had to swallow subsequently. There were two exhibitions of Rodin's drawings.

MATISSE

Matisse was unknown in New York. In 1907, after the Rodin exhibition, the Photo-Secession held the first show of Matisse's drawings and two years later a second exhibition of his drawings and sculptures took place. Matisse was the first Modern-ist who confronted the New York art public. He was soon declared the source of evil from which came all crimes against the sacred canons of academism. There was not yet any other artist to blame for the contagious bacilli of modernism. Of the first Matisse exhibition I have no records.[1]

Mr. Harrington in the *New York Herald* wrote about the second Matisse exhibition:

> As it was the fashion several years ago to call almost everything which was different from the Academic "Impressionistic" so now the tendency is to apply the name of Matisse to anything which is not understood.

An anonymous writer said in the issue of April 1910 of *Camera Work:*

> Coming at a time when the name of Matisse is being used indiscriminately to explain the influence to which any painter at present may have suc-cumbed whose work is unacademic, the exhibition of Matisse drawings and photographs of his paintings . . . was most opportune. . . . The exhibi-tion included drawings, etchings, watercolors, lithographs and one paint-ing. . . . "Influenced by Matisse" has become the common explanation of anything that seems queer, any departure from the old standards of artistic representation. The New York public was given a good chance for compari-son and study in the exhibition which followed the work of some of his sup-posed American disciples.

The exhibition of the "supposed American disciples" mentioned above was of the work of John Marin, Alfred Maurer, Max Weber, D. Putnam Brinley and Edward Steichen (1910). About this exhibition Mr. James Huneker said in the *New York Sun:*

> *We picked out Max Weber from the rest of the revolutionists in the Little Gallery of the Secession. Mr. Weber caught our eye (collided with it would be more truthful) with his dainty exposure of three ladies in search of the mad naked summer night. That their eyes are like casks, their hips massive as moons, their faces vitriolic in expression is beside the mark. The chief thing that interested us was to note the influence of Matisse.*

In spite of his great knowledge of the French poets of the 19th century, Mr. Huneker picked upon the wrong artist. Guy du Bois in the *New York American* did not fail to see Matisse all over the walls either. He said:

> *It is difficult to retain even a semblance of the individuality so important to an artist's fame when one's mode of expression is tagged with another man's name. There are "followers of Matisse" among the young men who exhibit during this week at the Photo-Secession gallery, and one may not but associate them directly and insistently with the usurper. What individuality they have is immediately merged, literally swamped by the overpowering suggestion in the big letters of the name of Matisse.*

About Matisse's own work Mr. Townsend said in the *American Art News:*

> *It is heresy, from accepted art standards, to admire or even see anything but fantastic and often vulgar vagaries in the so-called art of Matisse, and equally heresy, from the viewpoint of his band of followers, to decry him and his work. Around Matisse now wages the war of the suffragists and anti-suffragists, the vivisectionists and anti-vivisectionists of the art world—and he calmly pursues his path and is getting an enormous amount of advertising out of it all.*

The sculptures by Matisse did not make the conservative critics supremely happy, as you will see by the following criticisms:

> *The things that the Frenchman, Henri Matisse, has done in painting and drawing—and he has, curious to relate, a substantial number of followers—are as nothing to the concrete form his sculpture takes on, a display of which is now on view at the galleries of the Photo-Secession, 291 Fifth Avenue, which Alfred Stieglitz has arranged for the delectation of the cult, a cult, too, that is growing daily. Some of them, to put it very mildly, seem like the work of a mad man, and it is hard to be patient with these impossible travesties on the human form. There are attenuated figures representing women seriously offered here which makes one grieve that men should be found who can by any chance regard them with other than feelings of horrible repulsion, and their significance is quite beyond the ken of those not*

13 *Matisse in His Studio*, 1909. Photograph by Edward Steichen.

inoculated with the virus of post-impressionism. Indeed, it is quite unbelievable that sane men can justify these on any possible grounds. Yet, as seriously minded a man as Roger Fry, lately connected with the Metropolitan Museum of Art, takes this same Matisse seriously and has so expressed himself in black and white under his own signature. . . . It all seems decadent, unhealthy, certainly unreal, like some dreadful nightmare, and it is depressing to a degree.

(*Arthur Hoeber in the* New York Globe)

After Rodin—what? Surely not Matisse. We can see the power and individuality of Matisse as a painter, particularly as a draughtsman, but in modelling he produces gooseflesh.

(*James Huneker in the* New York Sun)

This is the way in which Matisse made his appearance in New York as a painter and as a sculptor. If the meaning of his work did not penetrate very deeply into the public mind, his interpretation of form and his treatment of color served at least to differentiate the academic from the non-academic art. That was at any rate a beginning.

THE CRITICS

Of course, I have only quoted the critics who were antagonistic to modern art. There were others who were intelligently favorable to it and still others who were sort of neutral.

It was officially stated in *Camera Work,* the organ of the Photo-Secession, that the second Matisse exhibition attracted over four thousand visitors. That, I am certain, was due to the adverse criticism.

The most conservative art critics at that time were Mr. Royal Cortissoz and Mr. Arthur Hoeber. Both honest gentlemen, loyal to their principles, and unable more than unwilling to see any possible salvation outside of the strict rules of the academy. They both made a very effective propaganda for modern art.

Here is an example of the attitude of an academic of that time and of his sensitiveness to Beauty.

In the *New York Tribune,* Mr. Royal Cortissoz wrote about an exhibition of photographs by Paul Strand:

At the Photo-Secession gallery, usually devoted to the vagaries of artists of the various modern "issues," are some noteworthy photographs of New York and other places by Paul Strand. This photographer has a good sense of composition and some of the pictures have a remarkably fine color suggestiveness in their tones. He has, too, the faculty for seeing possibilities of beauty in the most commonplace objects and places. In the snowy street corner the figures are well placed, and the top of a lamp-post at the bottom of the picture is a telling note. He has made splendid use of the line of foam against the rocks in the photograph of Niagara River below the falls. The base of the falls is veiled in the cloud of spray which forms the background, and the spots of dark are supplied by the pile of rocks on the left and the "Maid of the Mist" pursuing her valiant way on the right. It is a lovely photograph. The winding stream with a leafless willow in the foreground is exquisite in tone and texture. The artist has made a thing of great beauty of a railroad yard. The snow-covered hillock with its indefinite bushes, is a silvery picture of surpassing loveliness.

I have emphasized the "cliches" used by a critic who is only sensitive and moved by beauty. How could he use that sweet vocabulary in criticizing a Matisse or a Picasso, etc.? How could his brain, shaped to see loveliness, beauty, exquisiteness, good sense of composition, figures well placed etc. etc., see those things in modern art? It was physiologically impossible. But his criticism of modern art was nonetheless effective and constructive because he did his best to prove that those things did not appear in it, and therefore predisposed his reader not to look for them.

Mr. Arthur Hoeber who wrote for *The Globe* had a more modest intellect than Mr. Cortissoz. He also was more closed to anything but his art creed. He confessed his creed in what he wrote for the special number of *Camera Work* devoted to the question, "What does '291' mean?" (July 1914):

To me, the years have brought no order out of the chaos of the new men you have exploited. . . . Their utter disregard of form or beauty as I understand it, their stupidity in the arrangement of composition lines are all things my art notions rebel at, recoil from in disgust. . . . No, Alfred, pleasant as it has been to drop in the rooms and listen occasionally to a discussion, I have yet to find inspiring things on the walls in the way of paintings, or in sculptures on the shelves . . .

CÉZANNE

After Rodin and Matisse, Cézanne came next. I regret not to be able to give an account of how this artist was treated by the critics when in 1910 they were confronted with the first Cézanne exhibition.[2] Charles H. Caffin gives us an idea of their attitude when he wrote a "Note on Paul Cézanne" in the April–July number of *Camera Work* (1910):

Through the medium of the Little Galleries of the Photo-Secession, New Yorkers have had a chance of tasting Paul Cézanne's work in water colors. Since it was the first occasion of his work being shown in this country, the exhibition embarrassed the professional writers in the Press but interested a goodly portion of the public, both artists and laymen. As for the

14 Paul Cézanne, *Le château noir,* 1900–1904.

15 Paul Cézanne, *Toits de l'Estaque,* 1878–1881.

writers, they are in the state of the fuglemen, who are swept aside when there is anything actively adoing.

This exhibition was also due to the activities of Steichen who selected the watercolors with the collaboration of Félix Fénéon, writer, art critic, and head of the modern art department at Bernheim-Jeune and Co., who was the friend of Seurat. Fénéon lent the watercolors. Although they were for sale at very low prices (from one to two hundred dollars) not one was sold. A few years later, the Montross Galleries held another exhibition of Cézanne's watercolors, most of them being the same ones shown at the Photo-Secession. A few were sold at relatively high prices.

In 1916, the art critics saw Cézanne from an entirely different angle. His paintings were already selling at the art dealers. In that year the Modern Gallery exhibited two of the most important Cézannes which came from Vollard's cellar and had never before been shown to the public.

I mentioned that the pictures came from Vollard because it was no small triumph to get a picture from him before the time he had decided to sell it. The paintings he had from one artist had to be sold chronologically according to their intrinsic importance. One had to invoke and propitiate the spirits of Machiavelli and others to help perform the miracle of getting him to sell. One had to listen and enjoy his innumerable stories of all kinds for several days. He had to be absolutely sure that the picture he sold was leaving France and he had to be paid in cash, preferably in gold, and the picture taken then and there. His methods were unshakable. It took me two years to make him decide to sell the *Joueurs de Cartes,* the largest, if not the best, picture Cézanne ever painted. I had several subscribers willing to pay the price and present it to the Metropolitan Museum. The price he gave me was $15,000 with an option of one month. I offered it to the Metropolitan in the name of the subscribers, but the curator of paintings told me that although they would be glad to receive the painting they could not promise to put it on exhibition as it was against the rules of the Museum. The option was cancelled. Vollard was relieved and the painting was sold that same year at a much more substantial price.

ACADEMICIANS AND CÉZANNE

A retired academician was observed not long since working himself into a frantic state of wrath, and surely no one who learns the facts will withhold sympathy. Going into a gallery where he thought that nothing worse than Manet would ever appear, he found a Cézanne! Thereupon he repeated the cut and dried formulae that he had learned in Paris twenty years ago against modern art in general and Cézanne in particular. At that point he discovered that the Cézanne was sold—sold from the very wall on which he never expected to see such a sacrilegious sight!

Of course, it did not mean to the retired and angry academician that Cézanne was an artist merely because his pictures now sell on Fifth Avenue. It meant something much worse than that, it meant that more Cézannes will come to take the place of those that are now selling. For Fifth Avenue will have that which will sell! It meant that there will never be an end to this mad Cézanne epidemic, that America is as bad as Europe, as decadent, as misled, as gullible! Will you withhold your sympathy from an academician who after fighting against these dire meanings for twenty-five years can no longer find peace even on Fifth Avenue, always the last market to be captured by modern art?

Two impressive paintings, "Le Bouquet de Fleurs" and "Le Château Noir," as well as two water-colors and a lithograph, were placed on view this week at the Modern Gallery, 500 Fifth Avenue. They richly supplement the work of Cézanne, now at the disposal of the public, including the altogether beautiful still life that has been added to the Montross collection. The humility of soul which was one of the elements of Cézanne's greatness is made even more evident by the "Bouquet de Fleurs." It is profound, it has an air of permanence. The more obvious traits of Cézanne are not those which mark this specimen, and it is not, therefore, the type of Cézanne which has been most imitated. For one reason, to imitate it would be altogether too difficult for the easy methods of the average imitator.

No word analysis will ever catch more than a breath from this painting. It defies word analysis, as all great painting does. The best that can be said is a plea to every one who wishes to enjoy it to go and see it. Yet though so abundantly enjoyable, it is possible to imagine it even finer, to imagine that Cézanne did not leave it in its happiest stage, that he lost something of its earlier bloom in the persistency of his search.

Hardly less important is the landscape opposite, though this too is a little heavier than Cézanne at his best. It is, however, a painting that should always be at the disposal of the artists but it should be balanced by other works in which the master expressed himself more lucidly. To see these two paintings only would give but a limited idea of Cézanne, yet either one of them would be welcome additions to most collections of his work. (Evening Post, January 16, 1916)

MORE OF CÉZANNE

Two oil paintings of first-magnitude importance, two choice landscape evocations in water color, and a lithograph of a group of boys bathing which is a classic in its way, make up the latest and third consecutive Cézanne exhibition viewed by large and various congregations of New Yorkers within the last few weeks. It is at the Modern Gallery, No. 500 Fifth Avenue, at the intersection of Forty-Second Street—a place not to be discovered without some careful search, as it is on a mezzanine floor, reached by tortuous stairway from the street entrance, and only a casual unexpected stopping place for the lift. Once inside, however, one need not be surprised to find

16 Paul Cézanne, *Le bouquet de fleurs*, 1900–1903.

almost anybody there, gazing in tense silence upon cryptic pictures, or looking askance at horrific voodoo images from darkest Africa.

In addition to Messrs. De Zayas and Picabia, kindred brooding spirits who always pervade the place, the Christian Science Monitor's correspondent noted within a single quarter of an hour three such well-known artists as Robert Henri, Joseph Stella and Walt Kuhn. Each and all thought Cézanne "great," though they could in no way agree when it came to specifications. On one point, however, they were unanimous, and that was that the Old Man of Aix, when he expressed himself in his paintings, did not carry his heart on his sleeve. The meaning and merit of him lie deep beneath the surface. Henri thinks it time some one should take up cudgels and defend Cézanne from his present-day critics, especially the fullsome and transcendental ones. By the same wholesale process of elimination which they employ to put Cézanne at the head of modern painters, it will finally be necessary to eliminate most of Cézanne himself, until only one picture is left as his representative masterpiece—and then no two critics will coincide as to which picture ought to survive.

Meanwhile, the "Bouquet de Fleurs" and "Château Noir," the two big somber oils, are looking us in the face with their strange, disquieting insistence. They belong to Cézanne's latest manner, dating from the years 1900 to 1904, inclusive. Heavy masses of dark brown, blue and murky green are loaded on the canvases, especially the flower piece, which is outrageously varnished as well, until the patterns almost stand out in bas relief. The flower petals, pale blush roses, are summarily brushed in, but with a certain delicate freshness, against a rich and elaborate ground of textile fabric which, if one looks long and intently, make a vivid impression upon the senses.

The "Château Noir" is a more positive proposition—either you don't "get" it at all, or else you yield the imagination unconditionally to a powerfully romantic sway. It is a sort of a Childe-Roland-to-the-Dark-Tower-came presentment—a palace in a forest of Provence, or the scene of some Poe tale with every elemental detail clearly defined, yet the whole overhung with an unaccountable air of awe and mystery and unrest.

Such pictures compel a certain amount of thoughtful, studious attention, which it seems a considerable portion of the metropolitan public just now is willing to give, so all's not vanity in these sporadic Cézanne shows. (Christian Science Monitor, February 5, 1916)

"LE BOUQUET DE FLEURS"

The history of "Le Bouquet de Fleurs" by Paul Cézanne, shown recently at the Modern Gallery, was given in the catalogue of that show. We take the liberty to repeat it: "Le Bouquet de Fleurs" is considered by the very limited number of people who have had the privilege of seeing it, to be one of the paintings in which Cézanne has expressed to the very highest degree all his power and all his sensitiveness, and therefore as one of the masterpieces among his paintings.

To arrive at the result that he was striving for in this painting, Cé-zanne had to use as model for his researches, a bouquet of paper flowers. This was necessary in order that the subject might last long enough for him to succeed in finding the projection of himself expressed in this painting. It took three years of daily work to attain the desired result.

In 1902 he wrote to Mr. Vollard the following letter about "Le Bou-quet de Fleurs":

Dear Mr. Vollard:

I find that I must postpone the shipment of your canvas of roses to some later date, although I wished very much to send it to the salon of 1902. I shall delay for another year the completion of this study. I am not satisfied with the result so far obtained. Therefore I insist on continuing my studies which will force me to efforts I like to believe will not be sterile. I have had a studio built on a small piece of ground which I acquired for that purpose. I shall continue my researches and will inform you of the results obtained as soon as I gain some satisfaction from my efforts.

—Paul Cézanne.

That this picture was important to its author we are assured by this letter. The note on paper flowers serves to show that the great modern was the master and not the servant of his subject. It is not however a purely subjective work; it is not indeed more subjective than any canvas of Titian's whose "materialism" has disgusted the moderns. The difference is in the nature and not in the extent of the subjectivity. Cézanne's is intellectual—a matter of the organization of forms, a study of function, a realization of the organic coherence of everything in nature.

(Arts and Decoration, *March 1916*)

ROUSSEAU

In 1909 the Photo-Secession had an exhibition of lithographs by Manet, Cézanne, Renoir and Toulouse-Lautrec, a few drawings by Rodin and a few paintings by Henri Rousseau. Max Weber wrote the following note for the catalogue of the mixed exhibition. The note refers only to Henri Rousseau:

The work of Henri Rousseau, who died September 5th of this year, is shown here for the first time in this country. For many years his work was of a most interesting character in the Salon des Artistes Independents of Paris, in which he steadily exhibited since 1886, and for whose existence he fought from the beginning. The few pictures in this exhibition are loaned by Mr. Max Weber, who was a devoted friend of Henri Rousseau. He began his career in the custom house service of the French government, but gifted with artistic instincts, he eventually sought to express himself in plastic art. His work greatly interested the younger group painters and critics in Paris, known as Les Fauves, who were his greatest friends and ad-

17 Henri Rousseau, *Vue de Malakoff.*

18 Henri Rousseau, *Still Life (with Cherries)*, 1908.

19 Henri Rousseau, *House on the Outskirts of Paris*, c. 1902.

20 Henri Rousseau, *La mère et l'enfant.*

22 Henri Rousseau, *Tollhouse, Quai d'Auteuil,* 1885.

21 Henri Rousseau, *Quai d'Auteuil,* 1885.

23 Henri Rousseau, *Painted Vase.*

mirers up to the last. He was truly naive and personal, a real "primitive" living in our time. He loved nature passionately and painted as he saw it. His larger work is very fantastic and decorative, and recalls Giotto and other primitives. He lived a life of simplicity and purity, the spirit of which dominates his work.

In 1910, Stieglitz put on the walls drawings and lithographs by Rodin, Manet, Cézanne, Renoir, Toulouse-Lautrec and a few paintings by Henri Rousseau. It was the first appearance of paintings by the *douanier* in New York. The critics found all the good qualities that can be found in all these artists but not in Rousseau's paintings. Max Weber wrote the introduction of Rousseau to the New York public emphasizing the traits of character of the artist, the simple life he led, his naiveté, his candid expression, etc., etc.

The famous and learned critic James Huneker wrote in the *New York Sun:*

> *It would have been far better if Henry Rousseau had spent his nights in drinking and gaming and his days under the eye of the dreariest pedant of a drawing master (even at Julien's academy) than leading his simple life. As an artist he is a joke; as a joke, a mild one; to be sure, he was regarded in Paris by people who refused to take his earnest caricatures seriously. . . . Nor have the Yankees the monopoly in bad art. The superb Montmartre Jackass—literally—Boranali (wasn't that the name given him by the farceurs?) had a following, and it wouldn't be surprising if a school known as the Master of the Jackass had sprung into existence, tail and all. And when writers can speak of Henry Rousseau's work as "virginal, candid, ingenious" then it is time to ask yourself if the younger men aren't more humorous than their granddaddies. Virginal, fiddlesticks! Candid, twaddle! Ingenious stupidities! . . . Rousseau's ideas of paint, designing and composition are rudimentary. (And he bears the august name of the great landscapist of French art!)*

> *It seems impossible to believe that any man of artistic sense could have seen a villa and its grounds as Rousseau painted it; there is neither color, form, nor atmosphere in the picture.*
> (B. P. Stephenson in the Evening Post)

> *Henri Rousseau is too primitive by far for ordinary consumption. A little portrait of a woman and child is of unbelievable ugliness. But there is something seizing in a city landscape in which the telegraph poles are considerably bent to the wind, but it somehow warms and comforts the imagination to see them doing it in a picture. And in Rousseau's color there is something extremely fresh, quaint, delightful.*
> (J. Edgar Chamberlin in the New York Mail)

MANOLO

Of the Catalonian sculptor Manolo, we only exhibited two drawings at the Photo-Secession and one drawing and one bas-relief at the Modern Gallery. We could not get any other work by him because there was nothing more to get. His production was as good as it was limited, much to our regret. It would have been of interest to show his qualities as a modernist sculptor in contrast to those of Brancusi.

PICASSO

UNMIXED OR TRUE PLEASURES

Protarchus—"Once more, Socrates, I must ask what you mean."

Socrates—"My meaning is certainly not obvious, and I will endeavor to be plainer. I do not mean by beauty of form such beauty as that of animals or pictures, which the many would suppose to be my meaning; but, says the argument, understand me to mean straight lines and circles and the plane or solid figures which are formed out of them by turning lathes and rulers and measurers of angles; for these I affirm to be not only relatively beautiful, like other things, but they are eternally and absolutely beautiful, and they have peculiar pleasures, quite *unlike* the pleasures of scratching."

This quotation from Plato's *Philebus* was sent to Stieglitz during the Picasso exhibition in 1910 by a writer whose name I never knew. I have seen the same quotation several times since then from different translations.

The exhibitions in the Photo-Secession were mostly drawings and watercolors and sometimes sculptures, and the cost of packing, transportation and insurance was too high for its resources. Perhaps like Ingres, Stieglitz thought that drawings are "la probité de l'art" and were sufficient for his purpose.

The selection of the exhibits was a delicate and serious matter. In the case of Rodin and Matisse, I have said that the choice of the drawings and watercolors was made by Steichen and the artists, and for Cézanne by Steichen and Fénéon.

In 1910 we thought that the New York public was ripe enough to receive Picasso's cubist work. Picasso was then at the period when he had his studio at the Boulevard de Clichy. The proposed exhibition was to be of drawings only, and for their selection a real "jury" was composed by Picasso himself, Steichen, Frank Burty and myself, who most conscientiously performed our duties. Picasso brought out all the latest drawings he had, and there were many. I don't remember how many we took, but certainly enough to fill the Little Gallery, and you can be sure they were the best Picasso had done up to that time. The drawings were "cubistic," needless to say.

24 Manolo, *Drawing.*

26 Manolo, *Bas-relief.* Bronze.

25 Manolo, *Drawing.*

27 *Manolo,* 1914. Photograph.

I was designated to write for the catalogue an introduction of the artist to the American public, which I did after several conversations with Picasso about his ideas on "abstract" art.[3] This was my first attempt at "introducing" artists of the new tendencies. My article did not please a certain Irish editorialist of the *New York Sun,* who took me to task to prove that I was a perfect imbecile or words to that effect. I don't remember the name of the writer nor do I have his editorial, but I do remember that what aroused him most was what I said about Picasso's ideas on perspective: "Picasso has a different conception of perspective from that in use by traditionalists. According to his way of thinking and painting, form must be represented in its intrinsic value, and not in relation to other objects. He does not think it right to paint a child in size far larger than that of a man, just because the child is in the foreground and one wants to indicate that the man is some distance away from it. The painting of distance, to which the academic school subordinates everything, seems to him an element which might be of importance in a topographical plan or in a geographical map, but false and useless in a work of art."

"In his paintings perspective does not exist: in them there are nothing but harmonies suggested by form, and registers which succeed themselves, to compose a general harmony which fills the rectangle that constitutes the picture."

I believe it would be of interest to quote from that article a few ideas Picasso had on painting at that time:[4]

> Picasso tries to produce with his work an impression, not with the subject but the manner in which he expresses it. He receives a direct impression from external nature, he analyzes, develops, and translates it, and afterwards executes it in his own particular style, with the intention that the pictures should be the pictorial equivalent of the emotion produced by nature. In presenting his work he wants the spectator to look for the emotion or idea generated from the spectacle and not the spectacle itself.
>
> When he paints he does not limit himself to taking from an object only those planes which the eye perceives, but deals with all those which, according to him, constitute the individuality of form; and with his peculiar fantasy he develops and transforms them. And this suggests to him new impressions, which he manifests with new forms, because from the idea of representation of a being, a new being is born, perhaps different from the first one, and this becomes the represented being. . . . As it is not his purpose to perpetuate on the canvas an aspect of external nature, by which to produce an artistic impression but to represent with the brush the impression he has directly received from nature, synthesized by his fantasy, he does not put on the canvas the remembrance of a past sensation, but describes a present sensation. . . . Following the same philosophical system in dealing with light, as the one he follows in regard to form, to him color does not exist, but only the effects of light. This produces in matter certain vibrations, which produce in the individual certain impressions. From this it results that Picasso's paintings present to us the evolution by which light

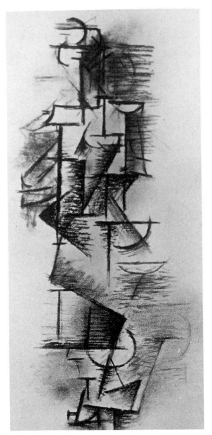

28 Pablo Picasso, *Nude,* 1910.

29 Pablo Picasso, *Violin,* c. 1912.

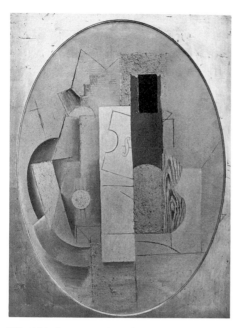

30 Pablo Picasso, *Violin and Guitar,* 1913.

32 Pablo Picasso, *Man Rowing,* 1910.

33 Pablo Picasso, *Two Women.*

31 Pablo Picasso, *Les pauvres,* 1905. Etching.

and form have operated in developing themselves in his brain to produce the idea, and his composition is nothing but the synthetic expression of his emotions.

The "clou" of the exhibition was the drawing I herewith reproduce (figure 28).

PAINTINGS BY PICASSO IN NEW COLOR SCHEME
ELEVEN SPECIMENS OF ART AT MODERN GALLERY ARE FOOLISH AND FUNNY

To those who are interested in the latest manifestations of the chief disciple of the art form that first began to be "News" eight years ago, the Modern Gallery will be full of lively and curious interests these days. The room is devoted to showing eleven paintings by Pablo Picasso and a marble sculpture that defies classification or name by Brancusi.

Most of Picasso's paintings are in a scheme of color that is much more cheerful than his older one, since they are in tones of bright green, white, red and brown. He calls them by such titles as "Jeune Fille" and "Nature Morte" which, to the normal eye and mind, mean nothing. The disposition of paint on canvas here produces little effect beyond the cheerfulness awakened by the color. Intellectual interest has no longer a part in these works.

A NOVEL ART INVENTION

One object numbered among these paintings is at least a novel invention, to be classed as such. It consists of a circle hung against a square of white watered silk and apparently made of plaster or some substance resembling majolica.

It is called "Nature Morte dans un Jardin," and the circle is enriched by some curious forms in high relief glazed with blue, white, green, red, and brown. One of these objects, arranged as "still life in a garden," resembles an ash tray fashioned like a playing card, with the pipe stamped out, and none of the other objects is more beautiful or elevating or intellectual than that. It is all so foolish it is mildly funny. The amusement will continue through January 3rd.

(New York Press, *December 1915*)

PICASSO'S ARID INTELLECTUALITY

A summary of Picasso's work during the past four years is being shown at the Modern Gallery, No. 500 Fifth Avenue. It represents the latest, and one may hope the last, word in the direction of abstraction. For unless I am mistaken, the effort of this artist is not to give the concrete an abstract interpretation, but to interpret an abstract idea by some formula that necessarily, if it is to be visible, partakes of the concrete. Instead of starting on earth with some basis of common understanding and feeling, he starts up in the air, where most of us can only guess of his intentions, while far be-

low we follow the seemingly arbitrary conventions that he selects to visual-
ize his imaginings.

Some people tell me they react to these abstractions both intellectually
and emotionally. I have no reason to disbelieve them. For my own part,
however, these diagrams recall the futility of the flagellants. They represent
the self-inflicted tortures of too ascetic an intellectuality.

(New York American, *December 20, 1915*)

PICASSO AT THE MODERN GALLERY

The Modern Gallery sits silently triumphant in the presence of Picasso's
latest, which is not the reactionary normal salonistic production recently de-
scribed, but a more than ever abstractly cryptic combination of little pieces
of substances and applications of pigment. Its name is "Nature Morte
dans un Jardin." The garden is a little round plaque, of wood perhaps,
painted green, and little cubes attached to this in a geometrically conceived
design stimulate your sense of touch as nicely as did the bits of sandpaper
in the old designs. It is quite impossible not to handle Picasso's paintings.
If there is any fear for their continued integrity under handling they ought
to be accompanied by "Keep Off the Canvas" signs. You run to them to
feel if the piece of something that looks like calico is calico or illusion. You
run your fingers over the piece of newspaper to see if the ink on it will
smudge as it does on your own last edition. You can't rest until you know
whether what looks rough is rough and what looks smooth is smooth.
That's Picasso. But quite all of Picasso. He is really to be admired for car-
rying it further than mere cheating of the eye, for such cheating is child's
play to his technical command.

Aside from the fun of trying to make out his absurdly complicated
riddles he offers you drawing of consummate skill and very nice color that
has no hateful quality of crudeness. Why should he go back to the sanity
required by deep thought and passionate feeling? Let us hope that he will
keep on with his play on line and color, his technical conundrums, his en-
tirely serious jokes. They constitute his method of expression, and so long
as we are comfortably ignorant of what he is trying to express, we are per-
fectly happy in the presence of his work—which is more than can be said
in the case of some of his followers.

(New York Times, *December 1915*)

PICASSO'S ART AND NEGRO WORKS IN SAME GALLERY
"PORTRAITS" BY LEADER OF EXTREMISTS SHOWN WITH IDOLS FROM AFRICA

Followers of the new art have a feast set before them at the Modern Gal-
lery, No. 500 Fifth Avenue, where seven paintings by Pablo Picasso are
on exhibition. The initiated, of course, will know what he means, or how
he feels, or how he expresses himself, or something of the sort, and the un-
initiated will get much amusement in trying to figure out these things.

There is nothing offensive in the exhibition, because Picasso is one of those "advanced" extremists who deal almost wholly in abstractions and so he does not do violence to the human body by disjointing it. In fact, in his "portraits" there is no suggestion of a human form. He tries to make one "feel" the person portrayed by means of color and curve and angle and such things. For instance, his "Jeune Fille" is just a bunch of many colored confetti divided into irregular planes by means of lines.

The artist, however, really does become objective in some of his still life subjects. In "Nature Morte" (Paris 1913), he uses real plaster and a strip of real wall paper, and in "Nature Morte dans un Jardin" (1915) he presents an actual limb of a tree and other sculptured objects, stuck on and then painted.

In the same galleries there is an exhibition of negro sculpture from the Ivory Coast, the Soudan, the Congo and Guinea. This is real art, because it is sincere. These negro sculptors mean what they did and the beholder gets some real "feeling"—the feeling of African superstition, for instance, because all of the sculptures are idols.

(New York Herald, *December 20, 1915*)

The exhibition referred to in the above article was the first one in New York of Picasso's paintings of his cubist period. It comprised paintings from 1912 to 1915.[5]

CUBISM

In 1916 Dr. Barnes published an article against Cubism in *Arts and Decoration*. I was asked by Guy Pène du Bois, one of the editors of that magazine, to answer the article. Unfortunately, I do not have Mr. Barnes' article.[6] In my answer, I quote the principal points of his attack. The two sides of the question are herewith expressed (*Arts and Decoration*, April 1916, pp. 284–286, 308):

CUBISM?

All art is composed of two elements, the fact and the idea. That is to say, one part objective, concrete, which is the work of art itself; and one part subjective, abstract, by which we take cognizance of the objective part.

In painting, the fact is the picture. The idea is the sentiment which it represents and which it gives the spectator. The fact is invariable, indestructible; the idea, that is to say, the interpretation which we give to the fact, is variable, destructible, mutable. It changes according to the extent of our knowledge and experience. In art the facts are sensorial realities, the ideas are intellectual realities. We give different interpretations to the same work of art; we have for it different theories according as our education progresses or our knowledge of art increases and our intellectual point of view changes. The work of art itself, its factual side, does not undergo any change and it is only the idea, the subjected thing, the theory that we have

34 Pablo Picasso, *Head of a Man*, c. 1910.

35

37

36

38

35 Pablo Picasso, *Female Nude*, 1910.

36 Pablo Picasso, *Woman Seated in an Armchair*, 1910.

37 Pablo Picasso, *Man in a Bowler Hat, Seated in an Armchair*, 1915.

38 Pablo Picasso, *Guitar Player*, 1916.

concerning the fact, that is variable; and this holds good for the producer as well as for the spectator and for the individual as well as for society. The interpretation that is given today to Greek art, to Egyptian art, to Chinese art surely differs from the interpretation given by the Greeks, the Egyptians and the Chinese themselves. To judge a work of art only theoretically, closing one's eyes to the factual side, is therefore as unreasonable as it is unjust.

Mr. Barnes, when he pronounces the "Requiescat in Pace" for cubism, in an article that appeared in *Arts & Decoration*, bases his entire judgement in condemning the whole new expression in art only upon its theoretical side, and when he says, "It was a wise man who said that great art speaks for itself and is independent of formulae," and adds that "Cubism was so choked up with formulae that it could not speak for itself," he proves that he is considering the question only theoretically and that he has completely shut his eyes to the reality of the facts.

Otherwise he would have felt and would have been forced to admit that this art which he defines as being "Composed of geometric planes, angles and cubes, with or without an element of representation to guide the observer in obtaining perceptions of forms of objects," has a natural *raison d'être*, is based upon a solid past, is in evolution logical and correct and brought to the field of art discoveries of real importance, and he would have seen that the theories to which he gives such attention have very little to do with the facts of this art.

It was the Spanish Pablo Picasso who discovered in the art of the African Negro a fact new to our art, sensorial reality, a reality unknown, or perhaps to be more exact, misunderstood by us, a plastic verity which can be called inherent in the human mind, since it was expressed by primitive intellects entirely free from any sophisticated influence. Negro art was for Picasso a revelation, as it has been for all who have studied it. It shows us comprehension of form under an aspect totally different from that which we are accustomed to entertain. This aspect, expressive rather than representative, grotesque and deformed, if considered from the naturalistic point of view, proves to us that there is a special anatomy of forms which are purely the expression of our sensations.

Picasso, an artist of extraordinary sensitiveness, took this discovery as a firm point of departure for a complete evolution of his exceptional sensorial faculties. He began by Africanizing his forms and succeeded after a short time in making his art the legitimate child of the most intensely impressive of all arts, namely Negro art. And this artist who in his naturalistic drawings has the photographic force of an Ingres, preferred to the expression of the reality of vision, the expression of the reality of sensation. And he introduced into European art new forms and new methods of expression.

It was Derain, according to Apollinaire, who first combined with Picasso to work in this new method of representation, soon following the path which his own personality imposed upon him. George Braque then became the working companion of Picasso. They collaborated in new researches exchanging discoveries which both employed in their pictures. Braque has of-

39 Pablo Picasso, *Bar-Table with Musical Instruments and Fruit Bowl*, 1913.

ten been accused of being simply the faithful copyist of Picasso. But if it is true that he has followed Picasso's method of painting, it is also true that he has paid his debt by bringing to Picasso contributions of a very personal nature.

Other painters followed this new conception of art which was then still anonymous. According to André Salmon, it was Henri Matisse, "with that feminine sense of the à propos of which his taste is formed," who baptised as cubists the works of two painters, inspired by Picasso. An art critic happened to be with him. He rushed to his paper, wrote with much chic his article of announcement and next day the public learned of the birth of cubism.

The word took like wildfire. The public needed a name for an art by which it was much intrigued. Many speculations followed. Cubism was theorized, codified and scientifized. Treaties were written on cubism; nor did it lack several inventors. Guillaume Apollinaire, in his book, "The Cubist Painters," says with a charming naïveté, "That which differentiated cubism from ancient painting is that it is not an art of imitation but an art of conception, which tends to become creation. In representing imagined reality or created reality the painter can give the appearance of three dimensions—can in some measure cubicise!"

He divides cubism as follows:

"Scientific Cubism is a pure tendency, it is the art of painting new ensembles with elements borrowed not from the reality of vision but from the reality of knowledge.

"Physical Cubism is the art of painting new ensembles with elements borrowed for the most part from the reality of vision.

"Orphic Cubism is the other great tendency of the modern painter. It is the art of painting new ensembles with elements borrowed, not from visual reality but entirely created by the artist and introduced by him with a powerful reality.

"Instructive Cubism is the art of painting new ensembles borrowed not from visual reality but from that reality which instinct and intuition suggest to the artist."

The division which Apollinaire makes in cubism shows only the diversity of theories which different painters who were inspired by the discovery of Picasso followed in search for new expressions, but they have nothing to do with the truth of the facts.

As an evolution of Picasso's art, which is purely sensorial, another art arose which is purely intellectual. This was the art of Picabia. Springing from a different source from that of Picasso, the art of Picabia leads him to a similitude of fact. By the elementary changing of the naturalistic form in colored volumes, this landscape painter whose drawing has won him in Parisian criticism the name of "worthy successor of Sisley," succeeded in finding abstract forms which were not a sensorial representation but a representation of ideas. In his art, more difficult to understand than that of Picasso, the factual side approaches more nearly to the intellectual side, without the one becoming exactly the expression of the other.

All these theories and others which he may have had, have surely blinded Mr. Barnes, or he could not have said that, "To enjoy or understand such pictures, there would be necessary not only new eyes but new systems of psychology, metaphysics, geometry and especially a new definition of aesthetics." Must we refuse all new discovery in art if it is not within the limits of the definition of aesthetics? The arguments of Mr. Barnes are far from agreeing with those of the great naturalist Fabre when he says, "The world of sensation is much vaster than it seems to our limited impressionability. For lack of organs of sufficient subtlety, how many facts escape us in the play of natural forces. The unknown, inexhaustible field that the future will discover has in reserve for us enormous stores next to which the actual known is but a miserable harvest. Under the scythe of science there will be one day fall sheaves, the seed of which would appear today a senseless paradox."

The sensorial possibilities of our eye have by no means been exhausted and we have no need of other eyes to enlarge our visual sensations. If the actual definitions of aesthetics are going to prevent us from making progress in art, it is necessary to change them rather than to deny the truth of incontestable facts. The work of art has always preceded aesthetics and aesthetics can never be more than an explanation rather than a theory of art.

Critics have wished to find in modern art a desire to destroy the preceding arts. Mr. Barnes tells us that, "Viewed in the light of its ancestral history, cubism has the birthmarks of present-day manifestation of that form of Rousseau-ism that is war against all law and order." Nothing is further from the truth. Modern art, that which Mr. Barnes calls cubism, has destroyed nothing and has not wished to destroy anything: nor was it created by any social theories but by the incontestable truth of plastic facts. For once Mr. Barnes has permitted himself to be taken in by the charlatanism of artistic demagogues. This new art follows a law and a natural law, and therefore it respects the existing order.

Those who like Mr. Barnes say that cubism is, "The vaguest mysticism, its symbolism more incoherent idiosyncrasy," take the chance of never understanding it.

It was Charles Sheeler who proved that cubism exists in nature and that photography can record it.

CUBISM JUSTIFIED

That Cubism exists, for the delight of the few and the mystification of the many, the many have long been aware, but that it could ever be justified or proved by mechanics or science, not even the delighted few were optimistic enough to believe—until quite recently. But science, it really seems, can prove anything, and according to the Modern Gallery, that familiar weapon of modern science, the camera, has proved Cubism. This gallery has just opened to the public an exhibition of photographs of Charles

Sheeler, in which the camera has registered certain effects and qualities hitherto seen only in the works of Pablo Picasso and his ablest followers. They will provide topics for debate to the progressives among the younger school of painters.

Mr. Sheeler's photographs are excellent photographs; that even a photographer would concede. He evidently has had great practice in the craft besides having aptitude for it. Then, too, his photographs are straight photographs—there is no blurring, no fog, no straining to pretend that the photograph has been accomplished with a brush instead of with a camera. Mr. Sheeler has been sedulous to permit the apparatus to work after its own fashion. He never forgets that the camera is a machine. The artist, however, who was back of his machine in this instance, had an excellent pair of eyes, a fine feeling for composition and an unerring sense of "values."

REMINISCENT OF MERYON

He found the subjects in an old farm house. A winding stairway, simple old windows and fireplaces, have been studied with a seriousness and the plates have been printed with an incision that would suggest that Meryon, the etcher, had been Mr. Sheeler's model, had we not been told that it was the cubistic master, Picasso, that he had set out to vindicate. He clearly vindicates him to the extent that an unprejudiced, open minded individual, inexperienced with Cubism and seeing it for the first time in these photographs—if such an individual be imaginable—would exclaim, "Why, if that be Cubism, Cubism is not so bad after all!"

For one thing, there is never a doubt in the mind of the beholder as to the subject. The title is not necessary for one to understand instantly that it is a stairway, or a door, or a window, and this is not always the case in regard to the paintings of Picasso. The qualities of the materials of the walls, floors, steps, etc., are astonishingly like the effects of the much discussed post impressionist of Paris.

(New York Sun, December 10, 1917)

"MODERNIST" PHOTOGRAPHS

Modernist photography by Charles Sheeler was exemplified in the exhibition held at the Modern Gallery, 500 Fifth Ave., to Dec. 15. Negro art has exerted considerable influence on the artist who has sought to prove by photography the reality of modern forms and values. The examples shown represented the exterior and interior of the artist's home and reproduced in a series of photographs the cold hard realities of stone, wood or iron so graphically that the "sensorial significance" of matter was vividly conveyed. From this point of view the exhibit was of interest, and its value in demonstrating a certain fundamental truth underlying the "modernist" theories is undoubted.

(American Art News, December 15, 1917)

41 Pablo Picasso, *Glass, Pipe, Dice and Playing Card,* 1914.

40 Pablo Picasso, *Portrait of a Girl,* 1914.

42 Pablo Picasso, *Studies of Apples.*

Photography has undertaken in the Modern Gallery, No. 500 Fifth Avenue, the task of proving that there is no pictorial realism more faithful than that of representative modernist paintings. Beholders are not yet through classifying as freakish much of the work of modernists. They endure it because of its persistence, but still usually wonder what it is all about.

Charles Sheeler, a disciple of modernism, has evolved a new advocacy for that cult by submitting typical pictorial puzzles to the exactions of the camera. Strange forms employed by the modernists, regarded generally as abstract, fantastic or imaginative, find now a kindly mechanical interpreter, for the photographs shown are surely of real and sane things, true in line and graceful in form and otherwise good, plain pictures. Sheeler says his object has been to prove that the principal elements in modern art are sensorial and exist in nature; that the impersonal lens has furnished proof of fundamental truths in modern art. It is an instructive exhibition.

(New York Evening World, *December 9, 1917*)

THE MODERN QUEST AFTER ABSTRACT BEAUTY

At the Modern Galleries is being exhibited a collection of drawings, etchings, lithographs and woodcuts by masters of the modern movement, by which may be understood the movement away from the subjective toward the objective. These modern masters date back as far as Daumier and Guys, men whose work in the middle of the nineteenth century was regarded as little else but clever caricature. It is, however, not the date of their birth or death which marks these men as modern, but their common search for the expression of abstract beauty, that is to say, beauty apart from the character of the thing represented. And in this respect a clue may be found which will assist the student to a better appreciation of the point of view in some very remarkable photographs by Charles Sheeler, which are on more or less permanent exhibition in this gallery.

For not only are they unusually beautiful examples of the platinotype process, but they are also of exceptional interest from the standpoint of motive and subject.

But the pleasure goes further than this. These points stimulate to a remarkable degree the tactile sense. In the phrase of the photographic studio, they are absolutely "straight" prints. The camera is allowed full play in its capacity of seeing and recording. Hence all the differences of material— wood, plaster and so forth—are distinctly realized, and the differences of surface-texture, with the varieties of ways in which they are affected by the lights and shadows. So clearly are the several plaster values represented that one's imagination is stimulated to feel that one can actually touch them as well as see them.

And then again, the pleasure that the forms excite is supplemented from that derived from color. The colors of these prints are comprised of tones of black and white. But they exemplify the fact that the beauty of color depends less upon the hues than upon the play of light and shade with which the hues are invested. And here the chiaroscuro is rendered so convincingly that one receives a vivid impression not only of the beauty of

43 *Picasso,* c. 1914. Photograph by George de Zayas.

color, but also of the actual structural relation between the colors and the forms. In fact, these prints of Sheeler's represent the testimony of photography to the truth and value of the modern evolution in painting. What Cézanne stands for in the structural use of colors is here certified to as being true to nature. So, too, are the studies of Picasso and others in the direction of abstraction.

Picasso has worked on the assumption that there are principles of organic construction beautiful in themselves, independent of the particular form in which for the time being they may happen to be manifested. In fact, that underlying the surface beauty of nature is an inherent beauty of abstract relations, harmonious and rhythmic. It is this abstract, organic beauty that the camera has revealed to Sheeler.

(New York American, *December 25, 1917*)

In 1917 Willard Huntington Wright wrote in *The Forum:*

Of the great number of men following in Picasso's footsteps it is strange to note that the great majority of them have their eyes focussed on the material success rather than on his failure to reach an exalted goal. They seem unable to view him as he is, insecure and uncertain, defeated by a versatility and talent which carried him forward, technically, so fast that his actual artistic ability was unable to keep pace. This cleverness—equalled only by a few men in history—developed unheedful to the weakness of the underbuilding. But the newer ultra-Cubists, for whose work, I regret to say, the Modern Gallery seems to have constituted itself the headquarters, see only the finished surface which is superimposed on an inadequate foundation; and they imitate and vary it, oblivious to the deeper needs of three-dimensional composition.

Mr. Huntington Wright had reason to say that the Modern Gallery had constituted itself as the headquarters for the work of the newer ultra-Cubists but he failed to see why. The newer ultra-Cubists were the consequence of the older ones (Picasso and Braque). The newer ones, with similar (not identical) abstract methods, were trying to make visual different psychological theories from those of their predecessors. They were entitled to be heard and seen.

Cubism was, indeed, the real "new art." It was the turning point from the old to the new in painting. Our job was to present to the American public the "new" in art, and we did not neglect to present cubism in all the different phases we could get hold of for exhibitions.

BRAQUE

An unpardonable sin committed by both the Photo-Secession and the Modern Gallery was not to have had a one man exhibition of the work of Braque. His contribution to modern art was, and is, one of the most valuable. When his work was first

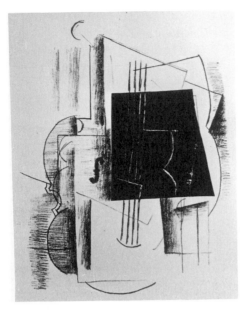

44 Georges Braque, *Still Life (Violin),* 1913.

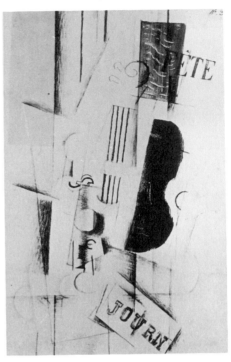

46 Georges Braque, *Musical Forms,* 1913.

45 Georges Braque, *Still Life,* 1913.

exhibited in New York at the Photo-Secession (1914–1915) it was in the company of Picasso's. The same thing happened at the Modern Gallery. Braque's work was always shown with Picasso's or with other painters. Picasso and Braque had parted company and they were no longer working together, exchanging ideas and practical innovations. The overpowering personality of the Spaniard overshadows that of the Frenchman in the public's mind. Some said that the difference between these two personalities was similar to the difference between Cézanne and Manet.

Strange was the fact that the critics overlooked Braque's part in the exhibition concentrating only on Picasso. In subsequent exhibitions Braque was invariably neglected. Was his work too subtle for the critics? Or did they see no difference between Picasso and Braque and took the latter as a satellite of the former? The public, I must remark, reacted differently and that was much to its credit.

Among other contributions by Braque to the association Picasso-Braque, was the "papier collé" which he discovered or invented in 1912.

THE ARMORY SHOW

In 1913 a great event took place: The Exhibition of International Art, better known as the "Armory Show" because it took place in the Sixty-ninth Regiment Armory. Arthur B. Davies and Walt Kuhn were responsible for it. Never before and never since has such a huge exhibition of Modern Art been shown under one roof. All modern art from all countries was represented. It was an avalanche of modern paintings and sculpture. It was overwhelming, colossal, stupendous, and best of all it was a tremendous success in all respects. It brought to New York all that could be known of modern art in Europe, and it also brought New York to the minds of modern artists. If its existence was transitory, I am persuaded that the effect it caused was permanent. It showed the American public that modern art was not limited to a small clique of Parisian artists but that it had taken root in all European countries.

The Photo-Secession by its limitations had only shown, we may say, the essential points of Modern Art; it had prepared an audience; it had paved the way for the "International Exhibition" to show it all and at once. If the Photo-Secession had awakened curiosity and hunger to know it all, the Armory Show more than satisfied that hunger.

Our conservative friend Mr. Royal Cortissoz wrote in the *New York Tribune*:

> *Visitors at the Armory, when they are studying Matisse and the rest, may recall that it was in the Photo-Secession Gallery that so many of the "revolutionaries" were first introduced to the New York public. With his delightful breadth of mind, his enthusiasm for liberty and all those who fight for it, Mr. Stieglitz has been an exemplary pioneer. He, too, like Mr. Davies and the other leaders in the Association of American Painters and*

Sculptors, has been content to show new things on his walls and leave the spectator utterly free to judge for himself. His liberality is a noble trait, and there is no better occasion than this one for offering it a public tribute.

We are living at a most interesting moment in the art development of America. It is no mere accident that we are also living at a most interesting moment in the political, industrial, and social development of America. What we call our "unrest" is the condition of vital growth, and this beneficient agitation is as noticeable in art and in the woman's movement as it is in politics and industry. "Art" has suddenly become a matter of important news. The New York "American" for instance, now devotes an entire page every Monday to art news and discussion. When one remembers what a great mass of people that newspaper is intended to reach, this fact seems significant. And the fact that Charles Caffin, one of our most conscientious and thoughtful critics, is writing that page would seem to indicate a serious as well as a wide-spread interest. That is only one of many journalistic indications of the popular interest. The coming great exhibition at the Armory has produced in a large public something like excitement. Moreover, there is surprising amount of curiosity and even stronger feeling about new and strange tendencies and experiments in art. Post-Impressionism, as it is called, has something of the same appeal as a bullfight.

(Hutchins Hapgood in the New York Globe, 1913)

Pablo Picasso, perhaps the leader of the Cubists in Paris, has here (in the International Exhibition) work in various stages of thraldom to or emancipation from objectivity. He is a painter of force and ability. At the extreme of his subjective range in this exhibition is a rather famous "Drawing" (No. 351) happily left without other title, which was for a time shown in the Photo-Secession gallery. It has been called a glorified fire escape, a wire fence, and other sarcastic names. It is undoubtedly rhythmic in high degree. There is a curious fascination about it. Based probably upon a human figure, it is still pretty thoroughly abstract.

. . . next to this drawing is another Picasso, a portrait of an old woman, in pen, which was done before he left accustomed paths, and next to this, in gallery J, is a pair of wonderful little portraits, drawings by no less a man than Ingres. You are surprised to see how well Picasso's drawing holds its own. Verily, an artist who has deliberately struck out a new path after acquitting himself so well in the old ones, commands at least your respectful attention in his new venture.

(Samuel Swift in the New York Sun, 1913)

The Armory Show was in fact an exhibition of contemporary art in which the most "significant" artists of the nineteenth century were represented, and among the three hundred artists whose work was shown, about ten percent were "modernists." The modernists, of course, were the main attraction of the show.

Walt Kuhn wrote a vivid description in his booklet *The Story of the Armory Show* (New York, 1938) of how the exhibition went during its one month of existence:

47 Entrance to the Armory Show.

48 General view of the exhibition.

49 Installation of painting and sculpture.

*Now came a surprise. The press was friendly and willing. Sides were
taken for or against, which was good, but in spite of this the public did not
arrive. For two weeks there was a dribbling attendance. Expenses went on,
a big staff of guards, salesgirls, etc. had to be supported. The deficit grew
steadily, when suddenly on the second Saturday the storm broke. From
then on the attendance mounted and controversy raged. Old friends argued
and separated, never to speak again. Indignation meetings were going on
in all the clubs. Academic painters came every day and left regularly, spit-
ting fire and brimstone—but they came—everybody came. Albert Pink-
ham Ryder on the arm of Davies, arrived to look at some of his own
pictures he had not seen in years, or maybe he too could not resist the Armory Show. Henry McBride was in his glory and valiantly held high the
torch of free speech in the plastic arts, as he is doing today. A daily visitor
was Miss Lillie Bliss who here first found her introduction to modern art.
Frank Crowninshield reveled in discoveries. He was a true champion and
is so today. Enrico Caruso came; he did not sing, but had his fun making
caricatures. Mrs. Meredith Hare, one of the show's ardent supporters, was
having the time of her life. Mrs. Astor, now Lady Ribblesdale, came every
day after breakfast. Students, teachers, brain specialists, the exquisite, the
vulgar, from all walks of life they came. "Overnight" experts expounded
on the theories of the "abstract versus the concrete." Cézanne was explained nine different ways or more. The then cryptic words "significant
form" were in the air. Brancusi both baffled and delighted. Matisse
shocked, made enemies on one day, developed ardent fans the next. People
came in limousines, some in wheel-chairs, to be refreshed by the excitement. Even a blind man was discovered, who limited to the sculptures, nevertheless "saw" by the touch of his fingers. Actors, musicians, butlers and
shopgirls, all joined in the pandemonium.*

BRANCUSI

It was at the Armory Show that Constantin Brancusi's work in sculpture brought
the attention of public and critics of New York, but I have a vague recollection that
previously Stieglitz had exhibited unofficially the first edition of the famous bird
which later Brancusi, in subsequent editions, corrected and diminished, each edition being more abstract than the previous one until he arrived at the quintessence
of abstraction.

The exhibits at the Armory did not present the highest qualities of workmanship of the artist; they were plaster casts.

In the season 1913–1914, the Photo-Secession held the first Brancusi exhibition. The critics unanimously praised Brancusi's sensitiveness for surfaces and material, and his technical skill in workmanship. Their opinion differed as to the form
or forms he had created.

50

52

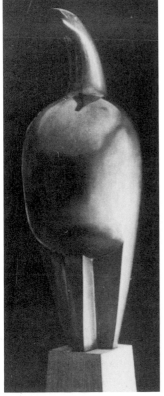

51

53

50 Constantin Brancusi, *Mlle. Pogany,* 1912. Marble.

51 Constantin Brancusi, *Maiastra,* c. 1911. Bronze.

52 *Brancusi's Atelier,* 1915. Photograph.

53 Constantin Brancusi, *Princess X,* 1916. Bronze.

. . . Mlle. Pogany appears at this exhibition in beautiful marble, and also in bronze. The beauty of this surface, of the mere workmanship, in this head is so great that it almost makes one forget the strange character of the head itself. Everything that is shown here, indeed, is finished in the same masterly way. Brancusi is a splendid artisan at any rate. Is he also a great artist? It doesn't appear so. . . .

(J. Edgar Chamberlain in the New York Evening Mail)

The sculptures are those of a highly accomplished technician whose mind works with symbols, not with explanation or representation. They are interesting and seductive, intellectual and mystic. Probably no other age could have produced them, and as expression of contemporary tendencies they are important, but they miss nobility of design.

(Elizabeth Luther Carey in the New York Times)

To me Brancusi's idea of the human head being as markedly egg-shaped as he makes it is a pure affectation and not at all an original one. For several years such a head has stood in one of the wall cases in a remote stairway in the Metropolitan Museum of Art, so that Brancusi's form has been antedated. And just why, in one of these marble heads, he should represent his original with a swollen face and a goiter is not easy of solution. But he makes the visitor forget much of his posturing by the sheer exquisite beauty of his "Sleeping Muse" in marble in a new fashion in sculpture which Rodin seems to have started.

(W. B. McCormick in the New York Press)

Visitors to the International Exhibition will remember his portrait of Mlle. Pogany which was jocosely styled "the egg shaped lady." That was in plaster, as also was the head of the "Sleeping Muse." Here both pieces have been rendered in marble by the sculptor himself, and the latter is also shown in a version in bronze. Among the other pieces are two female heads and a legendary bird.

Nothing so purely abstract in expression has been created in modern sculpture. . . . Those who admired the Pogany in the plaster—and they were many, despite the levity of the heavy-minded—will find in the marble even more sensitiveness of suggestion. . . . The bird is strangely Nervic. Its masses and curves are reduced to the utmost simplicity, and in consequence are the more salient in their actual constructiveness. It represents the most imposing kind of architectonics applied to a natural form. It is noble in conception and masterful in its technical rendering. And it is so because method and imagination alike are profoundly sculptural.

(Charles H. Caffin in the New York American)

But a few short months ago there were jeers for the Mlle. Pogany and the "Is it an egg?" witticism threw the philistines into such paroxism of uncontrolled glee that a consideration of the Sleeping Muse had to be postponed. . . . Those who can bear to look at Brancusi's sculptures will find it difficult to understand the shudders of the Philistines. They are, after all, so very abstract. . . . The "touch," to apply still another musical term to

54 Constantin Brancusi, *Princess X*, 1909–1916. Marble.

56 Constantin Brancusi, *Three Penguins*, c. 1912. Marble.

57 Constantin Brancusi, *Newborn*, 1915. Marble.

55 Constantin Brancusi, *Danaide*, c. 1913. Bronze.

58 Constantin Brancusi, *Prodigal Son*, 1914. Wood.

Brancusi's chisel, is extraordinarily caressing. Few pieces of modern stone cutting come up to it in "preciousness" and none that we have seen eclipse it. Certainly Rodin's do not. Sculptors who have any love for their trade as such and know in theory what "respect for the marble" is, will concede this success to Brancusi.

(H. McBride in the New York Sun)

SCULPTURE BY BRANCUSI

Several sculptures by Brancusi are at the Modern Gallery until November 11. In each of them you feel the intensity of the sculptor's interest in his material expressing itself in his skillful wooing of surfaces and the obedience of his tool to the character of what it works in. Compare his carved wood, his work in marble, and his work in bronze, and whatever you make of his unfamiliar conventions you find an extraordinary and exquisite sensitiveness to the properties of the substance under his hand. His marbles, so gracious and inviting in their bland smoothness, plead for contact with the hand, and his woods equally tempt the tactile sense with their delicate rugosities. He represents movement with the same subtlety. The lines of his abstract forms flow out sinuously or break into sharp angles and sudden changes of direction. The public still enamored of representation—and this is all but the most minute portion of the general public—will regret Brancusi's following of the modern gods. He is the gifted successor of Rodin in his treatment of marble.

(New York Times, *October 29, 1916*)

A FEW MODERNS

The decline of the modern movement, decline or return, lately so much discussed by the smug reactionaries, is not yet—whatever the promise of those blindfolded prophets. Brancusi at the Modern Gallery, over which Marius De Zayas presides, was the Brancusi of the Armory even perhaps a bit more abstract than we saw him in the portrait of Mlle. Pogany. In the Head of a Child through purity of craftsmanship he arrives at a spiritual purity quite equal to the sentimental conception we have of infancy. The Bronze Head of a woman with black hair drawn tightly into a nubbin at the nape of the neck is reminiscent of those Blue Stockings so fiercely satirized by the great Daumier. Daumier, himself, was here with another Third Class Carriage, rich and dark in tone, colorless except for fatness of the tonality, economic, direct, expressive in drawing. An etching by Picasso shows that he, too, at one time was an expressive, objective draughtsman, fond already of form though not yet driving it to the denial of local truth. In the Picasso of today the interest in form is supplanted by an interest in the color quality of surfaces. In this he may come closer to the old masters than he does to those negro creators of wooden gods—for spiritual

59 *Brancusi in His Studio,* c. 1915. Photograph.

worship—which attracted him so much at one period. When he shall have collected the results of his varied experiments about him and put them into a picture, we may expect a quite well-rounded, wealthy work.

(Arts and Decoration, December 1916)

In the weeks during which that exhibition lasted (the International Exhibition of Modern Art) the crowds stood and laughed in front of The Nude Descending the Staircase of Marcel Duchamp and the Procession of Francis Picabia. But the strange thing was that, instead of standing and laughing, they stood and wondered before The Kiss, The Sleeping Muse, the Mlle. Pogany, and the Torso of Constantin Brancusi. These sculptures were disturbing, so disturbing indeed that they completely altered the attitude of a great many New Yorkers towards a whole branch of art.

Brancusi has gone on and on since then. He has traveled further in the direction of simplification. He has got nearer to the expression of a pure idea the expression of the absolute in clay, marble or bronze. He is the great disillusioner. He puts you out of temper with the artists who modify Chinese and Egyptian ideas to suit modern tastes, and he has put the stamp of disapproval on the work of the so-called "portrait" sculptors.

It is astonishing to think that this man was once regarded by Rodin as the sculptor destined to carry the Rodin tradition. It was not to be. Like the proud soldier of Napoleon's time, Brancusi became his own ancestor. And it is safe to say that, just as he has had no predecessor, so he will have no descendant. He is hard to understand. But when the light comes on, it comes in a flood. He is certainly one of the most forceful influences in the art of our time. An austere influence, it is true, but one which helps those who realize the true beauty of line and form to escape convention, prettiness, and all sorts of compromise.

In his new Head of a Child, for instance, Brancusi has striven to place before us the feeling or sensation superinduced in us by a baby's head, stripping the concept of every detail which might please us as "representation" and leaving only the more gratifying pleasure of association.

The future of sculpture is veiled in darkness. Which road will it travel? What force in plastic art will dominate the sculptors of tomorrow? If simplification is to be the key of its future, then Brancusi must lead us to it.

(Vanity Fair, November, 1916)

PICABIA

Picabia came back to New York in 1914, bringing with him a few of his paintings to be exhibited at the Photo-Secession.[7] To these were added a few watercolors made in New York in the same style, and drawings of New York.

While in New York Picabia abandoned his former manner in painting and started his pictures of machinery in which he displayed all his ingenuity in their titles. Not that this was new to him, but it was new to apply them to machinery.

60 Francis Picabia, *New York*, 1913.

His mechanical style was first shown at the Modern Gallery.

Perhaps the last word of the futurist—and perhaps not. Picabia's develop-
ment from his pictures shown at the International Exhibition in 1913 and
his work shown this summer at the Washington Square Gallery is not
very great, yet one can easily see the great struggle and attempt he is mak-
ing for a newer form. A form of picture which would translate graphically
an emotion of music. In a small way this is quite possible, as his exhibi-
tion at 291 Fifth Avenue shows, but one is inclined to feel as though the
attempt is not as successful as it might have been. Of course, I speak only
for myself; some of my friends say that the work is successful in transmit-
ting the sensation of music, while, on the other hand, some say it is impos-
sible. One can only judge such things for one's self.

(Manuel Komroff in the New York Call, *1915)*

Picabia is now at the Photo-Secession Gallery, with an exhibition logi-
cally following that of Picasso last month. Three pictures with titles have
perhaps a direct bearing upon the artist's intention, but are not to be read
by one who runs except in their detachment: "Marriage Comique" is one,
and another is "Je revois en souvenir ma chère Udnie," both most unpleas-
ant arrangements of strangely sinister abstract forms that convey the sense
of evil without direct statement. A much breezier though still abstract com-
position is that entitled "C'est de moi qu'il s'agit." On the whole it is not
an agreeable change from Picasso, whose strangeness is more often than
not sheer beauty.

Probably we shall have another chance to appreciate Picasso. "If at
first you don't succeed. . . ." In time, no doubt, such is the assiduity of
those charged with the education of the public, we shall have all the Pi-
cassos, the many gifted personalities working through the one brain and
that one pair of hands. Perhaps of them all the most engaging is the Pi-
casso of "Le Lapin Agile," 1905, in which the painter in Pierrot costume
sits at table with a man and a woman in the famous Paris cafe.

(Elizabeth Luther Carey in the New York Times*)*

On the avenue yesterday I fell in with a young man, an assistant in the
gallery of one of the dealers, who told me that a cousin of his was holding
an exhibition in one of the rival establishments and that he was on his
way to see it. His cousin, he said, had passed a number of years in Paris,
and the family had been immensely relieved and pleased upon his return to
find that the young painter had been absolutely uncontaminated by "mod-
ern art" and painted nice pictures that anybody would like.

"It is terrible the sort of thing some of those fellows are putting over
on the public," he added. "Have you seen the Picabia Exhibition in the
Modern Gallery?"

"Yes, what do you think of them?"

"I think," and an expression of deep loathing passed over his young
face, "I think they are insincere. Don't you agree with me?"

"Hardly. On the contrary, I think Picabia is oversincere, if there be
such a thing as oversincerity. Look about you . . ."

We were trying to cross the roadway and the block of motors extending from the Forty-second street crossing prevented us. Immediately confronting us were the rubber and tires of countless automobiles, and the pistons and valves were shining brightly. Above against the sky could be seen the rectilinear lines of the steel beams of the new office buildings, varied by the zigzags of the derricks and softened here and there by an occasional rope and pulley.

"This is what you see every day. This is what countless thousands of New Yorkers see every day of their lives. These buzz saws, steel hammers, hard mechanical forms are recorded on your brain. Whether you know it or not they are there. It is impossible not to live incessantly in the midst of such things without being influenced by them.

"If you were to talk honestly from your own experiences, you would talk buzz saw talk, for that is all you've heard. Instead, you repeat like a mechanical doll or parrot formulas of beauty left over to you by ancestors who lived in the wilds of nature. If you really believed or understood what you say you would live yourself outdoors with nature.

"Picabia on the other hand, actually dares to use the shapes of discs and piston rods to express his emotions. It is amazing that you picture dealers won't look at them simply and unconcernedly, as a child or an engineer might, to see what you get from them. Why, that arrangement of four black discs with the connecting rods, in gold and red, has something of the simplicity and force of early Japanese art. I should hardly call it insincere."

"Now that you explain it to me," the young man said, and there was a note of fear in his voice, "I see it differently. Here we are at my cousin's show. Won't you come in? It is awfully nice work, I assure you. You won't! Well, I'll see you again soon. Good-by."

He saw it differently! I wondered if he really did. It struck me that the conversion was altogether too quick. He had yielded to my opinion precisely as he had previously yielded to the arguments of his unprogressive family. It really is one of the most difficult things in the world to induce people to think for themselves on subjects of art.

(Sunday Sun, *January 23, 1916*)

PICABIA'S CUBIST PICTURES

Fascinating bits of Negro Sculpture are shown at the Modern Gallery with the work of Picabia, which is a much less convincing demonstration of the cubist theory than that of his master, Picasso, shown there recently. There is absolutely no fundamental order, no tangible conception of the whole in these superficial canvases with absurd captions—"This Machine Laughing," "Daughter Born without a Mother," "This Thing is Made to Perpetuate," etc. Consequently there is nothing in the least impressive or emotionally impelling, while one who tried to comprehend really could find something personal and moving in Picasso's rhythmic figures. The observ-

er's mind was supposed to envelop the whole and receive a unified impres-
sion. The work seemed that of a serious experimenter with thorough
knowledge of what he was doing and a desire to do away with all superflu-
ities, making form an abstract force.

(New York Globe, *January 11, 1916*)

The Modern Gallery is showing a collection made up of works of Picabia,
who follows Picasso in exhibition. The current display comprises 16 ex-
amples of mechanical drawings, introducing color and largely showing ma-
chine parts and sections.

The colors used have been skillfully selected, with due regard to their
trade significance, and to the observer who is trained in reading plans and
diagrams the several catalogue numbers are full of informative vitality.

Circles, curves, rightlines, angles, rectangles, parallels, toggle joints,
cylinders, stopcocks, traps, siphons, and other mechanical units are offered
for observation in the more coherent frames, while into the frames with the
esoteric taint are introduced the various cubical devices with which the ar-
mory exhibition at least made us familiar.

(Minneapolis Tribune, *January 16, 1916*)

With the Armory Show, Picabia came to New York. He was, I understand, the first
modernist to cross the ocean, and soon found his center of gravity in the Photo-
Secession, where his torrent of art theories could be exposed. He soon went back
to Paris and began advertising the merits of the Photo-Secession among his friends,
the most conspicuous of whom were Apollinaire and Max Jacob. Both of them
had been the greatest propagandists of modern art, and they did not fail to make
propaganda for the Photo-Secession.

AFRICAN NEGRO ART

Through Picabia I met Apollinaire and Max Jacob, and through Apollinaire I met
Paul Guillaume, then a modest but ambitious art dealer and collector, or rather
importer, of Negro art. How he imported it will always remain a mystery, but the
objects he had were always genuine. When the First World War was declared and
desolation reigned among artists and dealers, Paul Guillaume was only too glad to
let me have all the African sculpture I could put in a trunk and bring to New York.
That was his first contribution to exhibitions of modern art in New York; many
others followed—if not with the same intention of making propaganda pure and
simple, with the hope of opening a market for them, which was just as legitimate.

We claimed, with justification, that the exhibition of African Negro Art that
we made at the Photo-Secession with those pieces was the first ever held presenting
Negro sculpture as Art.

There are several stories about how Negro Art was discovered; most of them agree, however, on one point: Maurice de Vlaminck was the discoverer. The story which in my opinion is the true one (although it might not have happened) is the one reported by Francis Carco in his book *De Montmartre au Quartier Latin*:

> *Vlaminck, the fauve, discovered in a "bistrot" at Bougival a negro statuette which he acquired by paying a round of white wine. Vlaminck was then an inseparable friend of Derain with whom he founded the famous school of Chatou. Vlaminck took his statuette to Derain, placed it in the middle of the atelier, contemplated it and said:*
>
> *"Almost as beautiful as the Venus of Milo, hein? Don't you think so?"*
>
> *"It is as beautiful," said Derain roundly.*
>
> *The two friends looked at it.*
>
> *"How about going to Picasso?" proposed Vlaminck.*
>
> *They went; carrying their piece of wood, and Vlaminck repeated: "Almost as beautiful as the Venus of Milo! Hein? Yes . . . almost . . . and some . . ."*
>
> *"Just as beautiful," repeated Derain.*
>
> *Picasso reflected. He took his time and, at last, having found how to outbid these two opinions, too daring for the epoch, affirmed:*
>
> *"It is even more beautiful."*
>
> *Thus negro sculpture was discovered and consecrated without delay as a great Art by the high priests of the modern movement.*

If Maurice de Vlaminck was the discoverer of Negro sculpture "materially," Picasso was its discoverer "intellectually." I wrote the following introductory note for the catalogue of the Negro Art exhibition which opened in the Photo-Secession in November, 1914:

> *Modern art is not individualistic and esoteric and even less an expression of spontaneous generation. It shows itself more and more frankly as an art of discoveries.*
>
> *Modern art is not based on direct plastic phenomena, but on epiphenomena, on transpositions and on existing evolutions. In its plastic researches modern art discovered Negro Art. Picasso was the discoverer. He introduced into European art, through his own work, the plastic principles of negro art—the point of departure for our abstract representation.*
>
> *Negro art has had thus a direct influence on our comprehension of form, teaching us to see and feel its purely expressive side and opening our eyes to a new world of plastic sensations. Negro art has re-awakened in us a sensibility obliterated by an education, which makes us always connect what we see with what we know—our visualization with our knowledge, and makes us in regard to form, use our intellect more than our senses.*
>
> *If through European art we have acquired the comprehension of form, from the naturalistic point of view, arriving at mechanical representation (by mechanical representation I meant photography), Negro art has made*

61 Francis Picabia, *Physical Culture,* 1913.

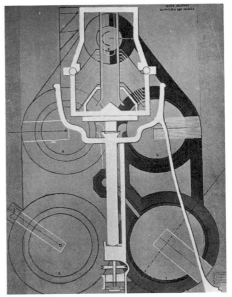

63 Francis Picabia, *A Little Solitude in the Midst of Suns,* 1915.

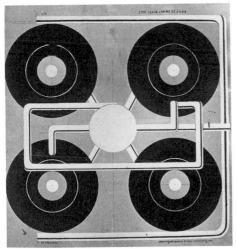

62 Francis Picabia, *This Thing Is Made to Perpetuate My Memory,* 1915.

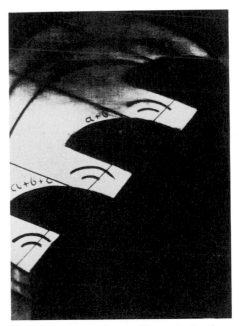

64 Marius de Zayas, *Portrait of Francis Picabia* (from *Camera Work* [October 1914]).

65 Installation view, exhibition of African Negro Art at the Photo-Secession Gallery, 1914.

66 [Unidentified.]

*us discover the possibility of giving plastic expression to the sensation pro-
duced by the outer life, and consequently also, the possibility of finding
new forms to express our inner life.*

*Negro art, product of the "Land of Fright," created by a mentality
full of fear, and completely devoid of the faculties of observation and analysis, is the pure expression of the emotion of a savage race—victims of nature—who see the outer world only under its most intensely expressive
aspect and not under its natural one.*

*The introduction of the plastic principles of African art into our Euro-
pean art does not constitute a retrogradation or a decadence, for through
them we have realized the possibility of expressing ourselves plastically
without the recurrence of direct imitation or fanciful symbolism.*

*The tenth season at the Little Gallery of "291" Fifth Avenue opens with
an exhibition of statuary in wood by African savages. Hitherto objects corresponding to such as are shown here have been mostly housed in natural
history museums and studied for their ethnological interest. In the Paris
Trocadero, however, their artistic significance has been noted by certain
French art collectors and by some of the "modernists" among artists—nota-
bly Matisse, Picasso and Brancusi.*

*It is as the primitive expression of the art instinct, and particularly in
relation to modernism in art, that the present exhibition is being held, and
it is said that "this is the first time in the history of exhibitions that negro
statuary has been shown from the point of view of art."*

*These objects have been obtained from the middle-west coast countries
of Africa—Guinea, the Ivory Coast, Nigeria and the Congo. Nothing is
known of their date or of the races who produced them, the natives in
whose possession they were found having come into some sort of contact
with white civilization and lost the traditions of the art.*

*I have talked with Marius de Zayas, the well-known caricaturist,
who for many years has been studying ethnology in relation to art
with the view of discovering the latter's root idea, and who accumulated
these eighteen examples during his recent visit to Paris. He begins by re-
minding one of the accepted premise in the study of the evolution of civiliza-
tions, namely that every stage in the progress of mankind, wherever it may
have occurred, has been characterized by a corresponding attitude toward
life and a corresponding expression of it in the handiworks.*

*While hitherto historians of art have looked for its roots in such direc-
tions as the lake dwellers and the caves of Dordogne, they have overlooked
the fact that the white race in itself represented an evolution in advance of
the black. Consequently, to get at the root of art one must dig deeper
than the white primordial and look for it in the black.*

*The objects, however, which are here shown do not go down to the
deepest elemental expression of the savage. They represent him at a comparatively advanced stage, by which time he had evolved a very marked
feeling for beauty.*

67 Baule figure.

68 Baule figure.

69 Baule figure.

70 Baule (?) figure.

71 Baule mask.

These specimens, when once you have got over the first impression of grotesqueness, are easily found to be distinguished by qualities of form, including the distribution of planes, texture and skillful craftsmanship that are pregnant with suggestion to one's aesthetic sense.

With what motive and under what kind of inspiration did the primitive artist carve these works? Mr. de Zayas explains that the savage looked out upon a world that seemed full of threats; that his imagination involved no idea of good, but only one of fear of mysterious agencies whose evil purposes he must avert.

Characteristic of all is the purely objective way in which the carver approached his subject. He set out to make his public see just what he saw in the object. But the way in which he saw it was entirely opposed to the photographic way. It was not representation, as in the case of white savage art; it was rather what we call today the caricaturist's way.

If he wished to objectivize the fierce bulging of the eyes, he makes them protrude like pegs; if a covert expression of the eye, he parts the closed lids by a decisive slit. Note, again, in one face the power expressed by the massive protuberance of the features and in another the refinement, actually subtle, obtained by varying the surfaces of the planes. And in almost every case it is not representation, but suggestion, that secures the objective reality. Here is the essential difference between this art and that of white savages.

In a word, the main characteristic of these carvings is their vital objectivity, rendered by means that are abstract. This or that objective fact has been, as it were, drawn out into constructive prominence, and has been given such a shape as would most decisively emphasize it.

And one other characteristic among many more that could be mentioned distinguishes these objects. To a greater or less degree all are expressive of movement, be it but the opening or shutting of the eyes. A feeling of static does not belong to the savage. He is ever on the move, encountering the changes of the seasons and weather. To him life is movement, which, by the way, brings his primordial instincts into touch with modern philosophy as well as modern art.

(*Charles H. Caffin in the* New York American)

We do not think of the wild African tribes as great sculptors, but the exhibition of their work which Mr. Stieglitz has been holding at the Photo-Secession gallery proves that they are real artists, expressing a definite idea with great skill—inherited, traditional skill. Their use of the rich, dark wood sculptures are remarkable. Forms are rude and conventional, but the expression is quite as successful as that of the archaic Greek sculptures.

Every one should see these African carvings. They are one of the few very real things now visible in this town.

(*J. Edgar Chamberlain in the* New York Mail)

One is tempted to think that the Primitive, the first barbarian moved to express himself in terms of art, has never existed. The further back we go the further he recedes until suddenly we come to something that looks so "modern" as to seem of today. The post-impressionist and the Congo savage have much in common, as the exhibition of African carvings at the Photo-Secession Galleries clearly demonstrates. The quality they share most obviously is the tendency to emphasize significance at the expense of representation. If an eye bulges make it bulge more; if a chin retreats send it back as far as it will go or obliterate it altogether; if arms are long make them like those of an ape. Certain of the carvings are, however, obviously of a much more advanced stage in art than others.

(Elizabeth Luther Carey in the New York Times)

In the case of these exhibits it was not necessary to explain that they are savages. Savage indeed! The rank savor of savagery attacks the visitor the instant he enters the diminutive room. This rude carving belongs to the black recesses of the jungle. Some examples are hardly human, and are so powerfully expressive of gross brutality that the flesh quails. The origin of these works is somewhat obscure. The gallery describes them as "the root of modern art," and this might be admitted in the same sense that the family of apes may be called the root of modern man. But to whatever period they belong, and whoever created them, there can be no doubt that they convey a sense of a race of beings infinitely alien to us.

(Forbes Watson in the New York Evening Post)

The most ancient of these carven masks are the most dynamic. The eyes, lips, nostrils, project from concave surfaces in these heads as surfaces are projected in modern cubistic art. The parallel was not long in being remarked; but just who among the cubists was the first to adopt the cult for it is not known. Matisse has some interesting pieces in his drawing room. Early in the game they were shown in connection with "cube art."

Last spring the little gallery started by Mr. Brenner in Washington Square held a few pieces, but this at the Photo-Secession is the first exhibition of ancient African wood carving, as such. This collection is owned privately in Paris. The museum at St. Petersburg was desirous of borrowing it for a show, but in spite of an "alliance" it was refused. It was owing to the effort of Mr. de Zayas, the caricaturist, that the carvings reached New York, and it also is worthy of record that he managed the shipment at the historic moment when most Americans abroad were parting from their luggage indefinitely.

(Henry McBride in the New York Sun)

Personally at the exhibition of "Statuary in Wood by African Savages" we found the root of Brancusi's handicraft more directly than that of Picasso. My interest in the works of the blacks may have been increased by the previous view of Brancusi while the interest of the work of Brancusi, who happens to be European, was entirely destroyed. It is very likely that without that grin Mr. Stieglitz would not have shown, in the works of the blacks, the ancient models of Brancusi's modern work.

(Guy Pène du Bois in Arts and Decoration)

Coincident with a display of carvings in ebony and other hard woods gathered from tribes in the interior of Africa, M. de Zayas of the Modern Gallery, No. 500 Fifth Avenue, has issued a pamphlet, entitled "African Negro Art: Its Influence on Modern Art," which represents with singular clearness the motives of the ultra-modernists, if they accept it as authoritative and final. Explanations of the new cults by their followers have often been so clouded by words as to lay them wide open to attack by opponents and to baffle the common understanding. M. de Zayas has at least spoken lucidly, and the statements of facts in his pamphlet are fully supported by quotations from travellers in the regions from which the carvings come. It is worth knowing also at the outset that these carvings, which had no value except as curios a few years ago, have become so much of a fad in France, the source of ultra-modernism, that sales of single pieces have been made as high as 30,000 francs ($6,000).

It is related of Picasso, one of the modernist apostles, that when a visitor to his studio remarked of a painting there that it might be the work of his child aged four years, he replied that no greater compliment could be paid to him, for it was his chief desire to have the innocent and pure vision of a child. M. de Zayas quotes several writers on the African tribes, who agree that in his earliest years the negro is ready-witted, docile and more precocious than the average European child, but at the age of ten or twelve years the negro intellect becomes stationary, slowly decreases in the following fifteen years, after which follows rapid decrepitude. This condition is attributed to the premature junction and subsequent ossification of the sutures of the cranium, which stop in that way the natural expansion of the brain. As the carving is supposed to be the work of adults, whose brain development was arrested and began to go backward in early youth, it does not strain probabilities to attribute to them in their art the sort of vision to which Picasso aspires. "Of all the arts of the primitive races," M. de Zayas says, "the art of the African negro savage is the one which has had positive influence upon the art of our epoch. From its principles of plastic representation a new art movement has evolved. The point of departure and the resting point of our abstract representation are based on the art of that race, which can be considered as being in the most primitive state of the cerebral evolution of mankind.

"It is known that in the evolution of the faculties of observation, man first notices the effect, the action, the movement of things, not the things themselves. The infant of the civilized races, indifferent at the beginning of life to static objects, fixes his attention on anything that moves. It is logical to believe that since the negro discovers his first criterion in movement, it will be movement and not objects that he tries to represent primarily. Movement cannot be represented except through the trajectories of the thing that moves, and these trajectories can only be represented by geometrical combinations of line. Hence, in my opinion, the geometrical structure of the negro sculpture. Negro tribes who practice drawing and painting express themselves only with geometrical figures, that being the only ornament known. The negro does not represent the concrete remembrance of form, but only the abstract image with which movement impresses him. Everything he conceives lacks objective or intellectual reality.

"Sense of color seems to be in accordance with primitive conception of form. Negro drawings and bas-reliefs resemble the work of primitives of white races, or the drawings of white children. Elements of direct imitation are either the salient points of the human form, which strike the primitive visualization of the negro, or the artificial decorations of the body, which he has the habit of making on himself and which he knows objectively. Symbolism does not exist in the art of the negro. His brain is in too primitive condition to attribute to a thing the significance of an idea. He gives form only to a feeling.

"It is certain that before the introduction of the plastic principles of negro art, abstract representations did not exist among Europeans. Negro art has reawakened in us the feeling for abstract form. It has made us conscious of a subjective state, obliterated by subjective education. While in science the objective truths are the only ones that can give the reality of the outer world, in art it is the subjective truths that give us the reality of ourselves."

Quotations from the pamphlet as given above are not continuous, but have been selected to trace the reasoning that connects ultra-modern and primitive expression in art. There is much of related interest in the pamphlet which the close student of the subject should read. So far as it goes it makes out a case that is at least intelligible. Whether or not all ultra-modernists will be willing to have their art linked up in this way with that of the junglemen, the Picasso ideal of childish vision would seem to be gratified in the negro work. There is, of course, much to be said of modernism, in respect to its intolerance of conventions and the impulse of trained talent to assert itself independently, with no thought or knowledge of jungle crudities, but visitors to the African exhibits cannot fail to be struck by the resemblance of some of it to the productions of modern cubists.

The carvings are mainly fetish figures of statuette size. They are intended as agents of propitiation. As the good churchman prays to the image of a saint, so the African invokes his fetish. In both cases there is full knowledge that the image is a man-made effigy, but it stands as the embodiment of a sacred entity, and the prayer is really addressed to the spirit thus clothed. A tutelary spirit inhabits the fetish, and the negro appeals to it to assure to him the favour of good influences and to appease the fury of evil. Indeed, he goes much further, for if his fetish does not respond to his entreaties he feels free to whip it or to force compliance by driving nails into it, or he may employ a tribal sorcerer to bring it back to sympathetic relation with himself. Belief in the fetish is not incompatible in the negro worship with faith in an invisible supreme being, or in various gods or devils, none of them represented in statues or symbols and none of them the object of intimate worship. In this view there is room without crowding for many deities in the spiritual world, and no reason to exclude any of them.

(Frederick W. Eddy in the Sunday World, October 29, 1916)

Considerable interest attaches to the exhibition of African negro sculpture which has been arranged by Mr. M. de Zayas in the Modern Gallery, No. 500 Fifth Avenue. Mr. de Zayas is the author of a brochure on the subject of this sculpture.

72 Kota reliquary.

73 [Unidentified.]

74 Senufo Mask.

75 Bambara figure.

76 Bambara figure.

A point he makes and one which the show brings out is the resemblance in point of primitive plan and design between these grotesque carvings of the negro of Africa and the work of the cubists and other schools of advanced art. To make his arguments more convincing he illustrates them by hanging in this exhibition several pictures in the cubist manner.

There is, however, a difference between the real primitive art and that practiced in civilized countries today. Real primitive art was not intended to be primitive. Its practitioners brought to their work everything they knew about art. They had no notion that it would ever be called primitive. They simply hadn't the technical knowledge of art to paint or sculpt otherwise than they did. That is the reason their work possesses a naive charm that the connoisseur loves. Modern "primitive" art, however, is not genuinely primitive but forced. Its naiveté has the effect of being studied, therefore is not naive at all.

If the primitives could come to life today they eagerly would seize upon all technical advances that art now could place at their disposal and the artists they would look most askance at would be their imitators. No doubt the best of them would eschew the conventional and the routine, but they would eagerly seize upon the sound, sane principles of art and practice them. Needless to say that African negro sculpture has the naiveté of the genuinely primitive. There is a great difference between the really quaint and the merely queer

(New York Herald, *December 24, 1916*)

NOTES AND ACTIVITIES IN THE WORLD OF ART

The close relationship of certain phases of modern art to African sculpture was quickly discovered and the taste for negro carvings, examples of which were to be studied in Trocadero, grew in Paris side by side with the development of the movement. Matisse and most of the other French leaders owned specimens of these curious works of art and undoubtedly were in turn deeply affected by them. If the sculptures could have been shown here in advance of the modern work it is safe to assume that the latter would have been more understandingly dealt with.

Mr. de Zayas has secured a notable group of these carvings for an exhibition in the Modern Gallery, and it is especially interesting to look them over with the help of an essay he has lately printed upon the subject. It seems that all these productions are fetishes meant to propitiate certain evil spirits. At first glance the strangeness of the carving is apt to divert the attention from the very real beauty of expression which the figures have, but the longer they are studied the more important they become.

Many pages of Mr. de Zayas's scholarly little book are taken up with the childlike characteristics of the producers of these fetishes, the exposition of their rare precocity as children and the unanimity of scientific opinion upon the atrophy that descends upon the faculties of the adults. Two short quotations can be made from this part of the essay. "Plastic evolution is the result of intellectual evolution. The savage of today, for example, would be incapable of understanding the work of the Greeks done over two

*thousand years ago." And this: "The small amount of direct imitation—
the almost abstract form of the plastic representation of the African negro—is nothing more than the logical result of the conditional state of his
brain."*

*In the conclusion of the study the direct relationship of the negro sculp-
ture to modern art is touched upon. "We have seen," writes Mr. de
Zayas, "that the first criterion of the negro is spontaneous movement in
which he sees the manifestation of life. It is known that in the evolution of
the faculties of observation man first notices the effect, the action, the movement of things and not the things themselves. The infant of the civilized
races, who is indifferent at the beginning of his life to static objects, fixes
his attention on anything that moves.*

*"It is logical to believe that since the negro discovers his first criterion
in movement and is an anamist it will be movement and not objects that he
tries to represent primarily. But movement cannot be represented except
through the trajectories of the thing that moves. And these trajectories can
only be represented by geometrical combinations of lines. Hence in my opinion the geometrical structure of the negro sculpture."*

(The New York Sun, December 10, 1916)

ART

*The exhibition of African negro sculpture in the Modern Gallery, 500
Fifth Avenue, shows how very old is called "Modern Art." The negro artist put into wood his primitive emotion, and there it stands, a vital remembrance of what the artist thought, felt and was at the moment.*

*This negro art shows the expression of emotion rather than the expres-
sion of vision, and this, the modernists say, is the truth, therefore the beautiful in art. However, the exhibition is very interesting, whichever
viewpoint one takes of it, and will be open to the public until February 9th.*

(Tribune, February 2, 1918)

*There is an exhibition of African negro sculpture at the Modern Gallery.
It has been said of modern art that the best of it was in its literature. That
may be true. I have often thought that one of the most convincing signs of
intellectual progress was in the possession of a real power to see without
prejudice, to see, let us suppose, as Degas did. It is quite possible that no
savage ever really knew what his brother looked like. Here is some "modern literature" upon the work of the African savage taken out of the catalogue of this exhibition:*

*"In a dim past, amid the stark and grim reality of primeval forest and
jungle, an artist puts into wood an emotion. He is a man of note among
his savage fellows, for he knows how to embody their tribal and personal
feelings. Today the artist is unknown, but his gesture lives, and the meaning of it inspires a vital development of plastic art. Such is the marvelous
history of negro sculpture.*

"At the time when the Modernists who followed the plastic reforms initiated by Cézanne were struggling to bring out of form its utmost power of expression, Maurice de Vlaminck, one of the fauves, discovered in an antique shop some negro carvings. The full extent of the constructive revelations of negro sculptures was immediately comprehended by the Modernists, who found in the fetish the realization of what their previous researches had divined.

"There is something talismanic in the influence which negro sculpture has wielded in modern art. The fetish has resumed its commanding position. It has pointed to our artists a new road to follow, inspired new creations, aroused new sensations and new pleasures in the domain of art. From the ateliers of the Modernists it has made its way into the collections of connoisseurs. It has shaped art's destiny."

(The Evening Post, *February 2, 1918*)

CONGO FETISHES AND FRENCH ART

Simultaneously, M. de Zayas has gathered at the Modern Gallery, 500 Fifth Avenue, nearly half a hundred more pieces of African Negro wood sculpture, statuettes and ceremonial masks, from the Ivory Coast, Sudan Guinea, Gabon and the Congo.

It might seem, at first thought, as if the fantasy of antithesis had reached the top of its bent, even for present-day New York, in this conjunction of French civilization's first product and that of innermost savage Africa. Yet the very contrast is typical of the curious, eager unrest of modern art. Moreover, this is an age of synthesis, rapproachement and fusion, not of differentiation and divergence. After all, is there such an abyss between the Gothic image-carver and the mystic black man of a primitive race making a symbolic elephant's head mask in the cathedral-like solitudes of a tropical forest in Gabon? The one puts his medieval religious passion into stone, the other translates his superstitious awe and unreasoned terrors or emotional transports into marvelously wrought wood or ivory, evolving at the same time an original formula for the plasticity of those materials.

VLAMINCK AND THE VOODOOISTS

Two or three of the intense, highly colored, spellbinding landscape paintings of Maurice de Vlaminck are hung at the Modern Gallery in juxtaposition with the weird, talismanic images of the African Negroes. One may feel no particular sense of incongruity, and yet ask, What is the connection? Well, there is no actual connection, yet a certain logical tie of personal association does exist. For this same irresistible "fauve" artist, Vlaminck, not much more than a decade ago, was first stirred to new awakening by the discovery of some neglected Negro carvings in a Paris junk shop. The famous ethnological exposition at the Trocadero opportunely confirmed the profound impression thus made, which went abroad spontaneously among the modernists, because it realized essentially what their

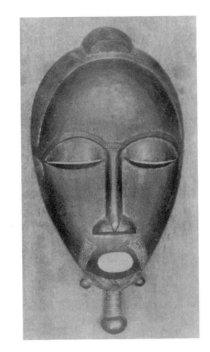

77 Baule or Guro mask.

79 Baule mask.

80 Giorgio de Chirico, *Portrait of Paul Guillaume.*

78 [Unidentified.]

previous independent researches had divined. It was at a moment when the heroic plastic reforms initiated by Cézanne and fomented by Matisse were bringing the power of direct expression to the point of violence.

So the Negro fetish has strangely and suddenly come into an influential position in modern art—alike in the ateliers of artists and the collections of connoisseurs. That "audacity of taste" which present-day conditions have fostered, makes us peculiarly appreciative of the expressive power of the darkest-Africa statuette. Here are forms and sensations absolutely unfamiliar in this handiwork of races without history, tradition or precedent, yet super-sensitive to the realities of the imagination. If you want a primeval passional vision expressed in terms of childlike naiveté, and at the same time in concrete forms of wizard craftsmanship, go to the Negro fetish-sculptor, whose culture is nil, but whose art-expression is 99 per cent efficient in expressiveness.

Twenty of the choice pieces at the Modern Gallery have been made the subjects of a limited-edition album de luxe of photographs by Charles Sheeler—a work which should take its place in art libraries beside the many sumptuous volumes already devoted to reproducing Egyptian wall-paintings. There is indeed, something vaguely Egyptian, and even archaic Greek, in the Sudanese, Congo, Sangha, Kissi, and other interior-African statuettes. In this Nile Valley category also belongs a beautiful little crescent harp or lyre, made from antelope horn, among the ivories at the Natural History Museum. And some of the wooden vases here have broad ivory bands and friezes etched with "pictographs," or line-drawings of human figures and animals with black pigment rubbed into them, after which the final brilliant polish is applied to the rich-textured surface of the tusk.

(The Christian Science Monitor, *February 4, 1918*)

AMERICAN MUSEUM OF NATURAL HISTORY
SHOWS AFRICAN NEGRO ART

Quite a different collection of African wood carvings is on view at the Modern Galleries. These carvings are shown because of their influence upon a certain group of extreme modernists. Maurice de Vlaminck discovered in an antique shop in Paris some negro carvings. At this time the modernists, who were following the plastic reforms indicated by Cézanne, were struggling to bring out of form its utmost power of expression. The discovery of these negro carvings was a timely one, as they seemed to embody in plastic form many of the ideas of the modernists.

The poet Apollinaire says: "By an audacity of taste we have learned to love the negro statuette; to understand its expressive power. Vast has been the benefit to us. He has taught us in art that the expression of emotion is more intense than the expression of vision; that feelings are more positive than understanding."

Modernists claim that, inasmuch as these statuettes were talismans in the dim past in which they were made, they have exerted a talisman's effect on modern art. They are interesting, of course, as the crude expressions of a primitive people. But I feel that the modernists claim too much for the crude statuettes. I cannot see where they are superior in the expression of simple emotion in simple form to the archaic Greek bronzes or primitive Christian wood carvings. The same quality is inherent in all primitive work. The African carvings are only a little bit more crude, and with the crudeness of a people, who have, in their native state, not developed beyond the savage.

(Brooklyn Eagle, *January 27, 1918*)

1915 was the golden year for modern art. The Carroll Galleries held early in the year the first exhibition in New York of Picasso's early work (paintings). The Montross Galleries had an exhibition of paintings by Matisse, and another of a group of American modernists called by the critics cubists, futurists and post-impressionists. This exhibition had a large attendance in spite of the fact that the entrance fee was twenty-five cents. The Photo-Secession began the year exhibiting paintings and drawings by Picasso and Braque (first appearance of Braque's work in New York). The Washington Square Galleries also exhibited paintings by Picasso. The Modern Gallery had an exhibition of Picasso's latest paintings.

Peyton Boswell wrote in the *New York Herald* in 1915:

> *Within the last few days five exhibitions involving the extreme in art have been opened in the New York galleries and these do not include the Matisse exhibition. So eager have been the galleries to show the new art that Alfred Stieglitz, of the Photo-Secession Galleries, No. 291 Fifth Ave., who showed the first extreme art seen in New York, said he might have to devote his gallery to exhibitions of academic work in order to escape being obvious.*
>
> *"If the worst comes to the worst," he said yesterday, "and the members of the National Academy of Design can find no other place to exhibit their pictures, I will cheerfully give to them the use of No. 291. An exhibition of work by Mr. Edwin Blashfield and Mr. Will Low might help a lot to start the pendulum swinging back the other way."*

In 1915, Willard Huntington Wright published his book, *Modern Painting,* the first book, I believe, published in the United States on modern art. He said in the foreword: "This book inquires first into the function and psychology of all great art and endeavors to define those elements which make for genuine worth in painting. Next it attempts to explain both the basic and superficial differences between 'ancient' and 'modern' art and to point out, as minutely as space will permit, the superiority of the new methods over the old."

81 Abraham Walkowitz, cover of *291* (May 1915).

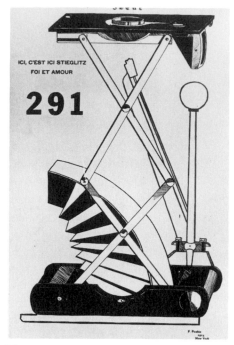

83 Francis Picabia, *Ici, c'est ici Stieglitz,* cover of *291* (July–August 1915).

82 John Marin, cover of *291* (June 1915).

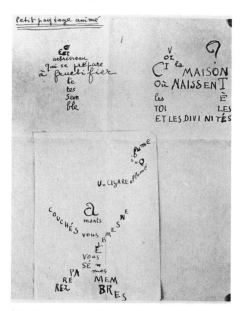

84 Guillaume Apollinaire, "Ideogram," original manuscript.

In 1915, Paul B. Haviland, one of the most active associates of Steiglitz, had the idea of starting a publication devoted to modern art in all its manifestations under the name of *291*. This was the first publication of its kind in New York and I believe the only one since then. A description of what it was appeared in *Camera Work* (October, 1916):

"291"—A NEW PUBLICATION

> *"291" is always experimenting. During 1915–16, amongst other experiments, was a series with type-setting and printing. The experiments were based upon work which had been done with type and printers' ink, and paper, by Apollinaire in Paris, and by the Futurists in Italy. No work in this spirit had as yet been attempted in America. The outcome of those American experiments has been a portfolio consisting of twelve numbers of a publication called "291." The size of the sheets were approximately 12 × 20 inches. Two editions were printed, one, the ordinary, on heavy white paper, of a thousand copies; the other, an edition of one hundred printed on very heavy Japan vellum. With the exception of the one picture in type by Apollinaire, all the matter and all the pictures in this publication have appeared nowhere else. One number is devoted to photography and includes a Japan vellum proof of "The Steerage" by Alfred Stieglitz. The new typography has already a name: "Psychotype," an art which consists in making the typographical characters participate in the expression of the thoughts and in the painting of the states of soul, no more as conventional symbols but as signs having significance in themselves.*
>
> *The chief contributors to this publication are Marius de Zayas, Francis Picabia, Paul B. Haviland, J. B. Kerfoot, Katharine N. Rhoades, Agnes Ernst Meyer, Pablo Picasso, Max Jacob (Paris), John Marin, A. Walkowitz, Eduard J. Steichen, Alfred Stieglitz, Apollinaire.*

These "Psychotypes," also called "Ideograms," were started by the Italian Futurists, but they did not go very far with them. It was Guillaume Apollinaire who brought them to a head in 1914 and published them in his *Les Soirées de Paris* (July and August, 1914).

I am giving you here Apollinaire's procedure in working out his "Ideograms," in which the design in printing-type corresponds with the idea expressed by the poet: first the original manuscript (figure 84), then the corrected proof (figure 85), and finally the "mise en page" (figure 86). I also reproduce the Ideogram published in the first number of *291* (figure 87).

Music had also a place in *291* (the publication). It was, naturally, the "last word" in modern music.

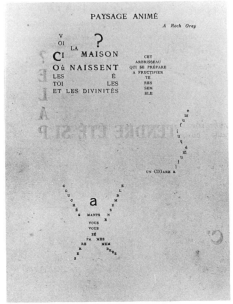

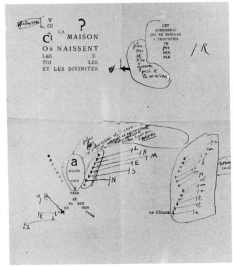

86 Guillaume Apollinaire, printer's proof of figure 84, with corrections by Apollinaire.

85 Guillaume Apollinaire, "Paysage animé," *Les soirées de Paris* (July–August, 1914).

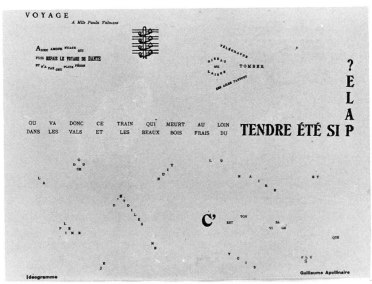

87 Guillaume Apollinaire, "Voyage," *Les soirées de Paris* (July–August, 1914); reprinted in *291* (March 1915).

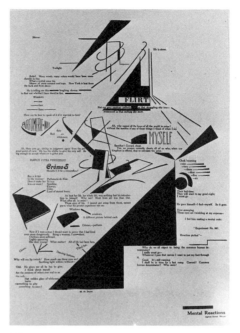

88 Marius de Zayas, *Portrait of Apollinaire* (from *Les soirées de Paris* [July–August, 1914]).

90 Agnes Meyer and Marius de Zayas, "Mental Reactions" (words by Meyer, drawing by de Zayas), *291* (May 1915).

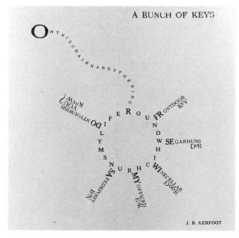

89 John Barrett Kerfoot, "A Bunch of Keys," ideogram, *291* (May 1915).

91 Max Jacob. Photograph.

92

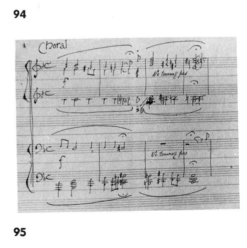

94

93

92–94 Alberto Savinio, "Bellovées fatales No. 12," musical score, *291* (May 1915).

95 Erik Satie, "Choral," musical score (previously unpublished).

95

SINCERISM

Just before the war a new tendency in music was initiated in Paris by the Italian musician Albert Savinio. He called it "Sincerism." Most of the music of Savinio is based essentially on music, his source of inspiration is music, music that has been written, and music that he hears. Instead of trying to translate life into music, he translates music into music. The sincerism consists in frankly acknowledging the musical motives which served as points of departure of his own compositions.

(*291, No. 1, March 1915*)

NEW MUSIC

The musical composition by Albert Savinio, published in this number of 291, should be called New Music rather than Modern Music.

Savinio has devoted himself to finding the place of music among the modern arts. He does not try to express in music either as a state of consciousness or as an image. His music is not harmonious or even harmonized, but DISHARMONIOUS. Its structure is based in drawing. His musical drawings are, most of them, very rapid and DANSANTS, and belong to the most discordant styles, for this composer thinks that a sincere and truthful musical work must have in its formation the greatest variety of musics—ALL THAT WHICH ONE HEARS—and all that which the ear imagines or remembers.

He does not invent; he discovers the significance of all sorts of sounds and uses them to create and as emotive source.

"La Passion des Rotules" is No. 12 in a series of "Chants Etranges" which has for its title "Bellovées Fatales."

(*291, No. 2, April 1915*)

We were to publish an original manuscript by Erik Satie, a few bars of a Choral, but *291* ceased publication. I am, nevertheless, including it in the illustrations (figure 94).

STIEGLITZ

Was Stieglitz a providential man to introduce Modern Art into New York? There is no possible doubt that Modern Art both in its principles or theories and in its accomplished work would have infiltrated itself into America. There were many American artists coming back from Paris who imported the ideas and new works of art done by themselves under the influence of those ideas. And there certainly would have been other ways of invasion.

Stieglitz had the gift to attract attention and the ability to get hold of that attention and develop it into genuine interest. He had the gift to promote publicity,

96 Marius de Zayas, *L'accoucheur d'idées* (from *Camera Work* [July 1912]).

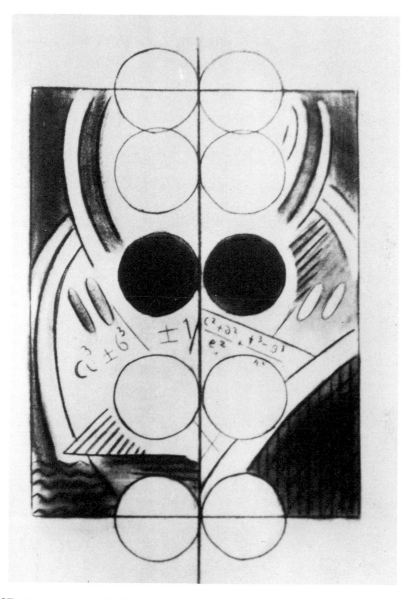

97 Marius de Zayas, *Alfred Stieglitz* (from *Camera Work* [October 1914]).

to raise controversies, and attract art critics of all creeds. He was above suspicion of working for his own ends. He was taken as an apostle worthy of consideration. In fact, he had all the qualifications of an unselfish promoter of ideas and a champion for the freedom of ideas. He was the right man at the right place at the right time. And it is an incontrovertible fact that the man responsible for the introduction of Modern Art in New York and its propaganda was Alfred Stieglitz.

In 1914, studying the ethnographical collection at the British Museum, I was impressed by an object invented by an artist from Pukapuka or Danger Island in the Pacific. It consisted of a wooden stick to which a few circles made of some vegetal material were fixed by pairs right and left to the stick.[8] It impressed me particularly because it reminded me of the physical appearance of Stieglitz. I say "physical" because the resemblance was also spiritual. The object, said the catalogue, was built as a trap for catching souls. The portrait was complete, and it caught my soul, because from it I developed a theory of abstract caricature, theory which I exposed together with a few caricatures called "abstract" together with a few others which were of the "concrete" style. Some of the critics took my theory of abstract caricatures seriously; others didn't.

I had previously made a caricature of Stieglitz with the caption "L'accoucheur d'idées." These two caricatures (figures 96 and 97) expressed my understanding of Stieglitz's mission: to catch souls and to be the midwife who brings out new ideas to the world.

The following anecdote collected by Paul B. Haviland and reported in *A Study of the Modern Evolution of Plastic Expression,* shows well the attitude of Stieglitz towards his hostile visitors:

> *A well known collector and connoisseur wandered into the Little Gallery at "291" while the first exhibition of John Marin decorated the walls. After a rapid glance at the watercolors he turned aggressively towards Stieglitz and in a tone which admitted no contradiction said "This is not Art and I am supposed to know something about art." "Yes," answered Stieglitz unperturbed, "but you have finished your education, I am beginning mine."*

The answer was by no means a "wise crack." Stieglitz was learning Modern Art, that is, he was learning to "see" his reaction to an art that was new to him; he was learning to look into himself and forgetting his art education which had taught him to look out of himself. The gentleman connoisseur had learned to circumscribe art within certain boundaries. Everything within those boundaries was *good,* and everything outside was *evil.*

Stieglitz was objectivist in art; he was a photographer, a champion of *straight* photography and was learning to become subjectivist, sharing with artists and with the art public in general the benefits of his education.

The art critic of the *New York Sun,* Samuel Swift, relates the following anecdote in his review of the exhibition of caricatures by Alfred J. Frueh at "291" in 1913:

There was once a young man making pictures and tying them together with strings of words for a New York newspaper. What he did was willingly paid for, but the work was not that which accurately expressed the personality of the young man himself. In his hours of leisure (this phrase will sound strange to many a newspaperman) the artist made pictures and drawings that were only to please himself. It happened that one of his colleagues saw some of the drawings, chiefly caricatures, and brought news of them to the unique man at the head of the Little Gallery of the Photo-Secession, Alfred Stieglitz.

Of course, Mr. Stieglitz, after seeing the modest youth and his work, said "Come." That is a way he has when he believes in anything; said Mr. Stieglitz to the newspaperman: "You have done these drawings in order to sell them?" "No." "Do you want them to be published?" "No." "You did them only for your own interest and satisfaction?" "Yes." "Good," said Stieglitz; for his gallery, as you know, is the one show place in New York where the matter of selling what is exhibited is of less importance than anything else connected with the enterprise.

The young artist went on to say that he was going to Europe to continue his art studies, and if Mr. Stieglitz would be good enough to keep his drawings, some fifty in number, until his return, he would be obliged. So he went and now Mr. Stieglitz has mounted these caricatures of well known actresses and actors under pieces of thick glass and placed them upon the walls of his little exhibition room.

A few days ago there came a distinguished man of middle age who looked hard and long at one of these clever and quite personal drawings. After a while he looked at Mr. Stieglitz. Pointing to the drawing of a well known actor, he said, "That, Sir, is my son-in-law."

"Indeed," said the courteous and cautious Stieglitz, moving a little further away.

"Yes," returned the visitor with solemnity, "that is he. I will buy it."

"But," ventured Stieglitz, in a relieved tone, "these drawings are not for sale."

"What," said the visitor, "do you mean to tell me that I can't buy the portrait of my own son-in-law?"

"Yes, that is exactly the situation."

The distinguished gentleman stared. "But I want the picture."

"No doubt," answered Mr. Stieglitz, "and so do others. But I can't let you have it." And so, after an exchange of cards, exit the visitor.

This authentic anecdote well depicts the attitude of the Photo-Secession in matters of sales. But this does not mean that Stieglitz was opposed to sales when circumstances demanded it. But it was done at his price and conditions. I remember that J. P. Morgan, the famous banker, once wanted "another print" of the photograph that Steichen had made of him. A masterpiece if ever there was one in pictorial photography. Mr. Morgan had to pay two thousand dollars for the new print. A record price, but worth it.[9]

Stieglitz knew how to sell, when, and to whom. But the cases were rare and exceptions to the rule.

That non-commercial, refined attitude helped also to inspire respect for modern art. It was shown for its merits and not for its value in dollars.

Now a few opinions on Stieglitz:

> *Mr. Stieglitz is on deck with sensational and sardonic theories that surmount the din of battles and shine above the dust clouds arising from crumbling Empires.*
>
> (*H. McBride in the* New York Sun)

> *Behind the masque worn by Alfred Stieglitz, which frowns from a tremendous height at visitors in the Little Gallery, No. 291, I am inclined to detect a somewhat sardonic grin . . .*
>
> (*Guy du Bois,* Art and Decoration)

Man Ray made a good picture of Stieglitz when he wrote the following in the special number of *Camera Work* devoted to "What is 291?":

> *A man, the lover of all through himself stands in his little gray room. His eyes have no sparks—they burn within. The words he utters come from everywhere and their meaning lies in the future. The Man is inevitable. Everyone moves him and no one moves him. The Man through all expresses himself.*

"A pleasing all-round paradox is Stieglitz" wrote Henry Tyrell in the *New York World* in 1911, "a dreamer who is so wide awake that he sees genius coming before it arrives, or maybe it never does arrive; a picture connoisseur who is always putting up a fight for the recognition of somebody or something, and yet is bored by success—who is a loyal lover of Rubens, and at the same time gives the glad hand to Matisse, who delights in showing things that nobody wishes to buy or would accept as a gift, and when he does occasionally trot out something that people would pay any price for, it is not for sale."

A lady visiting "291" during the second Marin exhibition became very much excited at not having been able to grasp the full expression of the watercolors after a five minute examination, and took Alfred Stieglitz severely to task:

> *Lady—Do you think these are good paintings?*
> *Stieglitz—I think they are excellent paintings.*
> *Lady—Well, I can't see anything in them, and yet I just adore art.*
> *Stieglitz—You do not surprise me. You probably like Japanese prints.*
> *Lady—Yes, I understand and adore Japanese prints. I begin to see something in this Marin over there; it looks a little like one of the Hokusai prints.*

Stieglitz—What you have just said makes me think that you are far-
ther than ever from understanding Marin's work. Perhaps if you for-
got for a few moments Japanese prints and other works you have seen
before and gave yourself a chance to relax while you are looking at
Marin's work you might perceive something of what he intended to
convey.
Lady—Well, I don't think an artist should . . .
Stieglitz—Excuse me, just a minute. Why should you presume to
tell an artist what he should do. When he is working he is not think-
ing of you or me, or anybody else; he is only satisfying a need of ex-
pressing something which is within him. When we are admitted to
look at his work, we are invited to look at his expression of his own
thoughts or emotions, not of what we would have thought or felt un-
der like circumstances. Therefore we are not to look for any part of
ourselves in his work. But if we are anxious to take advantage of the
occasion which he offers us to share his pleasure, we must try to under-
stand what he has expressed; and if we don't understand, it is proba-
bly more our own fault than that of the artist.
Lady—Do these watercolors mean anything to you?
Stieglitz—They give me a great amount of pleasure.
Lady—Well, won't you explain to me what pleasure you get out of
them?
Stieglitz—Let me first ask you a question. Some people are fond of
oysters and some are not. Are you among the people who like them or
among those who don't?
Lady—I am very fond of them.
Stieglitz—Well, I never could bear the idea of tasting one. Now, will
you please explain to me in words what pleasant sensation an oyster
gives you so that I will know what it tastes like?
Lady—I could not do it.
Stieglitz—No, you could not, no matter how eloquent you might be.
I must find out for myself. Neither can I explain to you in words the
pleasure I get from a painting or a statue. The plastic artist expresses
himself through his own medium and you must study him through his
medium to get what he wishes to express.

(*from* **The Modern Evolution of Plastic Expression**)

Such galleries (the Photo-Secession). . . . Alfred Stieglitz, we know, pays
for the galleries out of the hope of leading us to what he believes to be art of
the future, but he acknowledges he does not know where that art will
reach.

We are in somewhat of the same condition as they were in the early
days of the Renaissance, he will tell you, seeking for the unknown. I don't
know when it will be reached, but I do see that these men are alive and vi-
tal, and my object is to show to Americans who have no opportunity of go-
ing abroad, what vitality in art exists there.

(B. P. Stephenson in the Evening Post, *1909*)

> *. . . take the elevator [to the Photo-Secession Gallery] if you do not weigh over 90 pounds; and if you go there between 12 and 1 o'clock, midday, you may miss the grand panjandrum of the gallery, Alfred Stieglitz. This warning is not meant to depreciate that ingenious gentleman; rather it is a safeguard against the seductiveness of his golden voice. Once open the porches of your ears to his tones and ere long you will begin to believe that photography it was that originated impressionism; that camera and Monet rhyme; that the smeary compound of mush and mezzo-tint which they have christened the New Photography is one of the fine arts. There's no re-sisting Stieglitz. He believes what he preaches, a rare virtue nowadays; and he has done so much to open the eyes of the philistines with his little exhibitions that he ought to go into the Hall of Fame. . . .*
>
> *(James Huneker in the New York Sun, 1909)*

To justify the exhibition of Modern Art, Stieglitz published the following statement in *Camera Work,* April, 1910:

> *The exhibitions which have been held during the past two years and those which are announced for the season of 1910–1911 show the logical evolu-tion of the works of the Association. Its name, while still explanatory of its purpose, has taken a somewhat different meaning. The Photo-Secession stood first for a secession from the then accepted standards of photography and started out to prove that photography was entitled to an equal footing among the arts, with the production of painters whose attitude was photo-graphic. Having proved conclusively that along certain lines, pre-eminently in portraiture, the camera had the advantage over the best trained eye and hand, the logical deduction was that the other arts could only prove them-selves superior to photography by making their aim dependent on other qualities than accurate reproduction. The works shown at the Little Galler-ies in painting, drawing and other graphic arts have all been non-photographic in their attitude, and the Photo-Secession can be said now to stand for those artists who seceded from the photographic attitude toward representation of form.*

It would be a mistake to think that Stieglitz's purpose and objective was to make people understand modern art. Modern art to him was only an instrument to bring to the surface that which ought to come to the surface—a mirror to put before the public for them to see that the image reflected on it was not the image they thought they had. Modern art was to most incomprehensible; for that reason it was the best tool to make people understand themselves. Stieglitz believed and had faith in something he did not know and had he known it, he would not have be-lieved in it. And what was in his mind was "The Spirit of '291'." The exhibitions of modern art and pictorial photography were only the flesh and bones of the "Spirit" for everybody to see but only for the very few selected ones to understand. All this is not pure lucubration of my own—in a copy of *Camera Work* Stieglitz wrote the following dedication to one of his friends:

"291"—what is it?—to me it is the expression of all that has been—all that is—and all that will be. That at least is its Spirit. What has "291" accomplished? All that it has been given an opportunity to accomplish— and possibly just a little more—it is this more that is "291."

To one of the very, very few who has helped constructively to make "291" a visible something to many—in fact to all—to one who really understands the meaning of "291"—its meaning in its broadest, deepest sense—to one without whose understanding and ability "291" as a Visible Fact would not be what it is today—to my friend————the friend of "291."

—Alfred Stieglitz, January 27, 1915[10]

I think that in these few lines, Stieglitz, for once, showed a little bit of what was in his mind, showing the difference he made between the "physical" and the "metaphysical" sides of "291." In Stieglitz's hands modern art had transcendental value. He showed it not only for what it was but for what it could be for the individual to find his own real self. Without reference directly to modern art, Stieglitz made soliloquies which his friends, who sensed what he meant and did not listen to what he said, accepted as the utterances of an "illuminated," the unbelievers as the outburst of a "charlatan" and the practical ones as the twaddle of a "perfect bore." But both the practical and the impractical attitude of Stieglitz helped to land modern art in New York and stay and develop there.

Alexis Carrel once visited "291" and had, or rather listened to a long speech by Stieglitz. His comment when he left was: "I couldn't imagine that there were in New York a group of people living in the clouds." That after all was a compliment.

It was believed at the time that Stieglitz was the undisputed master of the group of men who worked with him, that his word was to them prophetic and final, in fact a moral autocrat in his surroundings. In Nos. 5–6 of the publication *291* dated July–August 1915, I said in part:

The press has established a false notion of American life. It has succeeded in creating in the American public a fictitious need for a false art and a false literature. The press has in view but one thing—profit.

The real American life is still unexpressed.

America remains to be discovered.

Stieglitz wanted to work this miracle.

He wanted to discover America. Also, he wanted the Americans to discover themselves. But in pursuing his object, he employed the shield of psychology and metaphysics. He has failed.

In order to attain living results, in order to create life—no shields!

Each manifestation of a progressing evolution must derive from an organism which has, itself, evolved. To believe that artistic evolution is indicated by artists copying Broadway girls instead of copying trees—is inane.

We have also moved on from the age of symbolism. It is only the day after that we believe in the orange blossoms of the bride.

Art is a white lie that is only living when it is born of truth. And there is no other truth than objective truth. The others are but prejudices.

Stieglitz tried to discover America with prejudices.

He first, and he alone, placed before New York the various foundation supports of modern art.

He wished to work through suggestion.

But soon, commercialism brought an avalanche of paintings.

Those lepers, those scullery maids of art, those Sudras of progress— the copyists, got busy. They even believed themselves to be part of the evolution because, instead of copying trees, they copied a method.

America remains to be discovered. And to do it there is but one way: DISCOVER IT!

Stieglitz, at the head of a group which worked under the name of Photo-Secession, carried the Photography which we may call static to the highest degree of perfection. He worked in the American spirit. He married Man to Machinery, and he obtained issue.

When he wanted to do the same with art, he imported works capable of serving as examples of modern thought plastically expressed. His intention was to have them used as supports for finding an expression of the conception of American life. He found against him open opposition and servile imitation. He did not succeed in bringing out the individualistic expression of the spirit of the community.

He has put the American art public to the test. He has fought to change GOOD TASTE into COMMON SENSE. But he has not succeeded in putting in motion the enormous mass of the inertia of this public's self-sufficiency. America has not the slightest conception of the value of the work accomplished by Stieglitz. Success, and success on a large scale, is the only thing that can make an impression on American mentality. Any effort, any tendency, which does not possess the radiation of advertising remains practically ignored.

America waits inertly for its own potentiality to be expressed in art.

In politics, in industry, in science, in commerce, in finance, in the popular theatre, in architecture, in sport, in dress—from hat to shoes—the American has known how to get rid of European prejudices and has created his own laws in accordance with his own customs. But he has found himself powerless to do the same in art or in literature. For it is true that to express our character in art or in literature, we must be absolutely conscious of ourselves or absolutely unconscious of ourselves. And American artists have always had before them an inner censorship formed by an exotic education. They do not see their surroundings first hand. They do not understand their milieu.

In all times art has been the synthesis of the beliefs of peoples. In America this synthesis is an impossibility, because all beliefs exist here together. One lives here in a continuous change which makes impossible the perpetuation and the universality of an idea. History in the United States is impossible, and meaningless. One lives here in the present. In a continuous struggle to adapt oneself to the milieu.

> *There are innumerable social groups which work to obtain general laws—moral regulations like police regulations. But no one observes them. Each individual remains isolated, struggling for his own physical and intellectual existence. In the United States there is no general sentiment in any sphere of thought.*
>
> *America has the same complex mentality as the true modern artist. The same eternal sequence of emotions, and sensibility to surroundings. The same continual need of expressing itself in the present and for the present; with joy in action, and with indifference to "arriving." For it is in action that America, like the modern artist, finds its joy. The only difference is that America has not yet learned to amuse itself.*

But I was wrong and unjust in saying all those things. As far as artists are concerned, the Photo-Secession had results or at least one result in John Marin.

MARIN

The American modernists whose work was shown to the public and who had "made their education" in Paris were Maurer, Weber, Walkowitz, Steichen—their ideas, theories, or principles were developed in the French capital, the capital of the world as it was then called. But Marin's case was different. He evolved under its influence, there he became a modernist, and what is still more important an American Modernist. He was the first artist to express the spirit of New York as he felt it. In his watercolors of the peculiar buildings created by the force of necessity he did not express, as others did, the impressive masses and their decorative combination of combined structures. The introductory note he wrote when he exhibited these New York watercolors is reproduced at the end of this chapter. It is a very impressive paper in which he described the emotions and feelings the buildings aroused in him, their pulling and pushing and raising hell among each other, and all that sort of dynamic behavior. And that was what he painted and did it masterfully.

> *Some of John Marin's most recent work in water-colors is being shown at the gallery of the Photo-Secession, No. 291 Fifth Avenue, between Thirtieth and Thirty-first Streets.*
>
> *This artist and this gallery are very intimately associated. It was here that Marin some five years ago found his mind directed toward more abstract forms of expression. Hitherto, in the years succeeding his actual student days in Paris, he had been seeing and feeling through the influence of Whistler. Then the exhibitions at "291" of Cézanne and Picasso water-colors and the talks in the gallery stimulated him to open up to the suggestion of abstraction as a motive. He spent a summer in the Tyrol, seeking to discover the principles of abstract expression in the study of mountain scenery. Then he returned to New York and for a while tested his experience and enlarged it by studying the colossal aspects of the city's skyscrap-*

98 Marius de Zayas, *Alfred Stieglitz and John Marin* (from *Camera Work* [October 1914]).

ers. He was represented by some of these water-colors in the exhibition in the armory in 1913. For the past two years he has been painting on the coast of Maine.

The most characteristic feature of Marin's evolution in this new direction has been his independence. Having sensed the idea that the most valuable element in paintings is expression and that expression may be made more expressive by disembodying it, as far as possible, from the direct representation of the concrete, he proceeded to fit the idea to his own temperament and to work it out in a manner personal to himself. The result is that his water-colors have shown not only a distinct individuality but also an unbroken progression in capacity, leading on step by step to the very remarkable advancement of this latest work.

(Chas. H. Caffin in the New York American)

One of the most comforting things about Mr. Marin, the artist, is that although he belongs unmistakably to this year of Our Lord, he yet escapes from complete identification with any of the various cliques or schools. Like Albert P. Ryder, he would be gladly claimed by all the factions. There is frequently in his work a breaking up of outlines and a recomposition of them in the "modern art" fashion, yet I should hate to call Mr. Marin a cubist, a post-impressionist, or any other term except "artist."

(Henry J. McBride in the New York Sun)

Here is the explanation Marin made of his new venture:

Shall we consider the life of a great city as confined simply to the people and animals on its streets and in its buildings? We have been told somewhere that a work of art is a thing alive. You cannot create a work of art unless the things you behold respond to something within you. Therefore, if these buildings move me they, too, must have life. Thus the whole city is alive; buildings, people, all are alive. It is the more they move me the more I feel them to be alive. It is this "moving of me" that I try to express, so that I may recall the spell I have been under and behold the expression of the different emotions that have been called into being. How am I to express what I feel so that its expression will bring me back the spell? Shall I copy facts photographically?

I see great forces at work; great movements; the large buildings and the small buildings; the warring of the great and the small; influences of one mass on another greater or smaller mass. Feelings are aroused which give me the desire to express the reaction of these "pull forces": those influences which play with one another; great masses, each subject in some degree to the other's power. In the life of all things come under the magnetic influence of other things; the bigger assert themselves strongly, the smaller not so much, but still they assert themselves, and though hidden they strive to be seen and in so doing change their bent and direction. While these powers are at work pushing, pulling, sideways, downwards, upwards, I can hear the sound of their strife and there is great music being played. And so I try to express graphically what a great city is doing.

Within the frames there must be a balance, a controlling of these warring, pushing, pulling forces. This is what I am trying to realize. But we are all human.

Marin was indeed the first American artist who decomposed the forms of the New York buildings, transforming them from their visual impressiveness into their sensational expressiveness.

THE MODERN GALLERY

Stieglitz's mission as an importer of French Modern Art was interfered with by the war. Most of the French artists had become soldiers. It was known that the art market in Paris was practically closed. An altruistic spirit invaded the Photo-Secession, inspiring the idea that the "moderns" should be helped in some way, most particularly those artists whose work had been shown at the Photo-Secession for "experimental purposes" only.

It was therefore proposed to open another gallery, a branch of "291" in which works of art would be used both for propaganda and for sale, in order to help the needy. The result of this suggestion was the opening of the Modern Gallery. The whole situation is perfectly explained in an announcement published in *Camera Work,* No. XLVIII, published in October, 1916, which says as follows:

> *"291" announces the opening of the Modern Gallery, 500 Fifth Avenue, New York, on October 7th, 1915, for the sale of paintings of the most advanced character of the Modern Art Movement, Negro Sculpture, pre-conquest Mexican Art, Photography.*
>
> *It is further announced that the work of "291" will be continued at "291" Fifth Avenue in the same spirit and manner as heretofore. The Modern Gallery is but an additional expression of "291."*

Underlying the above announcement, the circular reprinted below had been prepared for public dissemination. This was withheld because "291" felt it owed no explanations to anyone, and the above was substituted in its stead. But the course of events necessitated a recording in *Camera Work* of the genesis of the Modern Gallery. The withheld circular announcement read as follows:

> *"291" announces the opening in the first week of October of a branch gallery at 500 Fifth Avenue, called the Modern Gallery. Here modern and primitive products of those impulses which for want of a more descriptive word, we call artistic, will be placed on exhibition and offered for sale.*
> *We are doing this for several reasons.*
> *We feel that the phase of our work which has resulted in arousing an interest in contemporary art in America has reached a point where, if it is*

99 View from the window of the Modern Gallery, toward the intersection of Fifth
Avenue and 42nd Street, 1915.

100 View from the window of the Modern Gallery, toward the New York Public Library, 1915.

to fulfill itself, it must undertake the affirmative solution of a problem which it has already negatively solved.

We have already demonstrated that it is possible to avoid commercialism by eliminating it.

But this demonstration will be unfertile unless it be followed by another: namely, that the legitimate function of commercial intervention—that of paying its own way while bringing the producers and consumers of art into a relation of mutual service—can be freed from the chicanery of self-seeking.

The traditions of "291" which are now well known to the public, will be upheld in every respect by the new gallery.

It is the purpose of the Modern Gallery to serve the public by affording it the opportunity of purchasing at unmanipulated prices whatever "291" considers worthy of exhibition.

It is the purpose of the Modern Gallery to serve the producers of these works by bringing them into business touch with the purchasing public on terms of mutual self-respect.

It is the purpose of the Modern Gallery to further, by these means, the development of contemporary art both here and abroad, and to pay its own way by reasonable charges.

To foreign artists our plan comes as a timely opportunity. Their market in Europe has been eliminated by the war. Their connections over here have not yet been established.

Photography has always been recognized by "291" as one of the important phases of modern expression. The sale of photographic prints will be one of our activities.

We shall also keep on hand a supply of photographic reproductions of the most representative modern paintings, drawings, and sculptures, in order to give to the public an opportunity to see and study modern works of art that are privately owned in Europe and elsewhere.

The literature of modern art will also be dealt with.

Indeed, as time goes on, we propose that nothing shall be omitted that may make the Modern Gallery a helpful center of all those—be they purchasers, producers, or students—who are in developmental touch with a modern mode of thought.

To these products of modernity we shall add the work of such primitive races as the African negroes and the Mexican Indians because we wish to illustrate the relationship between these things and the art of today.

Marius de Zayas, who had been a very active worker at "291" for years past—as is evidenced in the pages of *Camera Work*—was, as the proposer of the idea and the chief believer in the need of such an enterprise as the Modern Gallery, naturally given the management of the experiment. The opening exhibition consisted of paintings and drawings by Braque, Burty, de Zayas, Dove, Marin, Picabia, Picasso, Walkowitz; sculpture by Adolf Wolff; photographs by Alfred Stieglitz; and Negro Art.

Mr. de Zayas, after experimenting for three months on the lines contemplated, found that practical business in New York and "291" were incompatible. In consequence he suggested that "291" and the Modern Gallery be separated. The suggestion automatically constituted a separation.

The intention of selling modern pictures was certainly a good one. But soon I found that "pictures do not sell themselves" was only too true, and that I did not have the qualifications of a salesman. Fortunately, the Modern Gallery did not depend on sales for existence. Eugene Meyer, Jr. had provided for it with the conviction that there would be no returns. And he was not disappointed. The commercial side of the Modern Gallery was, therefore, very negligible. In the three years of its existence there were only two buyers, Arthur B. Davies, who knew all there was to be known about buying pictures, and John Quinn, who just bought and bought. Neither of the two needed to be lured into buying. At the end of the life of the Modern Gallery, Walter C. Arensberg appeared as a buyer and made up for lost time. Davies and Quinn were old timers and knew the marked (French) value of modern works of art, and also knew that they were getting "bargains." Mr. Arensberg began collecting pictures from the Modern Gallery at a later date. You can well imagine that with that limited clientele the pictures were not selling like hot cakes at the Modern Gallery.

There would have been no reason at all to open a new gallery to show modern art if the same method and the same attitude of "291" were to be followed. I saw that also soon enough. Hence the "separation" announced by Stieglitz. I was not psychic enough to be a second Stieglitz. I thought that psychological experiments with the public had been done sufficiently. I thought that if pictures do not sell themselves, they could at least speak for themselves; and I thought the best policy I could adopt was to leave people alone to think for themselves. I wanted to bring the artist in contact with the public, the producer with the consumer without intermediaries; I wanted to feed the public with as much as I could get in quality and quantity, but not with pre-digested food.

The war favored the Modern Gallery in the supply of works of art. The Paris market had been almost closed; artists and dealers were willing to take a chance in letting their works of art cross the ocean in spite of the dangers encountered—I took full advantage of the situation.

In most of the exhibitions the catalogue had not the usual foreword to guide the visitor, and only occasionally I indulged in printing a few words when, in my opinion, the circumstances required it.

As you must have noticed, the succession of exhibitions both at the Photo-Secession and at the Modern Gallery did not follow a pre-established plan, didactic or otherwise. Pictures were exhibited when we could get them. We had discrimination but we did not have chronological order in the sequence of the progress on evolution of the modern art movement.

When the Modern Gallery opened I had the pretention of showing the public how that movement came about with a series of chronological exhibitions. I intended to begin with the work of Gauguin, who first introduced into European contemporary art the exotic element, and with the work of Van Gogh who started talking about the psychological meaning of color. Gauguin's paintings of Tahiti were not available even at that time. But I could get in Paris a few paintings by Van Gogh loaned by dealers. And the Van Gogh exhibition was in reality the opening one at the Modern Gallery.

The attitude of the Modern Gallery vis-à-vis the public was entirely different, in fact, quite the opposite of that of the Photo-Secession. Stieglitz experimented with the public; his place was, as he called it, a laboratory. I left the public to work out its own salvation; I left it alone. I experimented in combining most of the time the work of several artists, to suggest comparisons, combinations that I presented to the public for what they were worth. Besides, I do not have the ability, intelligence, and facility of speech that Stieglitz had and lavished on the public. Stieglitz had prepared the way, opened the roads, and I only had to let matters take their natural course—I let the pictures or sculptures do their own talking. Although, in truth, most of the exhibitions at the Modern Gallery were accompanied also by an introductory note.

The Modern Gallery, which is announced as "an additional expression of '291'" has been opened at No. 500 Fifth Avenue "for the sale of paintings of the most advanced character of the modern art movement, negro sculpture, pre-conquest Mexican art, and photography." The inclusion of the last may cause surprise until one reflects that a good deal of the modern art movement is concerned with the expression of pure objectivity, and a photograph, if it is a "straight" one, is the purest product of an objective process.

The Modern Gallery will serve a useful purpose as a "clearing house" not only of advanced ideas but of values. The question of how far the ideas of a comparatively small number of artists are biting into the consciousness of the community will be solved by the world's test of having arrived—the saleable value of the product.

This will be something, though it will not settle the real value of the ideas. Meanwhile, the permanent exhibition of the expression of these ideas will help toward estimating them. We shall be able to reach at least a personal conclusion as to what, if anything, they mean to ourselves and how far that something has a place for testing impressions of the "new art movement." Such as has not existed in New York before. I hope to return to the subject on another occasion.

(New York American, *November 1, 1915*)

Two important announcements are made by Alfred Stieglitz and the Montross Gallery. Both are of vital interest. Mr. Stieglitz announces that Marius de Zayas has secured for the Modern Gallery, 500 Fifth Avenue, a series of unusual examples of modern art. These include work by Van Gogh, the complete evolution of Picasso (including his very last paintings), Brancusi (his last piece of sculpture), important Cézannes, a new and rare group of negro sculpture, and other things.

On Monday, November 22, there will be shown the following eight Van Goghs: Berceuse, Les Baux, Nuages, Neige, Vase de Soleils, Fleurs-Lilas, Hollandaise, and Les Harengs. These will be on exhibition for three weeks.

This announcement, which will raise every young painter's expectation, follows close on the announcement by Mr. Montross that he will hold a small and select exhibition of works by Cézanne early in January. It has been insisted often in this column that a fuller opportunity should be afforded the Americans interested in modern art to study directly the works of Cézanne, Van Gogh, Gauguin, Picasso, and the other men who count, before the little men like Picabia and a host of others equally unimportant are thrust upon them.

(New York Evening Post, *November 20, 1915*)

VAN GOGH AT THE MODERN GALLERY

VAN GOGH AT THE MODERN GALLERY

The remarkable group of paintings by Van Gogh on view at the Modern Gallery until the middle of December, although comprising only eight examples, fairly represents the range of the artist's work, from the lacquered browns of "La Hollandaise" to the dry greens and synthetic outline of "La Berceuse." Between these lies a characteristic landscape with clouds that scud in loosely massed bundles across a blue sky above yellow field; and a flower subject not so characteristic, but one of the most beautiful and delicately organized pieces of color possible to imagine.

(New York Times, *November 20, 1915*)

IMPRESSIVE EXAMPLES OF VAN GOGH

A group of recently imported paintings by Vincent Van Gogh are being exhibited in the Modern Gallery. They include landscapes, still lifes, and an important portrait of a peasant woman.

The symbol of Van Gogh's life is a flame; at first coiling hither and thither in search of what to feed itself upon; then burning with concentrated heat and finally consumed by its very intensity. The elements of the flame were ardent sympathy with humanity and a need of self expression—a hunger to give out something that would serve his human sympathy. So, after working for some years as an art salesman, he became a clergyman and devoted himself to ministering to the miners of Belgium.

(New York American, *November 29, 1915*)

101 Vincent van Gogh, *La berceuse*, 1889.

THE MODERN GALLERY: 500 FIFTH AVENUE

The Modern Gallery makes an auspicious beginning in its plan to hold several successive exhibitions of important modern works recently secured in Europe, by showing eight of Van Gogh's paintings. The group presents the most striking contrasts imaginable, and on that account is particularly interesting, for, in spite of its tantalizing incompleteness, it gives illuminating glimpses of the richness of Van Gogh's genius. To him it was equally natural to express the intense excitement which exalted his spirit in [the] presence of wild mountain forms, and to put into visible color the lyric joy he felt in the most delicate harmonies in an arrangement of flowers.

(Evening Post, *November 27, 1915*)

VAN GOGH AT THE MODERN GALLERY
(BY THE SECOND VIEWER)

The "mad painter of Arles" is a sane and powerful master in certain of the eight pictures now on view at the new Modern Gallery. Mr. de Zayas is to be congratulated. His selection and arrangement of this little exhibition might have touched Vincent's own heart, so thoughtful is the selection and so modest the arrangement.

With what rare boldness had this expositor placed the most masterly of all the canvases against the light. Entering, one sees a blazing window—and a picture.

Sunlight streams from behind the canvas, around it and upon the floor. Light is everywhere but upon the picture. Yet the picture is luminous, for the light is "in" it. Here is a broad green meadow of Arles, with children half hidden among the grasses and the stalks of the field flowers they gather, lying under a sunny blue sky. Still leafless trees, slender, but firm, with roots well "struck" as Vincent used to say, into the earth, rise out of the moist green of the mid-distance, reaching in the spring air toward "the clouds" that churn above with a vigor not approved by Ruskin, but permitted by liberal and rather "old" fashioned mother Nature. What a marvelous vision in a mad man!

(American Art News, *December 11, 1915*)

The "rare boldness" of the expositor was due to force of circumstances. The wall space at the Modern Gallery was very small. The front wall was a solid window all glass from top to bottom. One felt it to be in the street (figures 99 and 100). The light which came from that window was not the ideal light for pictures, and the Van Gogh in question had to be put on an easel against the light or on the floor or nowhere at all.

The visitors at the Modern Gallery must have wasted a tremendous amount of mental energy trying to concentrate their attention on the pictures, for besides the distraction of the enormous traffic on the corner of Fifth Avenue and Forty-

Second Street, there were two bands in front of the Library playing the Marseillaise one right after the other from early morning until night.

MODERN SCULPTURE AT THE MODERN GALLERY

In 1916 I arranged an exhibition of comparative sculpture: Brancusi, Modigliani, Mrs. A. Roosevelt, Alice Morgan Wright, Adolf Wolff, three Americans who had started modeling with modern tendencies. A few Negro sculptures were around to complete the comparativeness.

> At the Modern gallery five sculptors of the newer school show pieces that exhibit their desire to make visitors use their imaginations in order to understand what meaning the creators of the works intend to convey. Mrs. A. Roosevelt in "Atoms" comes nearer to human warmth than the others, for, in a closely pressed together group of three almost human forms, only their backs being exhibited while their heads are brought together, she seems to express the agglutinative nature of atoms. Her "Tennis Player Serving" shows high action, as does Miss Alice Morgan Wright's "Wind Figure," only naturally more distorted. In his eight subjects Adolf Wolff, aided by geometrical suggestions in compressed form, would express such abstractions as struggle, revolt, relaxation, brooding, repose, etc. In the "Revolt" for instance, angles and points abruptly protrude, while in "Relaxation" the forms are constructed lower in stature. "New York" is presented as a series of truncated, tall pyramids, undoubtedly referring chiefly to skyscrapers and also to its aspiration and strife. A striking study is Brancusi's brass "Mythological Bird" which might haunt a superstitious person, and by Modigliani are two "Figureheads."
> (Brooklyn Eagle, *March 13, 1916*)

> Until March 22 the Modern Gallery will show sculpture by Mrs. A. Roosevelt, Alice Morgan Wright, Adolph Wolff, Modigliani, and Brancusi. From one point of view, the little "Wind Figure" by Alice Morgan Wright is the most interesting of the group, showing as it does the moment of passing over from an old and familiar convention to one as yet unfamiliar and new. It is a remarkably convincing little figure, keeping the gesture of life and its elasticity while adding the cubistic formula. In Adolph Wolff's work one encounters the long-recognized idea of certain linear symbols for repose and action, the horizontals, the diagonals, and the perpendiculars having their separate messages. The "newness" consists in the abstract treatment and avoidance of anything resembling imitation of nature. Brancusi is represented by a head and by his beautiful "Mythological Bird." Modigliani's "Two Figureheads" are very unequal, one having a monumental quality quite lacking in the other. Mrs. Roosevelt's "Tennis Player, Serving" is a happy conventionalization of a fine gesture in life. Most of the work seems to the outsider transitional in character, but most of it seems also on the way to something, and that is more than can truly

102 Adolf Wolff, *New York* [?], 1916, nickel-plated metal.

103 Adelheid Roosevelt, *Atoms.* Plaster.

104 Adelheid Roosevelt, *Tennis Player.* Wood.

105 Alice Morgan Wright, *Sculpture to Be Touched.*
Plaster.

106 Amedeo Modigliani, *Head.*

be said of the larger part of the sculpture placed in exhibitions in whatever school it finds itself.

(New York Times, *March 13, 1916*)

The Modern Gallery has chosen opportunely the present moment to offset, or rather to complement, the Forum exhibition of "isms" in painting with a showing of some of the latest evolutions in idealistic sculpture. Adolf Wolff's curious "block" or voluminal formulations of figures and architecture, which are also approximately characterized as polyhedral and "crystallic," dominate the small but vital assemblage. Mrs. A. Roosevelt has a geometrically organized statuette of a tennis player in the act of serving; and a vaguely twisted shred of plaster symbolizing "The Atoms." Miss Alice Morgan Wright's "Wind Figure" might indeed have been blown into its present formless shape. Two "Figureheads" by Modigliani would look well on the prow of some classic bark in architecture or on a monument, while Brancusi's well known "Mythological Bird" shown here in shiny bronze, has been often and aptly likened to a gargoyle.

It would be possible for a stranger to enter and walk around the cubist hung Modern Gallery and then make his dazed exit without noticing that a sculpture exhibition is installed there.

Nevertheless, there is sculpture, and more than a little of it, that should well repay study by the thoughtful seeker after artistic truth and beauty. Looked at more closely and with a certain responsive sympathy, Mr. Wolff's massed cubes of plaster and metal suddenly assume shapes of monumental dignity and grandeur. Their only lines are planes and many angles; their forms are material and mass, geometrically organized or "crystallized" into the symbol of an idea. This may mean nothing and yet the pyramidal pile representing a "New York" of skyscrapers, will. "Struggle," "Revolt," "Relaxation," and "Repose" are similarly expressed, in bare, angular, elementary arrangements that have a certain austere eloquence.

(The Christian Science Monitor, *March 25, 1916*)

DIEGO RIVERA AT THE MODERN GALLERY

In 1916 the Modern Gallery held an exhibition of paintings by Diego M. Rivera. After practicing several different styles of painting Rivera ingressed into the ranks of Cubism, bringing to it a few original contributions. Some of his styles including cubist pictures (which were his latest at the time) were represented in the exhibition.

In that year, 1916, Rivera wrote to me the following declaration:

Form exists in a plastic ensemble, as a relative entity changing into as many different expressions as the causes which limit the pace that surrounds it are modified. Example: the reformations of Cézanne, which people usually call "deformations." Form exists per se in everything, ever-

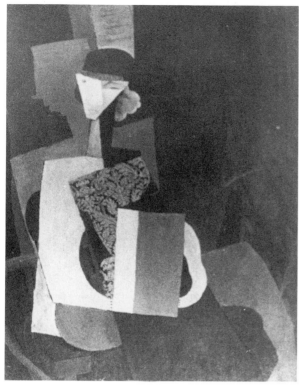

107 Diego Rivera, *Portrait of Mariewone (Madame Marcoussis)*, c. 1915.

108 Diego Rivera, *La terrace du café*.

lastingly immutably, independently from the perceptive accident, and without being under the influence of the surrounding space, and being only in relation with the Primary Form. Form exists as a quantity that participates in both the preceding dualities, that is to say, as belonging to one independent case of the physical space; in a portrait, for instance, the head exists as a generality common to all men; as a head it will have qualities of accidental form, its position in space, total roundness of the cranium, but in a portrait after making a head one must particularize and make of that head one head, and this individualization that will come over it will not depend upon the plastic accident but will be a determined ensemble of traits that would make a unique and personal facial cipher.

In the picture the accidental form carries with itself a mechanical taxation, its measure in relation to the other forms that accompany it, and the space that surrounds it; pure form does not carry in itself any relative dimension, therefore, for the picture; it will only be a starting point, a spiritual vista over the Universe, and this is the reason why it will live in the plastic ensemble, in the space created between the relative form and the super-physical dimension.

In plastic space, things have a super-physical dimension which grows or diminishes in direct ratio to the importance that its existence has in the spirit of the painter: For example, the change of the real size of the objects among the primitives: the Holy Virgin is far larger than the gift carriers; Saint Francis is as tall as the church he supports, and the fortress besieged and conquered by the condottieri could pass easily between the legs of his horse.

Color, like form, exists in the plastic ensemble as an individual accident: like the local color of the painting of all times; it exists per se: pure color, color-impelling-force; and exists also as a result produced by the reactions which are the consequence of the action of the color and local form, the pure color and form and substance, like in the work of Grunwald, Seurat, and the Impressionists, that is to say, color-derived-force.

"Matter," the substance, also lives as an accident: quality of painting; per se: as a substantial structure independent of the visual accident and its plastic consequences, and as derived force, giving the sensation of weight of lightness, modifying the representative quantities on the visual space, increased or diminished, multiplied or divided for the expression of their greater or less stability, as in the paintings of Giotto, Cézanne, Greco, Zurbaran, Velasquez, and in Oriental art—and above all in the negro and Mexican sculpture.

The plastic ensemble thus understood, the painter starts from two opposed and indisputable principles: the existence of things in the real, visual, and physical space; and their existence in the real, super-physical, and spiritual space.

The controlled and logical action of their primary elements would make possible the coexistence in the same plastic ensemble of the most complex and the simplest expressions. The painter is able to create the causes which produce them, and to find the true space in which they can exist without losing their purity nor destroying that plastic ensemble, which un-

*derstood in this manner, makes it possible for the expression of the most
visible and tangible thing and the most inner feeling to be within the
UNITY.*

—*Diego M. Rivera*

*The first comprehensive exhibition of the work of Diego M. Rivera, a na-
tive of Mexico, long resident in Paris, is on view in the Modern Gallery,
where it will remain through October 21. Mr. Rivera is a follower of the
most advanced schools of contemporary French art, his earliest canvas
shown here (it dates from 1911) being of the "confetti" type of pointillism,
and while it is lovely in color there is not a trace of originality in an inch of
it. The same may be said of his excursions into the school of Picabia and
Picasso, his chief offense in this line being a "Portrait of Mariewny" in
which the female original is made to resemble a violoncello, with the face
and head confined within the plane of a sharp triangle. The grotesque ab-
surdity of this picture is only excelled by the "Spanish Still Life" and the
"Sugar Bowl," all in half sections and askew at that. Obviously the gravity of the war abroad has not touched the inner spirits of the devotees of the
schools of pictorial art.*

(New York Evening Mail, *October 9, 1916*)

PAINTINGS BY DIEGO RIVERA

*Paintings by Diego Rivera are at the Modern Gallery, and their quality of
color and form will interest those for whom the non-representative character
of this school of modern art has no terrors. It should be kept in mind that
work of this kind expresses a certain philosophy, or at least a certain striving toward a philosophy, which is a part of modern experience and therefore inevitably is recorded in the art of the time. The religion inaugurated
by Buddha is written in a thousand carvings, and the system of thought
with its accompanying symbols of expressions that has grown up, no one
knows how, among a very large number of perfectly sincere painters today,
will be recognized historically as important evidence in the case of art in
the twentieth century. Many of these painters struggle with the written
word as a means of expression and a few of them conquer it. Rivera has
been clearer than the majority of these fellows.*

(Times, *October 8, 1916*)

*The Modern Gallery, 500 Fifth Avenue, shows a group of paintings by
Diego M. Rivera and an exhibition of Mexican pre-Conquest art. Mr. Rivera obligingly labels his productions 1911, 1912, and so on up to date.
Though, in fact, his paintings register their dates almost as unmistakably
as the brownstone houses of New York's crosstown streets. In 1911, Mr.
Rivera was doing quite nice Signacs, and every year this versatile painter
has imitated the work of some Frenchman; Cézanne, all of them have had
a year of it. The Aztec exhibit is so slight that it gives only the faintest
idea of muscular, original, and thoroughly interesting art.*

(Evening Post, *October 7, 1916*)

Impressions of an exhibition of paintings by Diego M. Rivera in the Modern Gallery are a bit confusing because, while the artist is highly imaginative and capable, he seems to let caprice guide him rather than set motions. Thus the display becomes one of versatility and its quality is uneven. Three kinds of modern work are represented in nine hangings, as if he would like to show that he understands each kind and is not certain which he prefers. He has studied the methods of the painters who aim at effects in color and line which produce the effect known as "abstract expression." Also he knows the devices and admires the technic of the cubists; and he has viewed with sympathy the landscape creations of the school of which Cézanne was chief exponent.

If he is feeling his way through those various methods in order to determine to which he should apply himself for permanent account, and if the present display represents his best accomplishments in each, it may be hoped that his taste leads him toward the school of abstract expression, for in that he excells and in the others he does not, aside from the consideration that cubism has had its day.

He has a canvas called "The Sugar Bowl" that gives full swing to his imagination and to his technic. It shows that when he had caught the spirit of the school, his creative powers evolved a product distinctively his own, in which his facile brush did its best work. One who can deal impressively in canvas abstractions needs to have behind him a reserve of technic and a creative impulse, and nature and training have well supplied Mr. Rivera with both. His "Sugar Bowl" and Spanish still-life on the same wall disclose equally an original fancy and a keen and discriminating eye for color effects. The still-life is concrete rather than abstract, but it has an inherent quality of deft color treatment, and that is one of the essentials in current progression. The new school will have a valuable acquisition in him if he will devote his talent to it.

(*Frederick W. Eddy,* New York World, *October 3, 1916*)

DAUMIER, GUYS, AND TOULOUSE-LAUTREC AT THE MODERN GALLERY

In 1917 I was able to borrow through Paul Guillaume, a few important paintings by Toulouse-Lautrec, belonging to Hessel, the Parisian art dealer. Lautrec's work at one time had impressed Picasso to such an extent that his paintings revealed his affection for Lautrec's. I borrowed also paintings by Daumier and watercolors by Constantin Guys—I made with the three an exhibition claiming them as modernists. I do not need to explain any further the meaning of that exhibition. Henry McBride in the *New York Sun* (February 11, 1917) could do it much better than I ever could:

> *The paintings and drawings by Daumier, Guys and Toulouse-Lautrec now exposed in the Modern Gallery form a highly interesting exhibition*

109 *Diego Rivera*, 1915. Photograph.

110 Honoré Daumier (?), *Third Class Carriage.*

111 Constantin Guys, *Le bel attelage.*

but it may be doubted if it be not—even after all these years—still in advance of public taste.

Mr. de Zayas, who directs the activities of this gallery, holds that these three great caricaturists were precursors of "modern art," and indeed but a hasty scrutiny of the drawings he submits leads one to acquiesce in his opinion. That is, those will acquiesce who already look upon modern art with respectful sympathy; those who feel, like the present writer, that the precursors of modern art were many, and that in fact signs of modernisms were to be discovered in almost all the sketch books of the leaders of a generation or so ago.

Those not sympathetic to the new aspiration, who refuse to recognize modern art and persist in thinking that nothing has happened since Jean Francois Millet and Edouard Manet, will not detect the contemporaneous note in Guys and Daumier because they do not know what the contemporaneous note is; and as for the signs of it in Toulouse-Lautrec which are decidedly pronounced, they will regard it as debauchery or perhaps insanity, or perhaps both.

However, Daumier as an artist is well accepted among us, even though his position as a modernist be disputed. Our Metropolitan Museum would be very glad to possess good works of art by Daumier, and that of course means that he is quite classic. Toulouse-Lautrec and Guys are not so well known.

That we have amateurs who appreciate Guys was illustrated amusingly at the Hayashi sale at the American Art Association some years ago. Hayashi was an especially erudite Japanese, who had excellent taste in western art, but it was his Japanese heirs who prepared the catalogue for his sale and they were not quite aware of the quality of all that their distinguished relative had bequeathed to them. Among some drawings labelled "artist unknown" was one that was unmistakably by Constantin Guys, and it did seem a heaven-sent chance for someone to acquire a Guys at bargain rates.

When the sale took place the engravings and drawings, some by fashionable artists of ten years ago, seemed not to interest the rather apathetic audience until, unfortunately, the drawing by the "unknown artist" appeared upon the block, when pop, pop, from all over the room came quick bids and the drawing fetched a price that would have been thought considerable even in Paris, where the admiration for Guys is practically a cult. It was quite evident that a few at least of our collectors were au courant.

Guys is certainly, as the French say, a "delicious" artist. His caricatures of fashionable ladies riding in the Bois or making themselves ready for the soiree are caricatures, but at this distance of time they make the effect upon us of realistic records. His work was so simplified (four strokes often sufficing him for the legs of the peculiarly Guys horses that he drew, one stroke a leg) that it is a double astonishment to find that one never gets to the end of it. Guys drawings do, in fact, wear excellently well.

Toulouse-Lautrec had his moment with us at the time of our great craze for posters; his, with Steinlen's and Cheret's, being the most sought for. Then and since an occasional picture by this artist has been seen and admired, but I doubt if his later tendencies as exhibited in certain of the canvases that M. de Zayas now shows us are known here at all.

They are not only "modern" but willful. If Guys was a "Man Child," as Baudelaire says he was, so too was Lautrec, but decidedly he was not a good child. So naughty a boy has seldom been heard of even in Paris, where all the naughty boys go before they die. I do not mean, however, the kind of naughtiness you mean, dear reader. Lautrec was just simply bad. Thackeray would have had him spanked along with the Rev. Laurence Sterne—but then Thackeray was confessedly old-fashioned in his outlook upon manners, was he not?

Lautrec apparently gave himself up unreservedly to the sway of the Muse. He made himself as limber as a willow branch in the effort to carry out the goddess's idlest fancies. Take the scene at the dinner table, for instance. It is not really shocking? Did you ever see the like? A gentleman at the head of the table, supposedly the host, rises and deliberately smashes the guest of honor, a lady, in the face. Two other guests apparently have already encountered the host's fist, judging by their faces, and only one of the diners preserves his corporeal investiture intact. What can a well bred Academician who sees in art nothing but the report of facts do in the presence of such work? Nothing of course but to depart from it as quickly as may be, calling down the wrath of heaven upon Mr. de Zayas, who brought the accursed thing hither.

Nevertheless it is artistic. That complicates the situation, doesn't it? But not for us Academicians! Mr. de Zayas kindly consider yourself cursed.

But perhaps you would like to hear Mr. de Zayas in his defense. Here is what he says in a preface to the catalogue of these artists' works:

"Baudelaire tells us that we must take Guys as a manchild, as a man possessing every minute the genius of childhood, a genius for which none of the aspects of life is worn out. And that if he often was bizarre, violent, excessive, he was always poetical, and knew how to concentrate in his drawings both the bitter and the exhilarating taste of the wine of life.

"If Guys had a passion to see and to feel, Lautrec had the love to live and the love to paint.

"Indefatigable observer, Lautrec was always in search of plastic documents, stenographing movements, and making notes of expressive lines. His paintings were never direct. They were composed, writes Arsene Alexandre, with great persistency, with the aid of documents taken from nature. Here is the way of his method of working: first, the direct sketch made at every occasion in the notebook; after, the study made from nature; after, the post, the illustration, the stamp, understood as a language of silhouette to converse with the public, and last, apart from it all, the painted picture, recommenced, reworked, enriched slowly and with the greatest patience.

"Daumier, Guys and Lautrec were essentially 'Modernist'; they were archivists of their milieu, and they knew how to draw the eternal from the transitory. They replaced the representative line by the expressive line, the intelligent line, which renders the sensibility with which the artist comprehended the object.

112 Henri de Toulouse-Lautrec, *Aristide Bruant.* Lithograph.

113 Henri de Toulouse-Lautrec, *The Red Divan.*

"They were the precursors of the modern movement of art. And in their work one finds the germ of all the art tendencies which have been developing in recent years."

An exhibition of singular interest is now being held at the Modern Gallery, 500 Fifth Avenue. It consists of paintings and drawings by Daumier, Constantin Guys, and Toulouse-Lautrec. To exaggerate what modern art owes to Daumier would be difficult. In a sense, all three of these artists are illustrative, but if those modern devotees of the orthodoxy of the movement are disposed to use the title illustrator as a term of disparagement, let them humble their haughty spirits by the study of Honoré Daumier. Daumier was illustrative, as Goya was illustrative. His genius expressed itself in caricature, full of a vast cynical laughter, yet the power of a great master is felt in the authoritative elimination of the superfluous, in the rich masses and big contours of his painting. Two of his paintings are included in this collection, compositions small in dimensions, but large in conception, and a number of his sardonic drawings.

A lesser talent was that of Constantin Guys, whose work appears in several witty drawings. His comment on life is satirical. His touch in handling pen and wash suggests the delicacy and distinction of Whistler. His little drawing Going to the Bois is touched with elusive magic that fascinates and tantalizes. If this is illustration, what a pity it is that more painters do not know how to be illustrators!

Toulouse Lautrec connects the tradition with that of the Impassionists. One cannot imagine him apart from his relation to Degas. His personality is assuredly very different from that of Degas, but without that influence his style would have been otherwise formed. Born of one of the great families of France, and a cripple all of his life, Toulouse-Lautrec's outlook on life was tinged with the bitter irony of the invalid.

There is nothing wistful or pathetic in his mocking spirit. In his presentation of the base human types he so often chose as subjects there is not the slightest hint of moralizing. His comment on their depravity is utterly free from sentimentality. Toulouse-Lautrec was a stylist, and a learned draughtsman, for all his occasional appearance of haste. He worked often on a sort of cardboard, using as much as possible the blank surface of the board as part of the color composition. A sense of volume is not one of his strongest points, but he made use of every expressive line in his characterization of gesture, and his color at times was rarely beautiful, as, for example, in The Red Divan and The Game of Cards. More fully represented on this occasion than either Daumier or Guys, Toulouse-Lautrec has probably never before been exhibited to this extent in America.

(The Evening Post, *February 11, 1917*)

DAUMIER, GUYS, AND LAUTREC

At the Modern Gallery until Feb. 28th may be seen an exhibition of paintings, water colors, and drawings by Daumier, Guys, and Toulouse-Lautrec, a curious trio to find associated as "modernists." The clever little catalogue of the exhibition gives them this title and explains it thus:

"They were archivists of their milieu and they knew how to draw the eternal from the transitory. They replaced the representative line by the expressive line, the intelligent line, which renders the sensibility with which the artist comprehended the object.

"They were the precursors of the modern movement of art. And in their work one finds the germ of all the art tendencies which have been developing in recent years."

If this is the test, there is many another nineteenth century artist to be listed with these admirable but not equally endowed masters. If we put Daumier at the head of the group it is not because he is wittiest, but because he is simplest with the profound synthetic simplicity of a richly mature mind. Lautrec's vision is thin and sharp, you think of him as the precocious child knowing more than his years warrant of good and evil. Guys looks at life gayly and inquisitively, getting only so far as the ripples near to the shore, however, and missing the stronger rhythms of the deep sea waves. These are for Daumier, in whose temperament ran a vein of blessed commonness, causing him to respond to universal human feeling not of Paris or of cities, but of places primeval, of jungles and prisons and public parks, wherever nature is off guard and free from self-consciousness.

(The New York Times, *February 11, 1917*)

PHOTOGRAPHY AT THE MODERN GALLERY

The Modern Gallery, following the traditions inherited from the Photo-Secession, also exhibited photographs. Three modernist photographers, Sheeler and Schamberg of Philadelphia and Strand of New York, had an exhibition of their work in 1917.

The Modern Gallery, for a change, is showing photographs by Sheeler, Strand and Schamberg. It is a fortunate thing that these three men are looking into the subject of photography, for all three are affiliated with the cause of "modern art," and "modern art" suffers grievously for the lack of proper interpreters among the photographers. Every one is aware, for instance, of how much Rodin and Cézanne owe to Druet, but no one had yet appeared to perform the same kind offices for Picasso, Braque, Gleizes and Duchamp.

Of the three new photographers, Sheeler keeps himself most severely within the limits of true camera form, and a photograph of a New York building has the incision of a Meryon print and the inevitableness of Cézanne's "Bouquet des Fleurs."

(The New York Sun, *April 8, 1917*)

The wish of the critic of the *New York Sun* was indeed commendable. No photographs of the paintings of the artists he mentioned had been done with the required understanding of the subjects and for commercial purposes. That would certainly have helped to promote modern art. But the photographs on exhibition were of an entirely different kind; they were pictorial photography for the recognition of which, as art, Stieglitz had been struggling.

These three artists were not "Photo-Secessionists"; they were independent and, to my knowledge, not attached to any photographic Society. The "real" Photo-Secessionists were a group of photographers devoted to "pictorial Photography" and were official members of the Photo-Secession. Nor were Photo-Secessionists the group of men who helped Stieglitz in his propaganda for modern art; they were just what they were, and did what they could to help the "movement."

An interesting exhibit of the works of three photographers is on at the Modern Gallery. Negro art from the Congo has furnished Mr. Sheeler with models for contribution, and if one cannot fully agree with those who claim superlative values for the artistic efforts of the dusky sons of the Ivory Coast, yet one finds in their work much to interest and surprise. One even sees a fundamental principle in these strange figures that may, consciously or unconsciously, have inspired the "Modernists," "Cubists," "Futurists" and "Vorticists." Be that as it may, Mr. Sheeler's reproductions leave nothing to be desired from the point of view of photography.

Mr. Strand has brought his camera to bear on some intensely realistic views of streets, back yards and such like, with marked success.

More conservative in his art than either of the above mentioned artists, Mr. Schamberg shows a number of charming portraits and photographic views that form the most attractive part of the little display.
(American Art News, March 31, 1917)

The Modern Gallery is showing a group of fourteen photographs by Sheeler, Strand and Schamberg, the alliterative trio.

Mr. Sheeler has specialized in photographs of the original African carvings that the Modern Gallery has constantly shown, in season and out of season, for some time and on modernistic motifs.

An obsidian mask, as executed in Mexico by a primitive, is superbly rendered by him. The same remark applies to a wood carving of a female figure from the French Congo, in which the free lines of the original are brought out in great shape. Brancusi's "Head of a Child," in marble (that looks like a hen's egg conventionalized, and executed in heroic size), is transcendently shown in photographs on its rectilinear base in superb shadow.

Mr. Schamberg has been very happy in his portraiture of a city backyard. The eucalyptus tree, the brick sidewalk, the neglected broom on the pavement and even the stalking cat are all admirably registered. The photographic composition is excellent.

Strand has been at his best in his catching of architectural themes; skyscrapers, apartments and entrances in charming chiaroscuro have engaged his skillful attention, although he has in at least one instance turned aside to record a magnificent mountain bit.
(Evening World, April 7, 1917)

MARIE LAURENCIN AT THE MODERN GALLERY

Marie Laurencin, the only female included by Guillaume Apollinaire among the French modernists, was also represented in 1917 at the Modern Gallery with a collection of her recent drawings and watercolors.

> Oh, how the wives of the New Hope Group of Artists would disapprove of the work of Marie Laurencin that is now to be seen in the Modern Gallery, just around the corner from the Arlington Gallery, and dangerously near. Marie would never do at all in New Hope. Fancy her attending the weekly meetings of the "Lapsed and Lost Society!" It wouldn't do. She'd be too disturbing. She knows too much. It's not good form in New Hope—what a delicious name for the new place that is—for a lady to know too much.
>
> It's a knowing age, though, and that cannot be denied. People these days seem to know everything, especially in Paris. Marie comes from Paris. See that portrait, isn't it awful, but interesting? That's the great danger in Paris, things seem to fascinate one that one wouldn't look at in New Hope. The hat perched upon the back of that woman's head like that is immoral. The hair descends about the pallid face in thin driblets as though the creature had been standing out on the corner in the rain all night.
>
> It reminds one of the spiteful things George Moore said about Madge Kendall's performance of Juliet. He said she didn't know what love was. He said no woman knew what love was who had not waited about for hours in the rain for a lover who didn't come. But this woman knows what love is. At least she has waited about in the rain.
>
> But Marie is an artist. Like Jules Pascin, she has the secret of the line that is vibrating with meaning. No wooden touches in her pictures. How fine those cats are, stealthily creeping through the soft fern! Perhaps they are Paris cats. But they have the same air of mystery and antique savagery that Henry Thoreau remarked in the city cats that drifted into Walden Wood. How knowing even those Picabia children are in their portraits! Here is what Marius de Zayas writes of Marie:
>
> "Marie Laurencin is one of the most conspicuous personalities of modern painting. An adventuress of thought, imbued with the essentially modern spirit, she has apprehended that in the life of the times there is an interloping, complex interweaving. With the manifestations of all races, forming new adjustments every instant, she realizes that there is no possible saturation of spirit that could in a final way express that flowering of life that is called art.
>
> "Derain chose the Italian and Spanish primitives as a medium of expression. Picasso found in the African art the means by which to render plastically his sensoriality. Marie Laurencin has found the terms that express her femininity and sensibility as an artist in the French paintings of the eighteenth century.

"She has embedded all her knowledge of the present in an olden mould. She manifests with purity her comprehension of the eighteenth century, and thereby reveals her personality without promiscuity.

"Marie Laurencin stands as a modernist in so far as her painting is modern. The fact is that the painting of today is not the expression of to-day's life. Modern painting is the interpretation of our comprehension of past performances.

"The work of Marie Laurencin is not the outcome of a theory but the representation of her life."

(The New York Sun, *May 6, 1917*)

A very delightful small exhibition has been arranged at the Modern Gallery of drawings by Marie Laurencin, a French artist, whose work has been shown before in New York only in isolated instances. This lady, whose name is well known to all those who are interested in independent art, is an artist through and through. She is endowed with charm and distinction, with a felicitous light touch, with grace and gayety of spirit.

One element in her independence is her fearless femininity. She makes no effort to disguise herself as a man. Apparently she never struggles with anything. It comes gayly and with facility or not at all, and the drawings seem a perfect vehicle for her delicate and elusive gifts. Those are the gifts that are displayed on this occasion.

Mme. Laurencin's drawings have the charm of mystery, the tang of willfulness, the courage of a lady who has her own ideas, and is not to be dictated to by a male confrere just because he is a man. She married a German, and lives in Spain, but she is French to the core, and the facts of her life bear out the testimony of her work that, first of all, she is herself. Her art is feminine, willful yet just, with the justness of an artist of exceptional sensitiveness, sometimes a little sardonic, often a little slight, tantalizing and alluring.

(New York Evening Post, *May 12, 1917*)

ANDRÉ DERAIN AT THE MODERN GALLERY

André Derain (his paintings) appeared at the Modern Gallery in 1917, unheralded and without any introductory note in the catalogue. Henry McBride supplied the omission to his readers. He wrote in the *New York Sun* (November 18, 1917):

DERAIN, THE MODERN FRENCH SOLDIER PAINTER

Those who have made a certain degree of progress in their modern art studies will relish the André Derain exhibition in the Modern Gallery, but not all of the newcomers to the feast will thrive upon it. Derain is truly one of the forces in modern Paris, but as he never makes the slightest concession to the spectator he is difficult. Every artist paints occasional pictures in

114 André Derain, *Alice in a Green Dress,* 1907.

116 André Derain, *Head of a Woman.*

115 André Derain, *Woman,* c. 1914.

117 André Derain, *Head of a Woman with Shawl.*

120 André Derain, *Still Life.*

118 André Derain, *Italian Woman,* 1913.

121 André Derain, *Woman.*

119 André Derain, *Still Life.*

which his character seems to be crystallized, and which he who runs may read. With this clue every other picture by the artist becomes legible. In the present Derain show there is no clarifying example for the stranger at the gates. There is plenty of diversion, however, for the initiated.

To assist beginners I append an appreciation of Derain, roughly translated from the article by the celebrated Guillaume Apollinaire:

"It is to German aesthetes and painters that we owe academistic art, that false classicism against which true art has struggled since the days of Winckelmann, whose disastrous influence cannot be too much deplored. It is to the honor of the French school that it has always reacted against it, and the audacities of the French painters during the nineteenth century were, above all, efforts to recover the authentic tradition of art.

"It is difficult to characterize the art of the young French school; one can say that it has at all times tended audaciously to adapt itself to the disciplines of great art.

"The future will tell us in what measure it has succeeded, but this one may say, that efforts so sincere, disinterested and brave cannot be in vain when they have been served by talent and knowledge.

"The case of André Derain, who conducts a heavy tractor of artillery at the front, and who may be considered as one of the most remarkable painters in the young French school, is altogether in the lines indicated.

"There are numerous works by André Derain in foreign museums. There is none in any French museum. I am not talking of one who is unknown, however.

"Derain has studied the masters passionately. The copies he made show the care he took to know things. At the same time by an audacity without equal he passed over all that contemporary art held as audacious to recover in simplicity and freshness the principles of art and the disciplines attached to it.

"After the noisy efforts of his youth, Derain turned toward sobriety and measure. At this time were produced works of a force that partook of a religious character, and in which some have wished to read traces, I do not know why, of archaism.

"In the works of André Derain, then, one recognizes an audacious and disciplined temperament. And in one part of his recent essays one traces the always moving efforts he is making to reconcile the two tendencies. He is near to attaining his end, which is a harmony full of realistic and sublime beautitude.

"It is in encouraging audacity and in tempering temerity that one realizes order. But for that a great deal of disinterestedness is necessary. André Derain is the completely disinterested artist. The path he has traced has been followed by a great number of painters, which signifies nothing except that some among them will never find themselves. Nevertheless may they follow his example, even to the end and stimulate their individual courage, for it is in audacity that that one finds the true measure of discipline!"

Mr. Apollinaire's favorite word, "audace," is not quite rendered by the "audacity" of the English, but for the purposes of the above article it will sufficiently serve.

AESTHETIC UNITY IS DERAIN'S MOTIVE

Oil paintings and water colors by André Derain are to be seen at the Modern Gallery. He is serving in the French artillery, so that all these examples were done in the time before the war. They show the artist experimenting with suggestions derived from Cézanne, Picasso, and African carving, intent on the problems of simplification and coordination, and inspired by a spirit singularly pure. He has much of the freshness of outlook and simple sincerity of purpose of the Primitives.

This exhibition well illustrates a remark of Roger Fry's, to be found in the October number of the Burlington Magazine. Speaking of the "movement in art" he says: "In general the effect of the movement has been to render the artist intensely conscious of the aesthetic unity of the work of art but singularly naive and simple as regards other considerations." Derain is not stirred to any emotional expression, and is preoccupied with technique, not for any delight in it, but solely as a means to an end—the attainment of a unity that in the simplest directest way shall stimulate the purely aesthetic faculty by its unity of conception and treatment. And in some cases the unity is so complete that one falls under the spell of it. The absence of the qualities usually associated with painting is forgotten in the sense of aesthetic completeness.

(New York American, *November 19, 1917*)

The Modern Gallery has an exhibition of the works of André Derain. The gallery passes from one extreme to another; one week there are shown the distinguished and significant works of Constantin Guys, and then, as in the present exhibition, the dreary works of a negligible modernist are on view. There is not much to say about these drab still lifes and muddy portraits. Derain was an experimenter in abstractions, which are not wholly successful.

(Brooklyn Eagle, *November 18, 1917*)

MAURICE DE VLAMINCK AT THE MODERN GALLERY

In January, 1918, the Modern Gallery showed a few paintings by Maurice de Vlaminck, paintings which, as usual, came through the agency of Paul Guillaume. I believe that this was the first time that Vlaminck's work was shown in New York, other than those that had been exhibited with the work of other painters.

Maurice de Vlaminck, another and perhaps a more powerful disciple of Cézanne, is represented by a half-dozen canvases at the Modern Gallery. In these the sight is more objective, and the themes of greater variety of content. Monsieur de Vlaminck continues the tradition which calls for creation of order out of chaos. We shall have something to be linked definitely with Cézanne, in his Mount Valerian, though in this canvas the color has less solidity than is Cézanne's wont, and the Vase of Flowers, where the imita-

122 André Derain, *Still Life [after Cézanne].*

123 André Derain, *Head of a Woman.*

tion amounts almost to plagiarism. But, having with these two pictures ac-knowledged his debt to his master, Mr. de Vlaminck goes forth upon his own errand, armed with the other's tools, to be sure, but so learned in the usage of them that they are no longer much of a hindrance. He makes them fashionable things—Marseilles, the Old Port, the Bridge, under which the coursing blue water catches reflections; the Old Street, in an at-mospheric disorder; the Port, on a stormy day, as examples—that better suit his own objective vision. That the fashioning should be a bit clumsy is in the nature of a foregone conclusion, when we remember that he is using the other fellow's tools.

(Evening Post, January 12, 1918)

The Modern Gallery is offering Maurice de Vlaminck a one-man show un-til January 19. Six of his paintings have been selected for assembling, and the Belgian artist, who was a pioneer in the modern movement, belonging to "the Fauves group," is offered a chance of impressing himself upon the gallery visitors, instead of being overwhelmed in a maelstrom of other paint-ings, as was the case when he had a sporadic picture "the Port" in the Soci-ety of Independent Artists' first annual exhibition at the Grand Central Palace last April.

(Evening World, January 17, 1918)

GROUP EXHIBITIONS AT THE MODERN GALLERY

It was the policy of the Modern Gallery before or after introducing a new artist in a one-man show, to exhibit one or two of his paintings together with the work of other artists. The idea was to invite the public to compare and see for themselves the common denominator which existed in that group of artists and at the same time the individual difference between them.

In October, 1916, we had an exhibition of sculpture by Brancusi and Manolo and paintings by Daumier, Cézanne, Van Gogh, Lautrec, Picasso, Derain, Picabia, Vlaminck, Braque, Rivera, and Burty. This was indeed the most complete or com-plex exhibition during the life of the Modern Gallery.

A FEW MODERNS

The decline of the modern movement, decline or return, lately so much dis-cussed by the smug reactionaries, is not yet—whatever the promise of those blindfolded prophets. Brancusi at the Modern Gallery, over which Marius de Zayas presides, was the Brancusi of the Armory, even perhaps a bit more abstract than we saw him in the portrait of Mlle Pogany. In the Head of a Child through purity of craftsmanship he arrives at a spiritual purity quite equal to the sentimental conception we have of infancy. The Bronze Head of a woman with black hair drawn tightly into a nubbin at the nape of the neck is reminiscent of those Blue Stockings so fiercely sati-

124 Maurice Vlaminck, *Flowers.*

126 Maurice Vlaminck, *Still Life.*

125 Maurice Vlaminck, *The Port.*

*rized by the great Daumier. Daumier, himself, was here with another
Third Class Carriage, rich and dark in tone, colorless except for fatness of
the tonality, economic, direct, expressive in drawing. An etching by Picasso shows that he, too, at one time was an expressive, objective draughtsman, fond already of form though not yet driving it to the denial of local
truth. In the Picasso of today the interest in form is supplanted by an interest in the color quality of surfaces. In this he may come closer to the old
masters than he does to those negro creators of wooden gods—for spiritual
worship—which attracted him so much at one period. When he shall have
collected the results of his varied experiments about him and put them into
a picture, we may expect a quite well-rounded, wealthy work.*

(Arts and Decoration, *December, 1916*)

In June 1917 the Modern Gallery held an exhibition of drawings in which were
represented only Daumier, Guys, Lautrec, Picasso, Braque, Derain, Laurencin,
and Picabia.

*The exhibition of drawings at the Modern Gallery is interesting—which
doesn't mean that they are all good. All interesting people are not good,
nor are all good people interesting.*

*These drawings are interesting because they have potentialities. Pi-
casso is, of course, the dominant figure, as is customary where two or three
"moderns" are gathered together. His active mind leaps from one experiment to another, and he has himself quite stopped doing the fiddles and
drawings on scraps of newspaper, which are in the present exhibitions, by
the time his imitators have prepared their first Baby Picasso for market.*

*Always he seeks restlessly for the intangible art of his dreams, and
the very gallantry of his search lifts him to a unique place.*

*There are, for instance, three sketches by Daumier which are rich, vir-
ile forecasts of the "abandon" of the present movement toward a richer,
freer art. The most impressive is a court-room scene, where a few swishing
lines, a few splashes of wash, suggest character and atmosphere more successfully than gallons of paint could do it. The smaller sketches are
miniature-size hands, very forceful and significant.*

Other exhibitors of interest are Derain, Manolo, and Lautrec.

(Evening Post, *June 23, 1917*)

ART NOTES

*Workers in the advanced schools are leading off in the parade of art for the
new season with an exhibition in the Modern Gallery, No. 500 Fifth Avenue, where such exponents of the new freedom as Brancusi, Braque,
Burty, Cézanne, Derain, Manolo, Picabia, Picasso and Rivera have
hung their offerings. Visitors have given real welcome to these unconven-
tionals. There is double reason for cordiality toward them. The work is un-
deniably good, to begin with, and one need not doubt that the persistency of
free assertion argues not only the sincerity of those who cling to it, but also
a clear purpose to stand firm.*

These men are real pioneers. None of them dissipates his talent in haphazard venture. The productions may not be easily interpreted, but none the less they carry wholesome appeal.

. . . At any rate, one has become familiar with such work and may judge it by new standards . . .

(*Frederick W. Eddy*, New York World, *Sept. 17, 1916*)

NEW YORK ART EXHIBITIONS AND GALLERY NEWS

MODERNIST ART IN VANGUARD OF SEASON'S SHOWS

SPECIAL TO THE *CHRISTIAN SCIENCE MONITOR* FROM ITS EASTERN BUREAU

New York, N.Y.—In the van of the art shows of the new season, shortly to be making their many voiced appeal for judgment before the popular and press tribunals, Marius de Zayas offers at the Modern Gallery, 500 Fifth Avenue, a small but significant exhibition of paintings and sculpture by such occult, but no longer entirely unfamiliar artists as Cézanne, Brancusi, Braque, Burty (Havilland), Derain, Manolo, Picasso, Picabia, and Rivera. This is significant, not because it is ahead in mere point of time, but because in the work of these "advanced" men, individually and collectively, we have the keynote of a whole conversion that is to follow. It is the "modern" idea, and there is no escaping it. Even the conservatives become more set and rigid in their conservatism because of an uneasy consciousness of this idea. What is it? It is the universal genii that somebody has let out of the magician's bottle, and that now pervades all the air, never to be reduced back and corked up again. Expression is the word that sums up its meaning, so far as a single word can. Intensive, subjective expression, the dynamics of emotion, chafing at the old and now mostly meaningless academic convention is the restless underlying force responsible for the new and strange manifestations at every hand. Making allowance for this, the things produced are found to be less unreasonable and baffling than we had thought. They may even thrill us with unexpected intimations of beauty, as we become accustomed to the new vocabulary they are using.

(**The Christian Science Monitor,** *Boston, September 29, 1916*)

Another one of these group exhibitions held in November 1916 gave Henry McBride an opportunity to make a few remarks on the attitude of the public toward modern art; he wrote in the *New York Sun* on November 26, 1916:

Derain, Vlaminck and Burty are the artists of the moment in the Modern Gallery, and the chance visitor not only has the opportunity to study works painted in the art language of the day but to see curious manifestations of various forms of human nature upon the part of the visitors.

There are those who seem to come simply for the purpose of shouting out their disapproval in a public place. There are others who just as ignorantly misbehave, for they profess an admiration merely to be in the fashion and give away their affectation in every speech.

Among the sincere spectators are many who appear to be just em-
barking upon a career of art study untrammelled by art habits of any kind,
and in this respect modern art follows the history of the Pre-Raphaelites,
the impressionists, and other innovators, all of whom acquired followers
from among the despised and lowly before the movement became
fashionable.

In the Modern Gallery the other day there was a uniformed porter
from one of the neighboring skyscrapers who evidently took a fearless sort
of pleasure in the novel paintings of Burty, Vlaminck, and Derain, and
who had brought his sister, a serious type of woman, to see them. The atti-
tudes of the two toward the pictures were natural and honestly critical.

This is the second exhibition of the season of the works of Derain.
Vlaminck's style is free and painterlike, full of suggestion. Burty, since his
exhibition of some years ago in "291" has gone Picasso-wards. He does
the Picasso business very well, it must be allowed.

From the first exhibition at the Photo-Secession to the last one at the Modern Gallery, the packing and shipping of all the modern art works shown in these two galleries was made by the firm of Lucien Lefebvre Foinet, Paris. In time of peace, the packing and shipping presented no difficulties, but it was quite a different matter during the war, when all shipping space was needed for war materials and private transportation of freight was practically forbidden, yet Monsieur Lucien Lefebvre managed somehow or other to send boxes containing works of art from Paris to New York, and what was still more difficult from New York to Paris. The Modern Gallery could not have existed without the collaboration of Monsieur Lefebvre, whose business was not mainly packing and shipping but the manufacture of artists' materials.

The friendship and devotion of Mr. Lefebvre for artists, especially American artists, was a very long duration. It was at his shop that Whistler supplied himself with colors and canvas, and since Whistler practically all the American artists, modernists as well as academicians, who lived in Paris did the same.

It must be remembered that the majority of the New York art public started its education in modern art, at the beginning of this century, from zero. It was very apparent that from 1908 to 1915 the art public in New York had gone from simple curiosity to being interested in modern art. I am speaking in a general way. Stieglitz dealt with the public individually, putting the visitor to the exhibition to a sort of third degree to get at their mental reactions. He tried psychological experiments.

It is true that besides the exhibitions at the Photo-Secession there was the "Armory Show." At the Montross Galleries there was also held an exhibition of Cézanne watercolors, several of which were previously shown by Stieglitz, although at the Montross Galleries the prices were greatly increased and several were sold. The Carroll Galleries showed in 1915 eleven early paintings by Picasso. All this, undoubtedly, reassured the public that all was not a joke or crazy stunt.

127 *At the Terrace of the Café du Dome,* Paris, ca. 1908. Photograph. Lucien Lefebvre (with a dog on his lap) with a group of American artists: standing at extreme left, the popular waiter who often lent money to the artists, André; seated third from left, Mahonri Young; continuing to the right, Bill Both, Phil Lawyer, Max Stall, P. Doùgherty, Glason, Morton Johnson, F. Friseke, McPherson.

These are the main points of our work for Modern Art during ten years. It does not seem to be much, but at any rate, a new manner of painting and sculpting was introduced and a new art vocabulary with them, besides a whole lot of new ideas and theories, which are still floating about.

With the Negro Art exhibitions in 1918, which I have already mentioned, the Modern Gallery came to an end, and also my career as a propagandist for modern art.

The war was over.

Sometime after the text of this account had been completed, de Zayas added the following note, commenting on the state of contemporary criticism:

There was at the time of the Armory Show perhaps more curiosity than interest among the general public, all due to the introduction of "Modern Art" into America. Nevertheless the fact remains that there was a demand for news and the papers supplied that demand. But at that time the demand came from a few thousand and now those few thousand have grown into millions. The demand has grown but the supply has dwindled.

One of the greatest of contemporary critics is Henry McBride. In his work during the last forty years he has done a great service to art. He had a large following. In spite of that, he was effaced from the daily papers without public apology to himself or to his public! Does this mean unconscious bad manners in today's press? I congratulate Art News for having opened its pages to a man like Henry McBride. Good judgment and good service to its readers.

I believe that good sound criticism is more needed today than ever before in the United States. Before, the public wanted to know what the artists did. The critic was a help to understanding. Whether they were right or wrong they helped. But now that the execution of art is practiced by the majority of citizens (at least it seems so), the critic is needed as an antibiotic—as a cure for self-delusion. To quote Henry McBride: "At a time like this when thousands of our young (and let me add: old) people are assiduously painting, composing and writing without actually creating anything at all . . . ," good sound criticism might possibly make them see their production in the light of truth.

128 Marius de Zayas, *Still-Life*, ca. 1936–1937. Oil on canvas, 66 × 79.5 cm.

129 Marius de Zayas, *Still Life (with African Sculpture),* ca. 1942–1943. Oil on canvas, 65 × 54 cm.

130 *African Sculpture.* Carved wood, 42 cm. high.

AFTERWORD

Curiously, de Zayas's account of "How, When, and Why Modern Art Came to New York" ends with the closing of the Modern Gallery. In actual fact, however, his "career as a propagandist for modern art," to use his words, was not over. After the Modern Gallery closed, de Zayas continued to deal privately and to organize exhibitions in New York. For the Arden Gallery, for example, he gathered an impressive collection of paintings and drawings from galleries and various private collections (including his own) to illustrate "The Evolution of French Art," an exhibition that opened in the spring of 1919.[1] With the backing of several friends, in the fall of 1919 de Zayas opened his own gallery at 549 Fifth Avenue. The De Zayas Gallery began its first season with a show of Chinese paintings, followed by an exhibition of African Negro art. During the three short seasons of the gallery's existence, de Zayas not only showed important works by major French artists (from Courbet to Derain) but also held solo exhibitions of selected American artists: Arthur B. Davies, Walt Kuhn, John Covert, and Charles Sheeler (Sheeler took over the management of the gallery when de Zayas was in Europe).

In a period of financial instability on Wall Street, de Zayas found selling difficult, and during the war years he had also encountered problems in securing high-quality works from his European sources. An exchange of correspondence between de Zayas and the Parisian dealer Charles Vignier clearly reveals the precarious state of the New York art market in this period. While de Zayas insisted that American collectors were interested in purchasing only works of exceptional quality (contrary to popular European opinion), Vignier tried to pressure his American colleague into the immediate sale of works he had sent on consignment. De Zayas revealed his unremitting integrity when he wrote Vignier, "I cannot accept that condition . . . if I push the sale of an object over another it is for its quality and not for where it comes from."[2] Breaks in communication caused by numerous postal delays resulted in further misunderstandings, and eventually de Zayas renounced not only his business arrangement with Vignier but also his friendship.

Meanwhile, other business relations that de Zayas had established in New York were also in the process of breaking down. He was pursued by a number of creditors, particularly Walter Arensberg, who through his lawyer initiated a suit to recover funds that he had advanced to de Zayas and works of art that Arensberg had consigned for sale to the gallery.[3] In an attempt to raise capital quickly, de Zayas held a sale of graphic work at the Anderson Galleries in 1920. Though financially unsuccessful, the sale allowed him to keep the gallery open for another season.[4] But, much to the regret of modern art enthusiasts in New York, he was finally forced to close it in the spring of 1921. Hamilton Easter Field wrote in *The Arts:* "Few things which have recently happened in New York have caused more gloom among art lovers than the closing of the De Zayas Gallery. In no other gallery was the work of art so absolutely allowed to speak for itself."[5]

Returning to Paris after the close of his gallery, de Zayas was left somewhat embittered by what he must have ultimately regarded as a lack of success in the decade he devoted to the promotion of modern art in New York. "I dislike the idea of getting in contact with the public," he wrote Stieglitz in 1922. "Neither the public nor I care a damn about each other," he remarked; "America is too young and Europe is too old to produce art."[6] In letters to Charles Sheeler, he announced that he planned to remain in Europe permanently. Sheeler was distressed by the news and, in October 1922, sent a letter to his old friend that contained, among other things, the following question: "Have you ever considered the resumption of your caricaturing, and if you haven't, why?" De Zayas's response, if there was one, could not have been very encouraging, for in Sheeler's next letter, he reports a conversation he had with the collector Miss Lillie P. Bliss, whom he had told about de Zayas's decision. "I told her of your expressed intention to return to Europe because of discouragement from the lack of response to your efforts during the past ten years," he wrote. "She expressed the opinion that no one in this country has the knowledge and intuition that you have, and that it would be a great pity to have you leave here."[7] Others surely agreed.

But the lack of sales in both of de Zayas's New York galleries left him in a somewhat precarious financial state, forcing him to sell at auction more works from his own collection. This second sale, held at the Anderson Galleries in March 1923, consisted of African Art, Old Master paintings, drawings of the Impressionist and Barbizon schools, and two important Renaissance drawings. In financial terms the sale was a success, and probably resulted in resolving some of the debts de Zayas left behind in New York.[8]

In spite of de Zayas's personal financial problems, those appreciative of modern art continued to benefit from his organizational abilities and his lifelong commitment to the art of this period. In the 1920s he made continual trips across the Atlantic, putting together a series of modern art exhibitions in New York and throughout Europe. In 1923 he organized several shows for the Whitney Studio Galleries in New York, where he featured the work of both modern American and modern European artists.[9] In Europe he organized a series of exhibitions that he called "The Tri-National," for they comprised work by modern artists from three countries: America, France, and England. De Zayas received backing for these exhibitions from Mrs. E. H. Harriman, the former wife of a railroad tycoon, whom de Zayas would marry a few years later. With her support, in the later 1920s these exhibitions were expanded to include modern artists from other European countries, whereupon they were re-entitled "The Multi-National." Through these shows—which toured in most of the countries where the artists originated—de Zayas continued to pursue his interest in presenting to the public didactic exhibitions designed to trace the evolution of modern art.[10]

In the 1930s and 1940s, de Zayas seriously took up painting; over a fifteen-year period the successive styles of his work curiously mirrored the various early movements in art, which he so thoroughly understood. Beginning with Cézanne-inspired still lifes (figure 128), his work progressed through the hermetic and synthetic phases of Picassoesque Cubism (figure 129). Withdrawn from active participation in the art scene of this period, he became involved in the production of documentary and educational films with diverse subjects, from Spanish themes of bullfighting and Flamenco dancing to the instruction of higher mathematics, jujitsu, and horseback riding. He also produced a film on the sources of modern art, which he illustrated with a painting of his own, designed to demonstrate the influence of African art on Cubism (compare figures 129 and 130).

Throughout his career, de Zayas possessed a keen comprehension of the aesthetic and historical factors that determine the degree of quality in a work of art. This knowledge is clearly exemplified not only in his own creative work but also in the art he introduced, supported, and promoted during the second decade of the twentieth century in New York. After World War II de Zayas moved to Greenwich, Connecticut, where he died on January 10, 1961, at the age of eighty one.

APPENDIX A

EXHIBITIONS AT THE MODERN AND DE ZAYAS GALLERIES

The exhibition schedule outlined in this appendix is based on the catalogues and reviews of exhibitions held at the Modern and De Zayas galleries that are preserved in the archives of Rodrigo de Zayas, Seville. The names of exhibitions that were accompanied by catalogues or checklists appear in italics and are followed by a reprint of the information provided in the catalogue itself (introduction, list of works exhibited, and so on). Reviews listed after the catalogue entry are from clippings that de Zayas collected and assembled in a scrapbook (also preserved in the De Zayas archives, Seville). Unless otherwise indicated, all newspapers and magazines were published in New York.[1]

THE MODERN GALLERY

1915

October 7, 1915–November 13, 1915
Paintings by Picabia, Braque, Picasso; Photographs by Alfred Stieglitz

"Advanced Modern Exhibit," *New York Press,* October 11, 1915; *Evening World,* October 11, 1915; *Las Novedades,* October 21, 1915; "Exhibitions in the Galleries," *Arts and Decoration,* November 1915, p. 35; "Modern Gallery of Advanced Art," *New York American,* November 1, 1915; *New York Evening Post,* November 20, 1915; *New York Sun,* November 21, 1915; *Evening Mail,* n.d.

November 22, 1915–December 12, 1915
   Van Gogh Exhibition

The following Paintings by Vincent Van Gogh will be on exhibition:

   I Berceuse
   II Les Baux
   III Nuages
   IV Neige
   V Vase de Soleils
   VI Fleurs—Lilas
   VII Hollandaise
   VIII Les Harengs

"Van Gogh Exhibition," *New York Press,* November 20, 1915; *Sun,* November 21, 1915; *Evening World,* November 24, 1915; *Evening Post,* November 27, 1915; *Sunday Sun,* November 28, 1915; "Van Gogh at the Modern Gallery," *Times,* November 28, 1915; "Impressive Examples of Van Gogh" (source not provided), November 29, 1915; "Exposiciones," *Las Novedades,* December 1915; "Van Gogh and the Zorachs," *Christian Science Monitor,* December 4, 1915; James Britton, "Van Gogh at Modern Gallery," *American Art News,* December 11, 1915; *Puck,* January 29, 1916.

December 13, 1915–January 3, 1916
   Picasso Exhibition

The following paintings by Pablo Picasso will be on exhibition:

   I Nature Morte (Paris, 1913)
   II Figure d'Homme (Sorgues, 1912)
   III Jeune Fille (Avignon, 1914)
   IV Nature Morte (Avignon, 1914)
   V Nature Morte Dans Un Jardin (1915)
   VI Nature Morte (1915)
   VII–XI Nature Morte (1915)

[V and VI are Picasso's latest works]

December 13, 1915–January 3, 1916
Negro Sculpture Exhibition

A series of Negro sculpture will be on exhibition:

Ivory Coast

Sudan

Congo

Guinea

Las Novedades, December 16, 1915; "Picasso's Here and 'Hark, Hark!
Dogs Do Bark,'" *Evening Post,* December 18, 1915; *American,* December
20, 1915; "Picasso's Art and Negro Work in Same Gallery," *Herald,* De-
cember 20, 1915; *Las Novedades,* December 23, 1915; *New York Evening
Mail,* December 25, 1915; "Paintings by Picasso in New Color Scheme,"
New York [illeg.], December ?, 1915; "Picasso at the Modern Gallery,"
Times, December ?, 1915.

1916

January 5, 1916–January 25, 1916
Picabia Exhibition[2]

I A Machine Without a Name

II This Thing is Made to Perpetuate My Memory

III Reverence

IV A Little Solitude in the Midst of Suns

V A Very Rare Picture on Earth

VI Altitude and Profundity

VII Paroxysm of Sorrow

VIII Behold the Woman

IX Ecce Homo

X This Machine Laughingly Castigates Manners

XI Catch-As-Catch-Can

XII Daughter Born Without a Mother

XIII Comic Force

XIV Horrible Sorrow

XV Mechanical Expression Seen Through Our Own Mechanical Expression

XVI The Saint of Saints

New York Evening Post, January 8, 1916; *New York Evening Mail,* January 8, 1916; *New York Tribune,* January 9, 1916; *New York World,* January 9, 1916; *New York Sun,* January 10, 1916; *New York Globe,* January 11, 1916; *Sunday Sun,* January 16, 1916; *Minneapolis Tribune,* January 16, 1916; *Las Novedades,* January 20, 1916; *Sunday Sun,* January 23, 1916; "Picabia's Puzzles," *Christian Science Monitor,* January 29, 1916; "Carlson Shown at Ease," *New York Press,* January ?, 1916.

January 25, 1916–February 9, 1916
Cézanne Exhibition[3]

   I Le Bouquet de Fleurs (1900–1903)

  II Le Château Noir (1904)

 III Le Village au pied de la Montagne (Watercolor)

 IV Le Chemin Tournant (Watercolor)

  V Lithographie

"Le Bouquet de Fleurs" and "Le Chateau Noir," two pictures by Cézanne done in his latest manner, are being shown to the public for the first time by the Modern Gallery.

"Le Bouquet de Fleurs" is considered by the very limited number of people who have had the privilege of seeing it, to be one of the paintings in which Cézanne has expressed to the very highest degree all his power and all his sensitiveness and therefore as one of the masterpieces among his paintings.

To arrive at the result that he was striving for in his painting, Cézanne had to use as model for his researches, a bouquet of paper flowers. This was necessary in order that his subject might last long enough for him to succeed in finding the projection of himself expressed in the painting. It took three years of daily work to attain the desired result.

In 1902 he wrote to Mr. Vollard the following letter about "Le Bouquet de Fleurs":

"Aix, April 2, 1902.

Dear Mr. Vollard:

    I find that I must postpone the shipment of your canvas of roses to some later date although I wished very much to send it to the salon of 1902. I shall delay for another year the completion of this study. I am not satisfied with the result so far obtained. Therefore I insist on continuing my studies which will force me to efforts that I like to believe will not be sterile. I have had a studio built on a small piece of ground which I acquired for that purpose. I shall continue my researches and will inform you of the results obtained as soon as I gain some satisfaction from my efforts.

*Paul Cézanne"**

*Translated from A. Vollard's book on Cézanne

"Le Château Noir" belongs to the very last period of Cézanne's painting, when he employed the manner that has given him his prominent place in the development of modern art.

"More Cézanne," *Evening Post,* January 22, 1916; *Sunday Sun,* January 23, 1916; "Cézanne Paintings at the Modern Gallery," *Brooklyn Eagle,* January 23, 1916; *Las Novedades,* January 27, 1916; "Still Cézanne," *Times,* January 29, 1916; *Globe,* January 29, 1916; "Academicians and Cézanne," *Evening Post,* January 29, 1916; "More Cézannes on View" (source not provided), January 29, 1916; "Exposiciones," *Las Novedades,* January 30, 1916; "Cézanne at the Modern Gallery," *Brooklyn Eagle,* January 30, 1916; *Sunday Sun,* January 30, 1916; *Tribune,* January 30, 1916; *New York Press,* January 31, 1916; *Globe,* February 4, 1916; *World,* February 4, 1916; "More of Cézanne," *Christian Science Monitor,* February 5, 1916.

February 12, 1916–March 1, 1916

Exhibition of Paintings by Cézanne, Van Gogh, Picasso, Picabia, Braque, Desseignes, Rivera

Cezanne

1 Le Village au Pied de la Montagne
2 Le Chemin Tournant
3 Lithographie

Van Gogh

4 Fleurs Lilas

Picasso

5 Nature Morte
6 Figure d'Homme
7 Jeune Fille
8 Nature Morte

Picabia

9 This Thing is made to perpetuate my Memory

10 A Little Solitude in the Midst of Suns

11 Catch-as-catch-can

12 Comic Force

13 Fantaisie

Braque

14 Nature Morte

15 Nature Morte

16 Nature Morte

Diego M. Rivera

17 A Spanish Still Life

18 Still Life à la Bonbons

19 The Sugar Bowl and the Candles

20 The Terrace of the Café

21 The Book and the Cauliflower

Ribemont Desseignes

22 Je ne suis pas intelligent

Tribune, February 13, 1916; *World,* February 13, 1916; *Evening World,* February 16, 1916; "An Art Clinic," *Christian Science Monitor,* February 19, 1916; *New York Herald,* February 28, 1916; *Arts and Decoration,* February 1916; *Forum,* March 1916; *Arts and Decoration,* March 1916.

March 8, 1916–March 22, 1916
Exhibition of Sculpture

Mrs. A. Roosevelt

1 The Atoms

2 Tennis Player—Serving

Miss Alice Morgan Wright

3 Wind Figure

Adolf Wolff

4 New York

5 Struggle

6 Revolt

7 Relaxation

8 Oppressed

9 Brooding

10 Repose

11 Embrace

Modigliani

12 Figurehead

13 Figurehead

Brancusi

14 Head

15 Mythological Bird

Evening Post, March 11, 1916; *Evening Mail,* March 11, 1916; *World,* March 12, 1916; "Sculpture in the Modern Gallery," *Times,* March 13, 1916; *Brooklyn Eagle,* March 13, 1916; "Ultra-Modern Art and Conventional in Two Exhibits," *Evening World,* March 15, 1916; "'Polyhedral,' Other Sculptures," *Christian Science Monitor,* March 25, 1916.

April 29, 1916–June 10, 1916
Paintings by Cézanne, Van Gogh, Picasso, Picabia, Rivera

Zoe Beckley, "Now Poor Cubists Get Blame for Some Folks' Bad Notions," *The Evening Mail,* June 12, 1916.

September 11, 1916–September 30, 1916
Exhibition of Paintings and Sculpture

Brancusi

1 Head of Child (marble)

Braque

2 Still-life

Burty

3 The Fortification
4 Still-life
5 Portrait (drawing)

Cézanne

6 Lithograph

Derain

7 Still-life

Manolo

8 Bas-Relief (bronze)
9 Head of Old Woman (drawing)

Picabia

10 New York
11 Music is Like Painting
12 Catch-as-Catch-Can

Picasso

13 In the Manner of Redon, Guys and Lautrec (drawing)
14 Salome (etching)
15 The Two Friends (etching)
16 Figure of a Woman
17 A Boy (drawing)

Rivera

18 Tree and Walls (Toledo)

African Negro Sculpture

19 Mask (Dahomey)

20 Fetish (Ogooué)

21 Carved Wood (Madagascar)

"The Fall Season Is Open at the Modern Gallery," *Evening World,* September 14, 1916; "Old and New Art Renew Struggle," *Brooklyn Eagle,* September 14, 1916; "At the Modern Gallery," *American Art News,* September 16, 1916; Frederick W. Eddy, "Art Notes," *New York World,* September 17, 1916; *Sunday Sun,* September 24, 1916; "New York Art Exhibitions and Gallery News," *Christian Science Monitor,* Boston, September 29, 1916.

October 2, 1916–October 21, 1916
Exhibition of Paintings by Diego Rivera

1 Landscape (Monserrat). 1911.

2 Landscape (Majorca). 1912.

3 Tree and Walls (Toledo). 1913.

4 Olive Trees (Majorca). 1914.

5 Portrait. 1915.

6 Portrait of Mariewny. 1915.

7 Portrait. 1915.

8 Spanish Still-life. 1915.

9 The Sugarbowl. 1915.

Exhibition of Mexican pre-Conquest Art

10 Stone figure of Quetzalcoatl (Aztec).

11 Obsidian head (Aztec).

12 Hermatite idol, mound type (Nahua).

13 Stone mask (Aztec).

14 Onyx mask (Aztec).

15 Volcanic stone Idol (Aztec).

16 Stone head of a priestess (Aztec).

17 Stone head of nahuatl (Aztec).

18 Nahua pottery.

19 Aztec pottery.

World, October 3, 1916; *Evening Post,* October 7, 1916; *World,* October 8, 1916; "Paintings by Diego M. Rivera," *Brooklyn Eagle,* October 8, 1916; "Paintings by Diego Rivera," *Times,* October 8, 1916; *Evening Mail,* October 9, 1916; "Dual Exhibition a Fall Show at Modern Gallery," *Evening World,* October 20, 1916.

October 23, 1916–November 11, 1916
Exhibition of Sculpture by Brancusi[4]

I   Portrait of Mme. P. D. K.

II   Head of Child

III   Bronze Head

IV   Carved Wood

"Dual Exhibition a Fall Show at Modern Gallery," *Evening World,* October 20, 1916; *Tribune,* October 24, 1916; *Evening Sun,* October 24, 1916; *Evening World,* October 26, 1916; "Sculpture by Brancusi," *Times,* October 29, 1916; Frederick W. Eddy, "Art Notes," *Sunday World,* October 29, 1916; "Brancusi Carries Simplification Further," *Vanity Fair,* November 1916, p. 75; *Sun,* November 5, 1916; *Arts and Decoration,* December 1916.

November 13, 1916–November 25, 1916
Exhibition of Paintings by Derain, Vlaminck and Burty[5]

Derain

1 Portrait

2 Still-Life

3 Landscape

4 Head of Woman

5 Still Life

6 Portrait

7 Still Life

8 Watercolor

9 Watercolor

10 Watercolor

11 Watercolor

12 Watercolor

13 Watercolor

14 Etching

15 Etching

16 Etching

17 Drawing

Vlaminck

18 Landscape

19 Still Life

20 The Harbor

Burty

21 Still Life

22 Table and Palette

23 Houses

24 Head

25 Head

26 Drawing

27 Drawing

28 Drawing

29 Etching

30 Etching

31 Etching

Evening World, November 17, 1916; *New York Times,* November 19, 1916; *Sun,* November 19, 1916; "Notes and Activities in the World of Art," *Sun,* November 26, 1916; Willard Huntington Wright, "Modern Art: Four Exhibitions of the New Style of Painting," *Studio,* January 1917.

November 26, 1916–December 31, 1916
Exhibition of African Negro Sculpture[6]

1 Statuette—Sudan

2 Wand—Ivory Coast

3 Fetish—Congo

4 Fetish—Ivory Coast

5 Fetishes—Sudan

6 Fetish—Loango

7 Fetish—Congo

8 Fetish—Nigeria

9 Fetish—Nigeria

10 Fetish—M'Gallé Ogooué

11 Fetish—Ivory Coast

12 Head of Elephant—Guinea

13 Ceremonial Mask—Guinea

14 Ceremonial Mask—Ivory Coast

15 Ceremonial Mask—Guinea

16 Fetish—Guinea

17 Head—Congo

18 Rattle—Dahomey

19 Urn—Dahomey

20 Bird—Ivory Coast

21 Fetish—Nigeria

22 Bell—Ivory Coast

23 War Tom-tom—Congo

24 Carved Wood—Madagascar

25 Carved Tusk—Ivory Coast

26 Fetish—Ivory Coast

27 Statuette—Congo

28 Statuette—Congo

29 Statuette—Nigeria

30 Statuette—Congo

31 Mask Baoulé—Ivory Coast

32 Mask Baoulé—Ivory Coast

33 Statuette—Nigeria

34 Fetish—Ivory Coast

35 Musical Instrument—Ivory Coast

36 Vase—Kamerun

37 Vase—Kamerun

38 Mask—Congo

39 Wand—Ivory Coast

40 Fetish—Dahomey

41 Ceremonial Mask—Dahomey

42 Ceremonial Mask—Dahomey

43 Ceremonial Mask—Dahomey

Evening World, November 29, 1916; *World,* December 3, 1916; *Christian Science Monitor,* December 8, 1916; "Notes and Activities in the World of Art," *Sun,* December 10, 1916; "Find This Gallery," *Globe,* December 15, 1916; *New York Herald,* December 24, 1916.

December 3, 1916–December 31, 1916
   Exhibition of Etchings by Hélène Perdriat[7]

   1 Confidence, No. 1
   2 Morning Song
   3 Sunrise—Invocation
   4 Full Moon
   5 Fishers, No. 1
   6 Ceremonial Dance
   7 The Shepherd's Shadow
   8 Confidence, No. 2
   9 Fishers, No. 2
   10 Among the Foliage
   11 The Bird
   12 Moon Song
   13 The Little Monkey
   14 The Twilight Dance
   15 The Two Sisters
   16 Bathing Girls
   17 The Deer and the Girl

The work of Mme. Hélène Perdriat is an example of spontaneous outburst. In January, 1915, she began painting portraits from memory. The results were singularly modern, of a striking simplicity and moving sincerity.

The drypoints in the present exhibition were produced six months after the beginning of her artistic career. They are the first work on copper which Mme. Perdriat engraved. In all of them she succeeded in happily expressing herself. Alphabetically her etched work has been characterized by strength and directness.

Her first steps as an artist are shown in the present exhibition. One can feel in the richness and precision of her vision, the fantasy and the fundamental firmness of her craftsmanship.

The "painting in little" entitled "The Deer and the Young Girl," was done one year after the drypoints.
   Henri Pierre Roché

Evening World, December 5, 1916; "American Craftsmen and a French Etcher," *Times,* December 7, 1917; *Christian Science Monitor,* December 8, 1916; *World,* December 10, 1916; *Globe,* December 15, 1916.

January 21, 1917–February 1, 1917
Paintings by Marion H. Beckett

1 Miss M. V. Pyle

2 Mrs. W. N. Tuttle

3 Mrs. G. C. Austin

4 Miss M. Hussey

5 Mrs. J. Draper

6 Mrs. Cord Meyer

7 Mr. Alfred Stieglitz

8 Mr. Eugene Meyer, Jr.

9 Mr. Seaouke Yue

10 Mr. Charles H. Beckett

11 Self Portrait

W. G. Bowdoin, "Modern Gallery Shows Portraits by Miss Beckett," *Evening World,* January 20, 1917; *Tribune,* January 21, 1917; *World,* January 21, 1917; *Christian Science Monitor,* January 26, 1917; *Evening Post,* January 27, 1917; "Marion H. Beckett's Portraits at Modern Gallery," *Brooklyn Eagle,* January 28, 1917, "Portraits by Miss Beckett," *Sun,* January 29, 1917; "Marion H. Beckett Shows Portraits," *American,* January 29, 1917; *American Art News,* February 3, 1917.

February 11, 1917–March 10, 1917
Paintings by Daumier, Guys, Toulouse-Lautrec[8]

Tribune, February 11, 1917; "Daumier, Guys, and Lautrec," *Times,* February 11, 1917; *Herald,* February 11, 1917; Henry McBride, *Sun,* February 11, 1917; *World,* February 11, 1917; "French Atmosphere in Works at the Modern Gallery," *Brooklyn Eagle,* February 11, 1917; *Evening Post,* February 11, 1917; *Mail,* February 12, 1917; W. G. Bowdoin, "Daumier, Guys and Lautrec at Modern Gallery," *Evening World,* February 17, 1917; *Pittsburgh Dispatch,* February 21, 1917; *Evening Post,* February 24, 1917; *Globe,* February 26, 1917; *Globe,* March 9, 1917; "French Art at Modern Gallery," *American Art News,* March 1917; *Arts and Decoration,* March 1917; Henry McBride, "Art at Home and Abroad," *Sun,* n.d.

March 12, 1917–March 28, 1917
Paintings by Patrick Henry Bruce

World, March 18, 1917; "New Exhibition at the Modern Gallery," *Brooklyn Eagle,* March 18, 1917; *Herald,* March 18, 1917; "Bruce's Exploits in Abstraction," *American,* March 19, 1917; *Sun,* March 25, 1917; *Christian Science Monitor,* March 30, 1917.

March 29, 1917–April 9, 1917
Exhibition of Photographs by Sheeler, Strand and Schamberg

"Photographic Art at Modern Gallery," *American Art News,* March 31, 1917; W. G. Bowdoin, "Modern Gallery Exhibits a Group of Photographs," *Evening World,* April 7, 1917; *Sun,* April 8, 1917.

May 5, 1917–May 18, 1917
Watercolors and Drawings by Marie Laurencin

"Works by Marie Laurencin," *American Art News,* May 5, 1917; "Drawings by Marie Laurencin at the Modern Gallery," *Brooklyn Eagle,* May 6, 1917; "Marie Laurencin Exhibition in Modern Gallery," *Sun,* May 6, 1917; *Mail,* May 7, 1917; *Evening World,* May 11, 1917; *Evening Post,* May 12, 1917; Gabrielle Buffet, "Marie Laurencin," *The Blind Man,* May 1917.

June 9, 1917–June 30, 1917
Exhibition of French and American Artists

W. G. Bowdoin, "Modern Gallery's June Exhibit Is Modern Imagery," *Evening Post,* June 9, 1917; *Globe,* June 11, 1917; "Drawings Being Shown at the Modern Gallery," *Brooklyn Daily Eagle,* June 17, 1917; *Mail,* June 18, 1917; *Evening Post,* June 23, 1917.

September 23, 1917–October 6, 1917
Engravings by Laboreur

World, September 23, 1917; *Sun,* September 23, 1917; *Evening Post,* October 6, 1917; *Arts and Decoration,* October 1917.

October 13, 1917–October 20, 1917
Drawings and Watercolors by Mell Daniel

World, October 14, 1917; *Sun,* October 14, 1917; "Drawings at the Modern Gallery," *American Art News,* October 1917.

October 17, 1917–November 3, 1917
Exhibition of Drawings by Constantin Guys[9]

Constantin Guys
(1802–1879)

1 Meeting on the Avenue du Bois
2 In Evening Dress
3 Lady for Sale
4 Promenading
5 A "Lorette"
6 "Those Bourgeois"
7 En Soirée
8 Women for Soldiers
9 Le Bel Attelage

It was Baudelaire who first gave to the work of Constantin Guys a Biographic interest. In his classic study of *le peintre de la view moderne,* he related the work to the character of the artist, and proclaimed the drawings that Guys made only to illustrate the passing of the second French empire, as an art without precedent, produced by a deeply observing character, with a rare sensibility and with a new comprehension of life.

Guys, like a cinematograph, left us the gestures of an epoch. With sincere indifference, with obstinate determination, he eliminated all personalism from his work, never stamping it with his name. His drawings were intended to live without any Biographic association.

In spite of his aristocratic contempt for all personal publicity, it has been known that Constantin Guys came from a family from the south of France. Born in Holland in 1802, from his early years he had the nomadic inclinations of the adventurer. He followed Lord Byron to Missolonghi and was a dragon under the Restoration.

He travelled in Europe and part of the Orient as an illustrator for *The Illustrated London News.* In Inkerman and Balaklava he was in all the engagements with the allied armies "always at the front with a cold indifference to danger, by nature and by dandyism." At his return to France he began drawing the social life of the second empire. His favorite themes being *la vie élégante* and *la vie galante.* He died in Paris at the age of eighty-seven.

His drawings, intended for the masses, were collected by the intellectuals of his time, who, after all, did not see in them anything but their historical interest and the romantic side of their technic. It was left to the modernists of today to discover a full understanding of their plastic and expressive qualities.

In the work of Guys there is no attempt to get at the human drama. He avoided Fiction. He grasped and rendered the expressiveness of the types of his time, looking for the movement that gives to form its living quality. He saw Reality, saw it really and found the manner to express its meaning.

Guys is classed today as one of the pioneers of the movement which brought art to abstract representation.

He had for his time and for his milieu "an open heart and what follows from the possession of such"; and as a modernist, he had the principle that "the pleasure of representing the Present has in it, not only the beauty with which it might be invested, but also the essential quality of being the Present."

"Constantin Guys," *Times,* October 14, 1917; *Evening Post,* October 20, 1917; "Modern Gallery," *Art News,* October 20, 1917; Henry McBride, *Sun,* October 21, 1917; *Herald,* October 21, 1917; "Constantin Guys at Modern Gallery," *Brooklyn Eagle,* October 21, 1917; *Evening Sun,* October 22, 1917; *Globe,* October 23, 1917; "Chic Drawings by Constantin Guys," *American,* October 28, 1917; *Arts and Decoration,* November 1917.

November 5, 1917–November 24, 1917
Exhibition of Paintings and Watercolors by André Derain

1 The Big Trees
2 Landscape-ceres
3 Still-life
4 Landscape
5 Portrait of a Woman
6 Still-life
7 Portrait of a Woman
8 Head of a Woman
9 Still-life
10 Head
11 Portrait
12 Still-life
13 Flowers
14 Pastoral
15 Woman with Basquet

16 The Blessed Ones

17 Still-life

18 Still-life

19 Portrait

"Art Notes," *Times,* November 15, 1917;[10] "Modern Gallery Exhibit," *American Art News,* November 17, 1917; "Derain's Modernist Work at the Modern Gallery," *Brooklyn Eagle,* November 18, 1917; "Derain, the Modern French Soldier Painter," *Sun,* November 18, 1917; "Aesthetic Unity is Derain's Motive," *American,* November 19, 1917; *Evening Post,* November 24, 1917; *World,* November ?, 1917.

December 3, 1917–December 15, 1917

Exhibition of Photographs by Charles Sheeler

Influenced by Negro Art, the Modernists have brought into painting pure expressiveness of form and the sensorial significance of matter.

Photography has now entered fully into the field conquered by Modern Art.

The unknown forms employed by the Modernists were called abstract, or creations of the imagination. The interpretation of the tactile values of matter was looked upon as fantasy.

The mechanical comprobation of the camera, untheoretical and fact-fetching, verifies the reality of the Modern forms and values.

Thus, the principle elements of Modern Art, elements essentially sensorial, are shown by photography to exist in nature.

Charles Sheeler, guided by his knowledge of what Modern Art has already revealed, has verified its discoveries by the precise, unbiased investigation of the impersonal lens. His photographs, on exhibition, are actual proof of the truths fundamental in Modern Art.

World, December 9, 1917; "Cubism Justified," *Sun,* December 10, 1917; *Evening World,* December 13, 1917; "'Modernist' Photographs," *American Art News,* December 15, 1917.

December 17, 1917–January 6, 1918

Drawings, Etchings, Lithographs and Woodcuts by European and

American Modernists

W. G. Bowdoin, "Extremists in Modern Gallery Exhibition," *Evening World,* December 20, 1917; *Sun,* December 23, 1917; *World,* December 23, 1917; "The Modern Quest after Abstract Beauty," *American,* December 24, 1917; *Sun,* December 24, 1917; *Evening Post,* December 29, 1917; "Art at Home and Abroad," *Times,* December 30, 1917; "The Camera in Modern Art," *Christian Science Monitor,* January 7, 1917; "'Modernist' Black and Whites," *American Art News,* December 1917.

January 6, 1918–January 19, 1918
Paintings by Maurice de Vlaminck

"A 'Modern' at the Modern Gallery," *American Art News,* January 12, 1918; *Evening Post,* January 12, 1918; *World,* January 13, 1918; *Evening World,* January 17, 1918

January 26, 1918–February 9, 1918
African Negro Sculpture

World, January 20, 1918;[11] W. G. Bowdoin, "Art of African Negro on View at Modern Gallery," *Evening World,* January 24, 1918; E. W. Powell, "Unique Art Exhibition," *Mail,* January 26, 1918; "African Negro Sculpture," *American Art News,* January 26, 1918; "American Museum of Natural History Shows African Negro Art," *Brooklyn Eagle,* January 27, 1918; L. J. F. Moore, "Sculpture in Africa and America," *Philadelphia Record,* February 3, 1918.

February 18, 1918–March 2, 1918
Exhibition of Paintings, Drawings & Etchings by Hélène Perdriat

"Hélene Perdriat at Modern Gallery," *New York American Art News,* February 23, 1918; *Morning World,* February 24, 1918; February 25, 1918 (source of publication not provided); "Symbolism in Parisienne's Works at Modern Galleries," *Brooklyn Daily Eagle,* March 3, 1918; "A War-Bride's Dream Pictures," *World Magazine,* May 12, 1918.

March 11, 1918–March 30, 1918
Exhibition of Paintings by Picasso, Derain, Gris, Rivera, Burty, Ferat

Morning World, March 17, 1918; "Modern French Paintings," *Sun,* March 18, 1918; *World,* March 18, 1918; *American Art News,* March 23, 1918; unknown publication, March 23, 1918.

April 4, 1918–April 13, 1918
Exhibition of Watercolors and Drawings

Marie Laurencin

1 Self Portrait
2 Birds
3 Portrait
4 Two Women
5 Portrait

Manuel Cano

6 Pastoral
7 Nud[e]
8 Apaches
9 Bather

André Derain

10 Flowers
11 Head
12 Bathers
13 The Adoration
14 Nud[e]

Gustave de Gwozdecki

15 Portrait
16 Nud[e]
17 Head
18 Nud[e]

Morton Schamberg

19 Woman Sitting Down
20 Still Life
21 Interior

Charles Sheeler

22 Windows

23 The Stove

24 Box Candy Barn

25 Gloxinias

26 Zinnias

27 One-Fortieth of a Second

American Art News, Saturday, April 6, 1918; W. G. Bowdoin, "Modern Gallery Shows Drawings and Watercolors," *New York Evening World,* April 8, 1918; "Modern Art at the Modern Gallery," *Evening Mail,* April 9, 1918; *World,* April 14, 1918; "Watercolors and Drawings at Modern Gallery," *Brooklyn Daily Eagle,* April 21 [?], 1918.

DE ZAYAS GALLERY

1919

October 26, 1919–November 1, 1919
Chinese Paintings

November 1, 1919–November 15, 1919
African Negro Art

November 17, 1919–December 6, 1919
Courbet, Manet, Degas, Renoir, Cézanne, Seurat, Matisse

December 14, 1919–December 31, 1919
Drawings, Etchings, Lithographs by French Artists

1920

January 26, 1920–February 14, 1920
Paintings, Watercolors and Aquatints by Arthur B. Davies

"The Art of Arthur B. Davies," *Evening Post* [?], January 31, 1920; Peyton Boswell, "Art of Davies Is Strange Mixture," unknown publication, February 6, 1920; "Arthur B. Davies, a Modern Idealist," *Christian Science Monitor* (date not provided).

February 16, 1920–February 28, 1920
Paintings and Drawings by Charles Sheeler

"Charles Sheeler at the De Zayas Gallery" (source of publication and date not provided).

March 8, 1920–March 20, 1920
Chinese Sculpture

March 23, 1920–April 3, 1920
Paintings by Walt Kuhn

April 5, 1920–April 17, 1920
Paintings by Paul Gauguin

April 19, 1920–May 1, 1920
Paintings by John Covert

September 1920–December 1920
Exhibition of French and American Artists; Asiatic Arts and African Sculpture

1921

January 22, 1921–February 12, 1921
Paintings by Henri Rousseau

February 19, 1921–February 25, 1921
Paintings of Ming and Sung Periods

February 26, 1921–April 9, 1921
Cézanne, Degas, Gauguin, Van Gogh, Toulouse-Lautrec

April 16, 1921–April 30, 1921
Paintings and Watercolors by Arthur B. Davies

APPENDIX B
STIEGLITZ–DE ZAYAS CORRESPONDENCE

The exchange of letters between Marius de Zayas and Alfred Stieglitz provides a rare, contemporaneous record of "How, When, and Why Modern Art Came to New York." Not only do these letters chronicle de Zayas's somewhat bewildered initial reaction to Cubism and his gradual conversion to the new art, but they demonstrate how the most current developments in the art scene of Paris were carefully observed, absorbed, and disseminated to a waiting audience in New York. They also provide insight into the nature of the relationship between Stieglitz and de Zayas, two relatively headstrong individuals committed to the advancement of the new art, but from different perspectives and with clearly different goals: de Zayas reported on the new art from his position as an artist and creative thinker, but he was by nature unassertive and worked best behind the scenes; Stieglitz, in contrast, thrived in the spotlight and continually sought public recognition for his promotional efforts. Finally, the portion of this exchange that pertains to the formation of the Modern Gallery represents a valuable record of an early attempt to open in New York a commercial establishment envisioned to capitalize on the growing interest in modern art that had been launched by the Armory Show and by exhibitions at Stieglitz's gallery.

Although most of the letters between de Zayas and Stieglitz date from between 1910 and 1918—the year when the Modern Gallery closed (and when de Zayas's account of "How, When, and Why Modern Art Came to New York" concludes)—all the extent letters of their correspondence are presented here (to 1926), for they represent the totality of their written exchange.

Letters by Alfred Stieglitz preserved in the De Zayas Archives in Seville are published here with the permission of Rodrigo de Zayas and the Georgia O'Keeffe Foundation, Abiquiu, New Mexico; letters preserved in the Stieglitz Papers, Yale Collection of American Literature (hereafter referred to as YCAL), Beinecke Rare Book and Manuscript Library, New Haven, Connecti-

cut, are published with the permission of Donald Gallup. "ALS" in the head-
note to a letter indicates "autographed letter, signed"; TL is a "typed letter,"
and TLS is a "typed letter, signed."

　　All letters are transcribed literally, with changes made only to facili-
tate reading. In most cases, grammatical mistakes have been retained, although
spelling errors have been corrected (unless considered relevant, whereupon
the mistake is noted). Brackets indicate insertions to the text.

De Zayas to Stieglitz, October 28, 1910
[ALS, Stieglitz Papers, YCAL]

24 Avenue Charles Floquet
Paris Oct. 28, 1910

My dear Stieglitz:

　　*It has been my good luck to arrive at this city [on] the 13th of this month, after
a trip of 13 days. Ever since I have been busy looking for a house to live in and
visiting the museums.*

　　*I have gone four times to the Salon d'Automne.[1] This exhibition has made me
realize once more the important work you are doing in the Secession, for thanks to
it, I was prepared to see with open eyes.*

　　*I expected though, to see each man follow their own way in painting, but I had
the disappointment to know that even these ultrapersonalists form groups, in which
you can only detect the individual through the catalogue. I found that the largest
group is composed by those who after [having] been influence[d] by Matisse have
taken refuge in [El] Greco. This group has gone beyond the japanese artists. Their
motto must be: repetition with no variation. They all have the same color, the same
composition, the same drawing à la Greco more or less spoiled or à la Matisse more
or less exaggerated.*

　　*There is one picture which took particularly my attention and a good deal of
my time trying to solve it. Its title is "Nu" and it is executed by Mr. Metzinger.[2] I
was lucky enough to find a reproduction of it in a magazine. The theory of this
gentleman is that he sees everything geometrically, and to tell the truth, he is absolutely consequent with his theory. To him a head represents a certain geometrical
figure, the chest another, and so forth. The fourth dimension was not enough for
him so, he applies the whole geometry. Afterwards I was told that this personalist is
also an imitator, that the real article is a spaniard, whose name I don't recall, but
Haviland knows it, because he is a friend of his brother.[3]*

　　*I saw too, two pictures by Maurer, which in my opinion are far better than those
he sent to New York.[4]*

　　*The two pictures Steichen has there, show too that he has improved greatly.[5] I
like specially one of flowers.*

　　*I was with Steichen last week. We went together with Karl to the Aviation Exhi-
bition. He seems to be very much interested in this deadly movement. We had lunch
together and we had a long talk about the Secessionists.*

For over a month before I left New York I wanted to have a talk with you concerning Weber's antagonism to Steichen, but I never had a chance.[6] *I really regret it.*

I know that in coming to Paris I had to tell him the truth about what is going on in the Secession and so I did.

You know very well, because you have known me long enough, that I am not inclined to play politics. I love the Secession, and I consider Steichen its most important and active member, after you; and I think it is unfair not to put him on guard about the damage Weber wants to do him as an artist and otherwise.

I saw Marin yesterday in the famous café du Dome.[7] *He intends to go to New York pretty soon. Steichen says he has done some wonderful work in the Alps.*

I think I will be able to manage to do some regular work for "The World." I saw the correspondent here, and he has planned a series of articles on Paris to be illustrated with caricatures. The first one will be The Café du Dome. In which I will be able to give some advertisement to our friends here.

I don't intend to show any work here until I produce something worthwhile showing.

I hope you have pulled through the troubles of your Buffalo exhibition successfully.[8]

Please remember me to my good friends.
      Yours sincerely,
      M. de Zayas

De Zayas to Stieglitz, December 22, 1910
[ALS, Stieglitz Papers, YCAL]

                        Paris Dec 22 1910

My dear Stieglitz:

I received your letter this morning. I think it is useless to tell you with what pleasure I read it. I began to feel myself forgotten. You know how very few friends I have, and how very few I care to have. Your silence made me feel kind of lonesome.

I am very glad to know that the Secession started its season the way it should. You forgot to tell me what the exhibition was of and made me curious and anxious to receive the catalogue.

I wish some of the fellows who have complained on the Secession would come to Paris, the greatest center of art to realize what the idea and importance of the "Little Galleries" are. To me they appear bigger than many of the colossal rooms of the Louvre. If they will only help instead of obstructing, if they would think a little more of Art and of humanity and a little less of themselves, the Secession would be the greatest institution of Art. My eulogy might seem exaggerated, but as far as I have been able to investigate, there is not such an institution here or anywhere else that would approach it.

I find here the same jealousies and the same egotistical fights among artists of all kinds than over there. And I begin to realize that to keep on I have to be a fighter too. I dislike the idea, and I prefer to quit the field. Art to me is the most refined expression of pleasure, and I don't think it is worth while to get the applause of the multitude and a few dollars, to soil it with spurious feelings.

Paris has affected me in a different way from what I expected. I have a general feeling of disgust. I have discovered too many frauds and robberies in art, too many ill intentions, and too much humbug. Humanity seems to be more nude here than anywhere else. That makes me lose a little my interest of personal caricature, and increase my interest on the caricature of the masses. What am I going to do? I don't know yet. But I will do something. I am getting a tremendous amount of impressions. They might fecundate in my brains and I will be able to deliver in a healthy way, or maybe I will only get an indigestion and will have to vomit. In either case, I will do something.

I saw Steichen lately. I am glad I have had the opportunity to know him better. He too, is little understood in the other side. Like the Secession he is too big to many a brain to understand. I saw some of the paintings he has done lately and I am glad to say, of him what you say of Coburn: he has improved wonderfully.[9] I remember I told you once that I felt in Steichen's painting something lacking, and as if he were still groping. In his recent pictures he shows all the qualities he initiated in his former ones, but fully developed. He is always a poet, but now he is vigorous and forceful. He showed one a picture of flowers in a crystal bowl, which I consider his masterpiece, and a masterpiece. This work does not show in any way the influence of the modern movement, for what I congratulate him. He is doing his own work.

I haven't seen Marin in a long time. Steichen told me that he is busy painting, that he is working now in oil, and that he is getting to be in the real mood for work. He told me too that he will sail at the end of the month, that he was only waiting for some money. So he will be there pretty soon.

It seems that I hurt Marin's feelings by publishing his caricature, because I put him playing cards. He doesn't know that I was limited to two pictures of the people in the Dome, and that I had my reasons to put him anyway, as a personality among the American artists in Paris. He ignores too that to play poker is a virtue in [the] U.S.[10]

I congratulate you on the success of the Buffalo exhibition. Haviland told me too that it was great.

I can imagine how tired you must be of struggling. But you can have the satisfaction that your work is not lost, and it is of more importance than what we can realize at the present. You have accomplished more than anybody else in the world of art in America, and I believe that the real thing is just beginning. So, for your own sake, for the sake of art and for the sake of humanity I wish you success in the coming year, and for may more years to come.

Yours,
M de Zayas

P.S. Thanks for the check which you say belongs to me, though you forgot to say on what account.

Dec 23

I send you back the check because I couldn't cash it. The Frank-American Bank which is the correspond for the Knickerbocker Trust said that they had to send it to New York and get another form there payable here. So, I think is better to send it back to you. I am sorry to cause you more troubles.

Yours,

M de Zayas

De Zayas to Stieglitz, January 25, 1911
[ALS, Stieglitz Papers, YCAL]

Paris January 25 1911

My dear Stieglitz:

I have certainly had today a fine time, I have been ill for the last week and unable to do anything or go out, what made my mood rather gloomy. Your letter, your pamphlets and Camera Work came to make me happy. These pamphlets are you all over, reading them I have realized once more all the things you have to fight every minute of your life, but in your fights you attain success upon success, and when you succeed the good cause goes a step forward. So, you don't have the right, I am afraid, even to get tired of fighting, and much more less to get discouraged.

This number of Camera Work is like all of them a bit, but to my opinion its literary part is more interesting than the pictorial one, though I fully realize the importance of this one. But the real point of the number I think is to be found like all points: at the end. "Our illustrations" is geme[?].[11]

The catalogue of the Buffalo exhibition made me realize what an important event in photography and art that must have been. I am sorry to have missed it.

You said in your letter: "I am going through a very critical period, a most trying one, and at times I feel as if I were not equal to it." This is not quite clear to me. I believe that what you refer to, is absolutely personal, of management, of the jealousies and quarrels of the people you have to deal with, and by no means [do] you refer to the evolution and development of the Secession, which has to be done in a path full of thorns indeed, but of thorns that wouldn't cover you with blood, but with glory. I sincerely confess that I have often thought, if you would be able to do with art in general what you have done with photography, and that if trying to do so, you were not putting upon your shoulders a burden that would crush you down instead of your being able to carry it to success. I have considered this point with the love of an utopist who believes that the true democracy of art will be born in the Secession, where the three words, that the French government uses to fool the people and spoil the walls of its monuments, will be a fact. And I have considered it too with the skepticism of a true friend who wouldn't like to see you fallen into ridicule for attempting something bigger than yourself. And I can tell you that I am convinced that if the Secession has changed route you certainly are the man, the only man that I know of, who can take it to a safe port. As we are not working for today, nor for tomorrow, nor for ourselves, but for all times, and for everybody, I hope that in order that your work would be complete, you would be able, now that you have realized a big idea, to find men who will construct it doing what you have done, so it will exist for "secula seculorum."

I wrote to Laurvik a few days ago, suggesting him an idea and asking him to talk it over with you.[12] Which consists in publishing interviews of the artists whose work you will exhibit. In this interview my principal object is to make them explain their point of views, and answer questions that I know will be asked when their work would be shown. I think this would save you a lot of trouble and make it easier for the public to understand the work of this man. At the same time, these interviews published in [a] paper that are an extension [?] to the Secession will create if not an interest at least a curiosity, which will make them go and see, and if they see, perhaps they might be compelled to think. I intended to send this week the first one with Picasso, but as I haven't been able to go out, I will send it next week.[13] Tell me what do you think of the idea. Steichen thinks it is a good one.

I have sent two articles to Laurvik on the new movements in French art. One of them is the one that Kennerly is going to publish.[14] In both my main object has been to suggest the way in which this work ought to be seen, and judged; not for what they actually are, not by their intrinsic merits, for people who haven't followed step by step this movement can't do it with justice; but for what they represent in the evolution of art.

I believe, and insist, that this kind of work needs explanation, especially in America, and that the exhibitions you are making of them wouldn't have their full value if some one doesn't take the trouble to do them. I am sorry that somebody else of more literary intelligence than I, wouldn't undertake this work.

As for my own work, I haven't done much either in quantity nor in quality.

I sincerely hope to see you here in the Summer, so we will talk over many important things. In the mean time, let me work my share for our ideal, and don't hesitate to use my services in whatever I can do.

I am sending you a monograph of Cézanne. I wanted to read something of this man who has left so many followers, admirers and fanatics, and the only thing I found was this book in german, which hasn't even been translated into french.[15] But Limantour the mexican minister of finances and the secondchief of the mexican mafia has been made lately member of the Academie de Sciences, and has almost daily all kind of eulogies in the papers.

It is time for me to stop. You are a busy man, and though I have yet too many things to tell you, this letter is getting too long.

Give my best regards to the fellows and receive my thanks for the check and Camera Work.

Yours,
M de Zayas

De Zayas to Stieglitz, March 7, 1911
[ALS, Stieglitz Papers, YCAL]

Paris March 7 1911

My dear Stieglitz—

Your most welcome letter [was] received the day before yesterday. It is sad to see how very little our own friends realize the good they have in the Secession. They are human, that is all, and no matter how they are or what they do they will not be able to kill the Secession. The real curious part is the financial one. Specially in New York where money means tyranny and as you say if someone will put up money in the S. they will simple profanate it and in that case it is better to quit. You are perfectly right not wanting to go beyond your limits. We have the right to sacrifice ourselves but not to sacrifice others and make the innocent pay for the sinner.

I am sending you an abstract of an article I wrote on Picasso for the Spanish magazine I work for. Maybe it will help you to get the point of view of this man.[16]

I have been sick and in a very bad mood for work. Nevertheless I have started in a new idea and made some caricatures and drawings for the philosophical collection.

Steichen too has been sick and feeling about the same way that I have. Maybe it is the weather.

I hope you will be here in June as you said, and that Haviland would be able to come too. Then we will be able to talk. Things can't go on like that forever, and there is not a reason why the just wouldn't have a place in this world. I am not usually optimistic, specially in art matters, but in the case of the Secession I am and I am sure we will succeed.

With my best wishes.

Yours,

M de Zayas

Stieglitz to de Zayas, April 4, 1911
Note written on an offprint of Marius de Zayas, "Pablo Picasso," **Camera Work**, no. 34
[ALS, De Zayas Archives, Seville]

Dear de Zayas: Exhibition a very great success.[17] We've again made a hit at the psychological moment. In a way this is the most important show we have had. The room looks very alive & swell. I am sure Picasso would enjoy the way we have presented his work. This little pamphlet is doing its work beautifully. Everything is just right at present. "291" is as it was before certain disturbing elements entered it. As you have heard we are well rid of them. Well soon we'll be able to have some good long chats. The future looks brighter than it has in a long while.

With kindest regards.

Cordially

St   April 4/11

De Zayas to Stieglitz, April 6, 1911
[ALS, Stieglitz Papers, YCAL]

Paris April 6 1911

My dear Stieglitz

I was very glad to hear the good news about the Secession and I certainly hope that it will grow bigger in its new address. As I understand from your postal, and for what Haviland told me, you will have the entire floor of a new building. I suppose that will enable the Secession to hold larger exhibitions than usually, what indeed will be of great advantage both for the Secession and for the artists.

I have had in mind to get up an exhibition of Spanish painters for New York, such as Picasso, Zuluaga Anglada etc. I spoke to Picasso about it and he thinks it could be easily gotten up. My first idea was to have it held in the Spanish Museum through the Secession, but now that you will be able to dispose of a larger space, I submit the idea to you for the Secession. I believe an exhibition of this kind will be of great interest, for it will show what eclecticism has done to the descendants of Velazquez and Goya. We will talk this over when you'll be here.

I am very glad that my notes on Picasso were of some use to you. He is very much interested in the idea of the Secession and curious to know the results of his exhibitions. I wish you would send me some of the criticisms of the press.

I have been reading lately the reproductions in Camera Work of the criticisms of the shows you have had, and I have come to conclude that after all there is more newspapers criticism in New York that there is in Paris!! It might seem incredible but it is so. The advertising dept. rules here more tyrannically than it does there.

It is a long time since I haven't seen Steichen. He lives now in the country and it seems that he comes to Paris very seldom.

As for myself I am ill most of the time, and have accomplished very little.

I heard from Haviland that Paul will leave New York about the same time that you will. I am really anxious to see you both, and I look up to the time in which you will be here with great expectation. With nothing of interest to tell you I close sending you my best wishes.

Yours,
M de Zayas

De Zayas to Stieglitz, April 21, 1911
[ALS, Stieglitz Papers, YCAL]

Paris April 21 1911

My dear Stieglitz

*I am sending you here with four criticisms of the Exhibition of the Artistes Independents: two in **pro** and two in **contra**. I think that reading both sides one can get a good idea of what tries Salon in this year, and I have hardly anything more to add. I only hope you will be here before it closes, for it really is worth the trip.*

I remarked more than ever the influence of the african negro art among this revolutionists. Some of the sculptors have merely copy it, without taking the trouble to translate it into french.

I am convinced one more of the necessity of having a show in the S. of the negro art. I suppose Steichen has already spoken to you about it.

I saw Picasso and showed him your note and gave him some of the pamphlets and announcements of his exhibitions. He was very much pleased. If you can send me some of the criticism of the press you will do us both a favor for I too am curious to see what they said.

Tell Steichen I began working in lithography with promising results. I see all the possibilities of the medium with which I can get all the effects of the charcoal and some others. I have the intention of making an album called "Paris" treating in it all that impresses me in this wonderful city. If it comes out the way I want I am afraid it will not be fit for publication.

Please give my regards to him, and to the neglectful Havilan[d], to the indolent Laurvik and to the rest of the rebels.

Yours,

M de Zayas

De Zayas to Stieglitz, July 10, 1911
[ALS, Stieglitz Papers, YCAL]

Paris July 10–1911

My dear Stieglitz—

Your welcome letter [was] received yesterday. I am glad to see that you haven't interrupted your pleasures in art. I suppose you have a lot to talk with Secessionists of Munich, and that you are getting more ammunition for future battles you still have to fight.[18]

It rather surprises me what you say about the production of art in that city. I thought they were following pretty close there, the movement of the frenchmen. I don't know where I got the idea that the "cubisims" had may adeps in Munich, and that there were many painters who move in the same track that Matisse follows.

Three days ago I received a letter from Picasso asking me [for] your address, and asking me to tell you to return his drawings because he was going to Céret and wanted to have them before leaving. I saw him this morning and explained to him that you had nothing to do with the drawings for you had sent them to Steichen, and if Steichen had not returned them already it was because he has been very busy in the country and wanted to do it personally instead of sending them. He seems to be very sore at the way he has been treated, and puts all the blame on Frank Haviland. He says that he never asked for an exhibition and that it is against his rules to exhibit, and if he did it this time it was to please Haviland, and after he gave his drawings nobody has informed him about anything concerning them. I gave him Steichen's address and told him to write to him. I fully explained what your position is in this matter and he understood that you are not to blame for any discourtesy.

If I gave him all kind of explanations it is because first I really think he is right and second because this fellow talks a good deal, and I believe that the Secession needs them. I don't want to tell anything to Steichen because I don't think he will take my attitude in the right way.

It doesn't surprise me that you haven't received a letter from any of the fellows in N.Y. The indians in Mexico say that people go to see the fruit trees only when they have fruits otherwise they don't even remember them.

Haviland (Paul) is in Paris, I read it in the Herald.

My father is leaving for Mexico next Saturday. He doesn't intend to stay and will try to fix matters to be able to live in Paris. I hope with all my might he will, for I don't like the idea to go back to America. The only way to be able to stand life in those countries where stupidity prevails is to be at perpetual war fighting that powerful enemy and I don't have either the character nor the strength that you have.

I am still working at my posters, one is already accepted, and the other has been accepted in principle. But I don't sing victory until I have the price of them in my pocket and know that they have been sold.

I will shortly write you about my answer to the Sun article.

Please give my best regards to your family and receive our best wishes from my father and myself

> *Yours,*
> *M de Zayas*

De Zayas to Stieglitz, July 22, 1911
[ALS, Stieglitz Papers, YCAL]

Paris July 22 1911

My dear Stieglitz

I am sending you a little book I bought at Bernheim's, which if you don't know it already I am sure you will enjoy. To me it is a clear view of the manner of every painter of importance at present. Anyhow I want to call your attention to this kind of literature which is written by young people and which gives a good account of the conditions of art in Paris. Don't you think it would be good to reprint some of it in Camera Work? For my opinion this is just what you need, that will help a good deal to make people understand a little. I translated some paragraphs of the little book, so you would appreciate more clearly what I mean.

I have been very busy working on the posters, at least I succeeded in making something that I like and that the manager likes too, which was rather hard. They are going to be delivered the 29 and the check will come from New York. Amen.

In my moments of rest I have been going to the Louvre. I have discovered quite a few masterpieces which are just as modern as modern can be. If you happen to see paintings by Fra Angelico in the Gallery there let me know what do you think of its color considering it from the modern point of view.

I hope you will make up your mind to come soon to Paris and stay here as long as possible for there is no question about it, here is where you have to get all your ammunition for your future fights, and you have to be more than ever perfectly sure of your ground.

My father didn't go to Mexico after all, we received news from there giving us awful information about the state of affairs. It is practically impossible to do anything there. But in exchange the business part of the spanish magazine is strengthening up.

With best regards.
Yours,
M de Zayas

De Zayas to Stieglitz, August 14, 1911
[ALS, Stieglitz Papers, YCAL]

Paris August 14–1911

My dear Stieglitz:

I have been wanting to write you for the last ten days and I haven't had the strength to hold the pen, and though I am in the same condition now I do it to let you know that if things continue to be like this Paris will be melted before long.

It has been worse than in N.Y. and I have suffered terribly.

For the last twelve days my father has been in a Sanitarium. He had an attack in the bladder from retention of urine and had to be taken there to be operated. He has suffered much, but is out of danger and most likely will be out this week. This has come to add more troubles. He had to pass all this hot days laying on his back without moving. He is half crazy. And so am I. No more Paris for us in the summer.

I haven't seen anything or anybody, and haven't been able to do my usual work. And the worst part of all this is, that there is no hopes of a change in the weather. My only ambition now is to feel cool. I have come to be quite animal.

I spoke to the N.Y. theatrical manager who ordered the posters about my "Theatre of Caricatures," he was very much interested in the idea and promised to help me along and produce it in N.Y. He left the 29 of July and asked me to write to him my idea in detail and send a play. And there you are! I am stung! I don't think I can do the whole thing myself, especially as far as the playwriting is concerned, and tho[ugh] my father could do that part, it would be to add too much work to what he already has. I don't dare to ask Laurvik again to help me. I know it would be valuable to him to get in touch with this man. But I am sure that if I write to him he wouldn't even answer my letter. So, I have to wait for a better chance. Nevertheless it is a pity to let this chance go by, and it pains me to go to somebody else where there is a chance for one of our group. Anyhow as soon as I feel a little better I will begin working.

Wishing you all kinds of pleasant temperatures and with my best regards to your family

I am yours,
M de Zayas

De Zayas to Stieglitz, August 22, 1911
[ALS, Stieglitz Papers, YCAL]

Paris August 22 1911

My dear Stieglitz

Sorry to hear that you are suffering again from your stomach, but I don't have anything to envy you, for, for the last week I have had serious troubles with mine too. I had to see a doctor, but don't feel any relief so far.

My father is getting along as good as possible under the circumstances. We brought him home today. And [he] feels happy anyway.

The same day I received your last letter I received one from Laurvik. A nice one too, together with the article he wrote on you.[19] I understand which force[s] make him shake his apathy and give signs of life. I will write him this week and ask him to see Tyler about the "theatre" idea.

The weather is almost pleasant but I still feel the consequences of the hot spell we had.

Hope to see you soon. With best regards.
Yours,
M de Zayas

De Zayas to Stieglitz, August 26, 1911
[ALS, Stieglitz Papers, YCAL]

Paris August 26 1911

My dear Stieglitz:

I wrote you to Lucerne the same day you left. I suppose they forwarded the letter to you.

Since then the only news is that I had the sweet experience of being poisoned by a pill of belladonna. The feelings weren't very nice, and I thought I was going to stop making caricatures for good. But it didn't go as far as all that and I am still alive, waiting for another chance.

My father is getting along alright. He is home and doing his business plentiful and easy. Now all his happiness consists in urinating!!

I wrote to Laurvik giving him all kinds of instructions on the matter of the "Theatre." Let us see if he knows how to take advantage of this chance. The man seems to be O.K. all along the line. He sends his check, praising my work once more, really more than it deserves.

I sincerely hope that Laurvik would make something out of this connection. He has a lot of plays that he might just as well try to do something with them.

Thanks for sending the clipping. I never receive the "World." I have asked for it several times, and about a month ago I subscribed to it through Brentano's but do not get it yet. They think that by sending the money I make with them I have to be satisfied.

Hope you have a good time and will profit of your rest. I think you needed it badly.

The weather here is very pleasant, but Paris seems to be rather dull. But it is always Paris.

Hope to see you soon.

With best regards.

> *Yours,*
> *M de Zayas*

De Zayas to Stieglitz, October 18, 1911
Cable Message / Western Union Telegraph Company [Stieglitz Papers, YCAL]

From London
Received at 26 West 31 St———Oct 18 1901
Stieglitz,
291 Fifth Ave, NY
Need 150 get New York Cable American express london return at arrival urgent.

> *Zayas*

> *Oct 18th, 1911 8:24 am*

De Zayas to Stieglitz, September 14, 1912
Written on stationery of: The Mount Sinai Hospital (Private Pavilion) / Fifth Avenue,100th to 101st Streets / New York; [ALS, Stieglitz Papers, YCAL]

> *Sep. 14 1912*

Dear Stieglitz

Your letter found me still in the Hospital where I expect to leave today. I am doing very well and feel quite proud of my disease for it has been declared by all doctors as "most unusual." I feel I am a Secessionist even pathologically.

I have been treated most kindly by Dr. Berg, partly by his natural disposition and partly by a letter that Dr. Stieglitz gave me for him.[20]

I am glad to hear that you are taking up exercise. That's the trouble with all of us, we spend too much energy in thoughts and don't make up for it. The result is "most unusual" diseases.

Well, our pantomime has been an artistic success, and the only judgement we lack is yours. Which I hope we will get soon, for it really has been a great disappointment to all of us not to have your opinion.

As for the financial part of it, I think we will be able to make something. Anyhow, to pay expenses is not bad for the first venture.

The Dr. just came in here, dress[ed] my wound up and told me to go home!!

The pains of the dressing seemed sweet.

Best regards and hopes to see you soon.

Yours,

M de Zayas

De Zayas to Stieglitz, September 7, 1913
[ALS, Stieglitz Papers, YCAL]

Sep. 7. 1903[21]

My dear Stieglitz

Received your letter which came in the good company of one from Haviland. It was good to hear from you both.

I have been living in a perfect state of imbecility, and have enjoyed it so much that I intend to keep it up as long as I possibly can. That is the reason I haven't written to you. I was afraid to lose the good opinion I know you have of me. This is one proof of my imbecility. Otherwise I have been working hard for the paper. The theatrical season has began with an avalanche of plays. All bad of course. Moral New York is crowding two of them which take place in houses of **pleasure** of different prices. They are not so naughty as they say they are. They do not go any further than the parlor, what disappoints the respectable feminine audience.

I believe the time has come for the Secession to have the exotic show you have in mind. If you don't do it now maybe next season will be too late. New York is growing rapidly.

I hope you will soon be back for I really feel lonesome with the crowd I have to see.

With best regards from the family and myself

Yours

M de Zayas

De Zayas to Stieglitz, May 22, 1914
[ALS, Stieglitz Papers, YCAL]

Paris May 22 1914

My dear Stieglitz

Here I am since the 13th hunting for people without very much of a success. After many calls I saw Picasso, and Picabia. I didn't see any of Picasso's latest work his studio being all upset. Picabia's latest work is more simple and direct but still complicated and arbitrary.

Paris seems to be more beautiful than ever, and I really regret not to know the use of the camera.

I was introduced to the crowd of the "Soirées de Paris." A rather interesting bunch of artists headed by Appollinaire [sic][22] *I told Picabia he ought to send some copies to you. I believe it would be good also that you should send "Camera Work" to them. They have seen some copies and admire them greatly.*

I spoke to Picasso about an exhibition in "291." He is willing, but all those matters have to be treated with Kahnweiler.[23] *I will see him about it.*

Picabia says there is nothing really "new" in art. Anyhow I will look around and if I find something new and worth the while to us I will let you know.

I will leave for London next week to get through with the caricatures I have to make and hurry back to Paris.

Picasso would like to have three copies of the supplement Matisse-Picasso, and one of the other special number with the article of Mrs. Picabia. I will show him tomorrow your photographs and the drawings of W.[24]

I am waiting to hear from G. Stein to go and see her. I will work at her caricature immediately, so you will have it on time.

>*With best regards*
>>*Yours*
>>*de Zayas*

1 rue Jacques Offenbach.
(Passy)

De Zayas to Stieglitz, May 26 and 27, 1914
[ALS, Stieglitz Papers, YCAL]

My dear Stieglitz:

I have been very busy these last few days and have seen quite a lot of important people. Picabia has been a great help to me, and in all our excursions we make propaganda for "291" and "Camera Work." You would be very much pleased if you would know the high appreciation of the few people who have seen Camera Work, not only of the work done in it, but of the effort it represents and of its meaning.

I believe it would not be at all a waste to send regularly copies to four or five people who understand and appreciate your work and who have no money to pay for the price of it but who certainly will have a great deal of pleasure in knowledge of it. Apollinaire is one of them, he is one of the editors of "Les Soirées de Paris" a center very much in the spirit of "291." They are very willing to get in contact with you in order to be of mutual service. If you approve of the idea, and have confidence in my judgement I will try to establish our relations with them. They have, in an indirect way, a salon de exhibition for paintings the galleries of a young man Paul Guilla[u]me with whom I have had a long talk. He seems to be of the right kind in every respect, and is also willing to communicate with you. He said he was going to write to you.[25]

I saw Kahnweiler and ask[ed] him about the Picasso exhibition. He said he was very sorry not to be able to be of any service to you, because he has a contract with Brener [sic] who has open[ed] a galerie in Washington Sq., N.Y., that he has to be his sole agent.[26] That Brener Galerie from what I can see is going to be a danger to modern art in America. Kahnweiler also is taking a decided attitude of commercialism and pure commercialism.

Nevertheless you can have an exhibition of Picasso's latest work which in my opinion would be of great importance to 291. Picabia and Mrs. Picabia have about 18 of his paintings 8 of which are of his latest style and very well selected they are willing to let you have them and sell them if there are any offers.

Picasso's latest pictures are to me the best and deepest expression of the man, with a remarkable purity that his other work lacks.

If you want the pictures that Picabia has let me know at once so I will arrange to bring them to N.Y. with me. Also give me full particulars about the Customs House entree and the form of the affidavit.

I believe I can also arrange an exhibition of Marie Lorencin [sic] and another of remarkable negro statue[t]ts. Guilla[u]me, the art dealer, has a very important collection and is willing to let you have them. I have always believed that a show of the art of the negroes would be a great thing for 291. Tell me if you want them.

I saw Gertrude Stein last Saturday. I was very much pleased with her. For the first time in my life I have had the pleasure of laughter with a woman, and I don't know of any one who has a deeper sense of the comic than she has. I was with her for over two hours. There was also her companion in life a california girl with a very interesting indian type, she is, physically, the reverse of Gertrude Stein.

I have changed my mind about sending you her caricature. One caricature would be without meaning. I have in mind a triptych in which the indian girl plays a big role. So, I think we better wait.

I spent the afternoon yesterday with Matisse, in his Paris studio. His latest work is very moderate both in color and form. He showed us some interesting lithographs. I spoke to him about his photograph in Camera Work.[27] He told me he hadn't seen it.

May 27

We had lunch today at Vollard's. I asked him to let me make his caricature and he invited us (Picabia and myself) to his house so I would know him better. We spent four hours with him. He read part of his work on Cézanne that will soon be published.[28] It really is very interesting. Among the many remarkable paintings that he showed us he pulled out what he considers the best picture of Cézanne, a still life which indeed makes the rest of the work of Cézanne look pale. What I call a real masterpiece. I never even suspected that Cézanne had reached that note. He also showed us about fifty rotten Renoirs that he tried to make us believe they were wonders.

So far I don't complain of my trip to Paris, I have learned a few things, and I intend to keep on.

I have shown Walkowitz drawings to several people. I will write to him the opinion I have gathered all important and all favorable.

It must be well understood that when I speak to people, like those of "Les Soirées de Paris" and Guilla[u]me the art dealer, about "291" I only try to establish a friendship and by no means any relationship that might appear like if we were looking for correspondents or protection of any kind.

I haven't seen Steichen yet. I will probably see him tomorrow and will talk things over with him. If you can spare a copy of Walkowitz number I would like to show it here.

With best regards.

Yours,

de Zayas

Stieglitz to de Zayas, June 3, 1914
[TL (retained carbon), Stieglitz Papers, YCAL]

291 Fifth Ave., New York
June 3, 1914.

My dear De Zayas:

Day before yesterday your letter of the 22nd ult. came to hand. I was glad to get it. It is too bad that you haven't seen the people you are after as readily as you expected. But that is always so, and I trust that you have made connections more easily since. I can imagine how beautiful Paris must seem. I often think of it and think of all the wonderful photographs I could make there. And all the real pleasures I could have there. But somehow or other in spite of all the temptations, all the desires, something keeps me sticking to New York. I wonder if I will ever get away. That the "Soirées de Paris" crowd must be interesting goes without saying. Haviland, you know, gets its magazine. And I have heard about it from other sources. I would only be too glad to send "Camera Work" to them. To whom should it be addressed?

I hope you will be able to make connections with Kahnweiler for a Picasso show. I am more eager than ever to have him. "291" needs it badly. That is New York needs it. This morning I had a letter from Paul Guillaume in which he tells me that you had told him to write to me. He says that he would be glad to let us have a show of negro art. Has he really very good things, and what do you think about it? Of course I would like to have a show of Negro art as you know. I want to make the next season at "291" a very live one. I have decided to open up about October 16th with several photographic shows. I will run more shows during the year than I did last year. I have been doing a heap of thinking about lots of things. As a matter of fact I have been obliged to. The situation becomes more and more complex. But I suppose I will be equal to the task of keeping things moving in the right direction as I always have.

Of course I am curious to get your impressions of London and of Gertrude Stein, and of anything else you may see. Haviland as you have probably heard is to remain in this country for the summer. It is his father's wish. It is rather rough on Haviland

and he was quite upset about it. He had looked forward to his trip abroad.

Just as I was about ready to do a lot of printing at "291" I was called on Jury duty. That meant two whole weeks and a day cut out of my life. It was very tiresome work, uninteresting, uninspiring. Otherwise there is no special news. With kindest regards from the two-ninety-niners, Always,

Yours,

N. B. Walkowitz is going abroad for a six month trip. He leaves within a few weeks and goes to Greece and Italy.

Marin is booked for Maine in about ten days. You see I will be pretty much alone at "291" for some time. I take the family to the Jersey coast next week and then my three and one-half hours commuting daily will begin.

Puck is decidedly uninteresting, very commonplace. But they are doing a lot of advertising and they claim to be printing an edition of 2700.

Stieglitz to de Zayas, June 9, 1914
[TL (retained carbon), Stieglitz Papers, YCAL]

291 Fifth Ave., New York
June 9, 1914.

My dear De Zayas:

Your long letter arrived yesterday morning, and I immediately dictated a reply. But somehow or other the reply seemed stupid and unsatisfactory, owing probably to the fact that my mind was on a thousand and one different things at the same time. And so instead of mailing it in the evening I had Marie tear it up.[29] I am going to make another try now and I hope I won't be disturbed. Although I thought that at this time of year I would have quiet at "291," somehow or other I have been overrun with visitors. I suppose a lot of the people have nothing to do so they come around to "291" where they know that they are always welcome, even if they do keep me from attending to those things which ought to be attended to. And now as for your letter.

I am glad to hear that you are on the go for fair. That Picabia should be an immense help to you goes without saying. He is a fine generous chap. The right kind, no matter what they say of his art. I am glad that "Camera Work" means something to some of the people in Paris. And by **meaning** *I mean that some people realize what it represents. In other words* **feeling** *the spirit in it. I will be only too glad to send copies to those whom you think ought to have them. You know how I feel about circulating "Camera Work." It should get into the hands of the right people. The money end means absolutely nothing to me. Above all I will be only too glad to know Apollinaire gets it. I would have sent copies to him long ago, but I did not want to make it look as if we wanted to get something out of him. You know how easily decent motives are misconstrued even by the most decent of people. But now that you have brought about the connection between "291" and those little "crowd," we are not so apt to be misunderstood.*

As I wrote to you Guillaume dropped me a letter telling me that you had been to see him and in this letter he expressed his willingness to cooperate with me. Of course we want that Negro show. But more about that later.

As for Kahnweiler I am not at all surprised at what you wrote me. As a matter of fact I expected nothing else. I had heard that Brenner and Cody, an old friend of Max Weber's (they have had a falling out lately), had opened a little gallery on Washington Square. Brenner was to be in Paris and send things over. Cody was to stay in New York.[30] I was informed that Kahnweiler had given Brenner a sole agency. But I hardly could believe that Kahnweiler would be so devilish[ly] stupid. If he only knew how slick and irresponsible, how absolutely without conscience the average American is, Kahnweiler might spare himself some great disappointments. For these disappointments are in store for him, I am sure, as far as this special little gallery goes. But perhaps I am mistaken. Well, as far as we are concerned it makes no difference. Washington Square is to be purely commercial, and as long as Kahnweiler has become purely so, the less we have to do with him the better. Of course I feel that "291" ought to have a Picasso show. And so it is doubly gratifying that the Picabias are in a position to help us out with a fine show of what you say is the right Picasso stuff. I shall write you within a few days exactly how the things can be brought over, so that you can bring them with you yourself when you come. And when do you expect to come? That is when do you expect to leave Paris? Have you any idea? Yes, Marie Laurencin's work I have had in mind ever since I saw it first. I would like it shown at "291." So you can arrange to have that sent over too; or bring it over yourself. Of course let these people know that the shows cannot all take place at once and that the things ought to remain over here for some time. It will be to their interest as well as ours. Of course I know that you are giving all these people a full understanding of what we are doing. "291" could not be in better hands than yours.

Say, that must have been a great time with Gertrude Stein. I wish I had been present. As for her caricature, your idea is a capital one. I have heard about that Indian like girl. The pair must be wonders. I have a hazy vision of that triptych. I see a great show of your's at "291" for the coming year. There is hardly a doubt that the season will be a hummer. Probably the most exciting we have had as yet. I have already made up my mind that no exhibition would be run longer than sixteen days. I shall force issues.

So you also saw Matisse. I suppose that Steichen has not given him "Camera Work" as yet. You see Steichen did not have his numbers when he came to America, and since he got back to Voulangis I suppose he has been engrossed in his garden, to the exclusion of everything else. I wonder how you find him looking. I hope alright again.

We had a great day at Mt. Kisco. Eugene Meyer was unfortunately not there, but between Mrs. Meyer, Haviland, Marin, Katherine Rhoades, Walkowitz and Mrs. Stieglitz and myself and three cameras, including a moving picture one and a magnificent day as far as weather was concerned, the outing proved to be about as perfect as one can imagine. You will undoubtedly see Mrs. Meyer in Paris.[31]

And so you had lunch with Vollard. He is a great fellow. I have heard about that Cézanne book. It goes without saying that it will prove interesting. Although Vollard has a habit of not making entirely good when it comes to his publications. There is always just a trace of "business" back of it all. But only a trace. He is a shrewd old fellow. But of his type a masterpiece. You make my mouth water when you speak of that Cézanne. I know how chary you are with the use of the term masterpiece. And when you say it in conjunction with something you saw of Cézanne's at Vollard's and that it makes all other Cézanne's seem pale, it is a wonder that I am eager to see this piece. I wonder if I did see it that afternoon when Steichen and I were at Vollard's.

I saw a marvelous still life there, which at the time, was a question in my mind whether it was not finer than the ones the Meyers finally got. But I had seen so much that day before going to Vollard's and so much marvelous stuff at Vollard's that I did not consider myself fit to judge. I do remember a lot of inferior Renoirs. Renoir has done a lot of potboilers, and I think Vollard has a goodly batch of them.

I am glad that the Walkowitz drawings are approved of by the people to whom you've showed them. He had done a few new things. And I think they show a distinct development. He is certainly the real article. I am glad he is going to make this trip to Europe. It will do him a great deal of good. He leaves next Wednesday for Greece, Athens. From there he goes to a little place near Rome where he had been some years ago. Later on he will go to Paris and expects to be back to America end of October. He is going to see quite a bit of the world and on very, very little money. Marin goes to Maine a week from today. He is in fine shape. I have managed to do a good turn for him, so that his mind is at ease for some time to come. I induced Daniels [sic], the ex-saloon keeper, to take quite a few of Marin's outright.[32] Daniels came down to see me and spent several mornings with me. I had long talks with him. Important for him, important for the fellows, important for the public, and consequently of importance to "291." I will tell you all about it when you come back. There is somebody waiting for me and so I must stop. As ever,

>Your old,

N.B. Under separate cover I am sending you a batch of "Camera Work," Special Numbers, Walkowitz Numbers, a Rodin Number. You can place them where you think they can do most good. If you want more Numbers just say so and I will send them.

De Zayas to Stieglitz, June 11, 1914
Written on stationery of The Imperial Hotel / Russell Square / London
[ALS, Stieglitz Papers, YCAL]

June 11th 1914

My dear Stieglitz

    Here I am since the 4th displaying an activity quite strange to my nature. I had the good fortune to go and see Bayley as soon as I arrived.[33] *He certainly is as fine a fellow as there ever was. He has done all in his power to help me along. I spent last Sunday with him at his country place. He showed me over one hundred of his photographs which are rather interesting. He has a big print of a bull's head which I think is very remarkable and according to my understanding of photography one of the very finest things I have ever seen. In this particular print all the qualities of the man are expressed purity of expression, a clear view and perfect honesty in rendering it. It reminded me in its effects of light, that still life of de Meyer of the crystal plate and the flowers. I wish you could see it. I told him so, but he answered that he was not a photographer, to which I replied that that was the kind of people that interested you.*

    I am very sorry I didn't bring the three photographs you gave me. He spoke of the ones published in Camera Work as wonders he would have enjoyed seeing the big prints, as there really is a great difference between them and the small ones.

    I also saw Muir, and I am glad to know him better. He also is a fine fellow and a great admirer of the head of 291. It is really a pleasure to see how people appreciate you in these neighborhoods. I was lucky to catch Shaw.[34] *I saw him the day he was leaving for the country. I was quite a long time with him and I only hope I will be able to express exactly my impression of him. He didn't look to me like any of the photographs I have seen of him. He acted very nervously, like if he wanted to get away from me, he jumped all over the place, spoke of every possible subject, showed me a million things, etc., etc. I had a hard time catching up with him. But I got him. And I got him good. I believe that with his caricature and the one I want to make of Gertrude Stein I will become a real caricaturist, or at least start on the right road. I have seen some other important people among them Browning the printer. He seems to be very much interested in my way of working and said that he could arrange an exhibition here anytime I wanted to have one.*

    I also saw Roger Fry the head of the modern movement of art in London as you probably know.[35] *He spoke very highly of you. I saw him at Holland Hall where he was fixing a room for the exhibition of the work of his shop. This exhibition is the Independents of England. I saw all the paintings. Not a single thing worth while and lots of very, very, very bad stuff. Kandinsky has three pictures there. One is good the other two pretty poor.*

    I also saw Coburn.[36] *He treated me very cordially but I received still a more cordial treatment from his mother. She was exceedingly nice to me. So nice, that not even once she made the slightest reference to you or the Secession. Coburn showed* me his latest work some of which, or rather most of which, is very good. I believe he has moved quite a long way. I feel that he has realized that honesty in photography is one of the essential qualities. I hope that realization will not stop at photography.

I have yet a lot of people to see. Most of them live out of London what makes it more difficult.

The day I left Paris I was with Picasso for quite a long time. We had a very interesting and intimate talk on art and on his latest manner of expression. He open[ed] himself quite frankly. I will try to write down what he said because it will interest you. The sum and total of his talk was that he confesses that he has absolutely enter[ed] into the field of photography. I showed him your photographs and Walkowitz drawings. He came to the conclusion that you are the only one who has understood photography and understood and admired the "steerage" to the point that I felt inclined to give it to him. But my will power prevented me from doing it.

About Walkowitz drawings he made quite a conscientious criticism that I will also try to write down for him because he went quite deep in pointing out the things that according to him are on the wrong way. That might help Walkowitz—at least for looking at his work from another angle. I am glad I brought those drawings.

I might possibly make connections with a magazine here, what would be a very good thing for me. I haven't sent yet anything to Puck though I have almost all the material for the thing I have to send. Of course I will not send to them the real stuff for that does not interest them nor the readers of Puck. That I will reserve for us.

I am very sorry Haviland could not come to London as we had planned. We would have had a very interesting time.

I am anxious to hear from you about the thing I told you of Paris.

With best regards.

  Yours,

  de Zayas

Stieglitz to de Zayas, June 22, 1914
[TL (retained carbon), Stieglitz Papers, YCAL]

       291 Fifth Ave., New York
       June 22, 1914.

My dear De Zayas:

Your letter from London was positively refreshing. It arrived at a time when I needed something like it very sorely. I am delighted to know that you may make some connections in London. That would be really great to have some of your things published there. That you would like Bayley I knew. He is so much of a man. And besides that has such a keen sense of humor and is a thoroughbred sport—sport as I understand that term—of the finest type. Of course I would like to see that bull's head you speak about. Bayley has been photographing for many years and he has been very modest about it. I am glad you told him what you did about me and for the kind of work I am looking for. I shall write him in a few days. I am glad too that *you saw Muir. I was amused at your description of your visit to Shaw. I can well imagine what he was like. He is very quick in realizing what he is up against. And I don't think that he was quite as easy at heart with you about as he is with the photographers and even people like Rodin. Shaw and Gertrude Stein! What possibilities! And what probabilities! And as for your Coburn visit, that too I could picture to myself most vividly. I can see the old lady's face, I can hear her voice. And I know exactly what she thought even though she didn't express her thoughts. How amusing. How small. And yet without her Coburn would never have gotten where he is. And as for Coburn and his photography, without seeing what he has actually done I can fully believe that he has made decided progress. He has always had talent and ability. And his ability is bound to develop as he is constantly on the job, both in work at his photography, and working for his photography. That his photographs are honest I do not doubt. After the Buffalo Show he realized that that was the only way. He has always been keen enough to feel how the wind was going to blow. For his sake I am assuming that he is really honest now, at least in his photography. Lord, how I hate trickiness. I loath[e] deceit. Whether in photography or whether in life. And the Coburn pair have shown that they were blessed with a goodly portion of those lovely attributes. I had always hoped that Coburn would outgrow them,— and I still hope he will, as he seems to have in his photography,—and that his mother would achieve a certain amount of sense. A sense which would let her know that people never were quite as blind to her methods as she imagined. Her ambition was to put Coburn at the "top." And now that she has achieved this end, to her satisfaction at least, she ought to dissemble a little wisdom. But why bother about her, except that I always felt that Coburn could never become honest while under his mother's influence.*

It was mighty interesting to hear what Picasso had to say about my photographs. Of course I value his opinion tremendously. I am specially pleased that he liked the Steerage. To me the Steerage has always been a great favorite. As a matter of fact it comes nearest to expressing the thing I wanted to express. There are only two or three photographs that I ever made which I consider really successful from my point of view. And what Picasso had to say about his own work is tremendously significant and it does not surprise me. As a matter of fact I saw exactly at what point he would have to come to. And that he has arrived at this proves to me, if proof were necessary, how honest he is with himself. What he said about Walkowitz interests me quite as much as what he said about me. I feel a little as he does. But knowing Walkowitz and knowing all his work, I also feel that Picasso does not see the whole of Walkowitz. And how can he? Not having had a chance to see what I have seen.

On the day that your letter arrived I also had a surprise in receiving a letter from Leo Stein. Walkowitz had sent a number of Camera Work to Stein. And as there was no inscription, and no name of any kind, Stein assumed that I had sent the Number to him. He wrote me quite a letter analyzing the Number. Your article interested him, but he thought it was "unentertainingly presented" and badly written. I laughed when I read this. Thank God we have some bad writing! The Weichsel he could not go at all.[37] He took it on trust, he said. As for the Walkowitz drawings, he thought "prettily melancholy." The two last he could not abide. He hates everything appertaining to "cubism." The letter at least shows that Stein is very intelligent. It also shows that in some things he does not feel below the surface. He has just a little of the Berenson quality in his makeup. At any rate I am glad to have the letter.

And now for the Picassos, Negro art, etc., etc. The best way I think in handling this matter is to have Lucien Lefebre Foinet be the agent for us and the packer and shipper. He is the man who sent over the Brancusis. Steichen will give you his address. Undoubtedly Picabia knows the address. Foinet is well known. Now my advice in order to save any trouble at this end is to have each person's work packed in separate cases and separate shipments made. With each shipment there must be a Consular Invoice of each article contained in the shipment, and there must be an artist's affidavit attached to the invoice, which affidavit is to attest that the work sent, as per invoice is the original work of the artist and that there are no duplicates. This affidavit must be sworn to also before the American Consul.

Now in case that Picasso should not be in Paris when the affidavit for his work is to be made, an affidavit can be made by the owner of the goods (Picabia in this case)—or if Picabia is absent, by the Agent, M. Foinet. I am enclosing copies of instructions for such affidavits. They will explain themselves.

In the case of the Negro art, M. Paul G[u]illaume will have to make the affidavit, for which I am also enclosing a copy of the instructions. For any other show, Laurencin for instance, please follow the same course of action. The American Consul ought to be able to help you in case you have any doubts as to what to do. This will all entail a certain amount of trouble and work, but if it is done right it will save money and later trouble. Of course Foinet should insure the shipments.

The shipments are to be made to Alfred Stieglitz, 291 Fifth Avenue, New York. The Consular Invoices should all be made on Consignor's blanks. Don't fail to see that this is done as there are two kinds of forms. The goods in question are not bought by me, but are consigned to me.

I want to get this off with the steamer so I am going to stop dictating. With kindest regards, and the hopes that you will continue to have an interesting time, as always,

Your old,

De Zayas to Stieglitz, June 30 and July 1, 1914
Written on stationery of América / The Illustrated Spanish Magazine / The Thirty Third Floor / Metropolitan Tower / New York [ALS, Stieglitz Papers, YCAL]

Paris June 30th 1914

My dear Stieglitz

I have been wanting to write to you for several days, but since I am in Paris my activity has left me. Nevertheless I have been doing some work, a lot of thinking, specially about the exhibitions we are to have.

It is all arranged with Mrs. Picabia to send all the Picassos she has. After a long talk with Picabia we have agreed that in order to make the exhibition complete some paintings of Braque ought to be shown at the same time. These two men really complete one expression, and in order to be entirely just both of them must be shown together. It is true that Braque is a satellite of Picasso, and it is true also that up to the present it hasn't been found what is the actual use of satellites but they must have one otherwise they would not exist. Braque would have never existed without Picasso but Picasso owes very many things to Braque. I am sure that you will not hesitate in exhibiting both together so I have asked Mrs. Picabia to lend us the Braques she has.

Studying the significance of this exhibition in 291, and by what I see in the latest work of Picabia I also feel that you ought to have an exhibition of Picabia's work. My reason is the following: Picasso represents in his work the expression of pure sensibility, the action of matter on the senses and also of the senses on matter while Picabia's work is the expression of pure thought. Picasso could never work without dealing with objectivity while Picabia forgets matter to express only, maybe the memory of something that has happened. He expresses the object the other the action. To me, it is very interesting these two cases of plastic expression. And I believe that exhibiting them at 291 this point could be brought out clearly. The latest paintings of Picabia are very large. One that I especially care for is 2 1/2 meters high. I believe if it could get into the room at 291 it would make quite an impression to have only three big paintings in it, covering almost the entire three walls from the floor to the ceiling.[38] Tell me as soon as you can if the idea interests you, for I will probably leave Paris by the first of August. I have told Picabia about it and my reason for exhibiting his work and also made him understand that it was not by friendship or by sensationalism that I would like to see his work in New York but only to show the psychological case we might say, of two men like Picasso and himself both products of the present time working through entirely different channels and arriving to similar conclusions and also to show clearly to the public the difference of the expression of abstract representation. I also made him understand that I was only looking around for things of this sort and that you only could decide about showing the things. You can be perfectly sure that if you don't think it worth while he will not resent in the least not showing at 291 for he understands and says it himself that ours is not a place to hang pictures that do not have in them a meaning that would carry out and develop the idea that you are trying to express. This very point has made me think after careful consideration that an exhibition of Marie Laurencin's work would not have any meaning at 291. I have come to the conclusion after studying her work more clearly that this clever girl is doing exactly what Davis and his bunch did with "Cubism" in the exhibition at Montross. She does not express the present, she has the spirit of the XVII century represented by one of the formulas of modern art. You might see it from a different angle if you think that we ought to have her work I believe it will be easy to get it. She also is in the hands of an art dealer, but this one has not contract[ed] with any New York dealer. Let me know your decision.[39]

As for the negro art I believe that if you haven't made up your mind about having a special exhibition of it it would be good to have some good specimens of it around the place. I will try to take along as many things as I possibly can.

July 1

I received your interesting letter of June 22 with the instructions to send the things for exhibitions. I will follow them to the letter.

I have started working at the Trocadero, taking photographs of the negro art. My brother is the one who takes them and of course they are not very good but good enough to help me. I have been talking with several people about my studies in the Evolution of Form, among them with the conservateur of the Trocadero. They all seemed to be very interested in the theory. I will make an effort to accomplish as much as I can in this work.

I received the copies of "Camera Work" and sent to Picasso the ones he asked for. He is now in Carcason [?]. The rest I will place in good hands. I told the people of the "Soirées de Paris" that you were willing to make the exchange. They will send you their paper from the first number.

The last word in art in Paris is the "Simultanism" in literature. Apollinaire is the father of it. I recommend you to read in the last number of the Soirées his Carte-Ocean. It is really very amusing. This Apollinaire is really the deepest observer of superficiality. We have become good friends.

I am very glad to hear that Walkowitz is coming to Europe. I believed he really needed it.

What has become of Hartley? G. Stein told me that he seemed disappointed about his exhibition in New York, from the artistic stand point.[40]

I feel very enthusiastic about the coming season at 291. I am sure we will reach a higher standing and do very effective work. Well we will see.

Yours,
de Zayas

Stieglitz to de Zayas, July 7, 1914
[TL (retained carbon), Stieglitz Papers, YCAL]

291 Fifth Ave., New York.
July 7, 1914.

My dear De Zayas:

Just a couple of lines to tell you that I have given a letter of introduction to you to a young girl, a dancer whose name is Roshanara. She is very young and very beautiful. She is an English girl born in India.

I wonder if you had any opportunity in view of the terrific amount of work you are doing to think of your little article on "291," which is to appear in the Special "291" Number. I hate to bother you about this matter, but I know that if it is delayed too long that the Number will never materialize. I would like to have the MS not later than September 15th and earlier if possible. I have so far received but one, from Mabel Dodge.

Mrs. Meyer wrote to me that she had seen you and that she had bought a Picasso.[41] That is great. And she also writes that if her husband will let her she will buy a Cézanne which is a beauty. I suppose this is the one you wrote so enthusiastically about. Of course business is still rotten over here and I don't know how Meyer will feel about the pictures. I hope he will see his way clear to let his wife get the picture. And if she gets it we must, by hook or brook, show the two Meyer Cézannes at "291," even if it is only for two or three days. A batch of the fellows can sleep up in the place and act as guard.

O yes, to come back to the "291" Special Number business. I wonder whether you could explain to the Picabias what I want to do, and I would like it if either one, or both of them would write something about what "291" meant to them. I would write to them directly, but I think they will understand if you explain. I often think of Picabia and his work, and also of Mrs. Picabia and their stay over here. They both meant a great deal more to me than they can ever realize. And as they meant something to me then they mean something to me as long as I live. If you think it best that I should write directly, why I will do so. Of course if they want to write in French, because it may be easier, we can have the matter translated.

We are having infernal weather, cold and dreary. I have never seen anything like it in this country. Of course in Paris such weather would be considered beautiful. Over here one is somewhat spoiled in regard to sunshine. I shall write again shortly. I see Haviland nearly every day. He wishes to be remembered. With greetings,

Your old,

N. B. I am hard at work at the De Zayas Number. It ought to be out end of September.[42] I look forward to it with great glee.

De Zayas to Stieglitz, summer 1914

[undated text published in the Special Number of Camera Work *devoted to the question: "What 291 Means to Me," no. XLVII, dated July 1914, published January 1915 (de Zayas contribution on p. 73)]*[43]

291.

I belong, or at least I believe to belong to that class that Carlyle describes as cause-and-effect speculators, with whom no wonder remains wonderful, but all things in Heaven and Earth must be computed and "accounted for." Mental attitude that indeed is not at all romantic, but which I believe to be just as good or just as bad as any other one. At any rate, that is the criterium with which I form my opinions, though I must confess that I am, like a certain writer, not always of my own opinions.

Liberty, Freedom, Individualism, Self-expression, To-live-ones-own-life-in-ones-own-way, & I think to be nothing else but the tool with which the strong draws out of the timid things that the latter would not do but under the influence of the toxic of those ideas.

I owe to 291 all that I have given to 291.

291

Not an Idea nor an Ideal, but something more potent, a Fact, something accomplished, being of a nature although perfect, by no means final or conclusive, but much to the contrary.

291

Expression of the Present brought out by one man, to keep in constant evidence the spirit of the time, apparently, only in its artistic production and in its artistic judgement.

291

A Gallery of Effects to be taken as points of departure to get at the Causes and at the Mechanism.

291

Laudable work of He who in matters of art does not cast looks filled with extasis to the Past nor of dreams to the Future but does with what the Present puts into his hands and makes the World realize its own worth through its own deeds and through its own thoughts.

291

Magnificent school for Autobiography and. . . . Caricature.
        M de Zayas

De Zayas to Stieglitz, July 9, 1914
[ALS, Stieglitz Papers, YCAL]

Paris July 9 1914

My dear Stieglitz:

I received today the new Camera Work. I am sure that you will feel better for a while now that the baby is out. But for the sake of the World I hope that your autogenesis will never stop. I haven't read this number but [the] child certainly looks clean and pretty and deserves to belong to the family.

I have been working hard in spite of a beautiful cold that has taken possession of my nose, chest, throat, etc. I have kept on taking photographs of the negro art in the Trocadero. The photographs are indeed very bad, but very helpful to me. The conditions in which one takes them cannot be worse, but at any rate they show the form and I can make my studies from them. I have already taken 50 and there are still 40 to take.

I have also done some progress in getting interesting people for the album.

The other day I was in the house of a russian girl who had the most interesting collection of paintings by Rousseau. I don't know what I wouldn't do to induce her to lend them to you for an exhibition, they would make the season complete. But for what I can see it will be a very difficult task to make her do it. But I will try to do my best to get them. I have gotten from Apollinaire a series of articles he published on Rousseau with many of his letters. If they interest you and want to publish them in a booklet (they make only about 80 pages) he will be able to get about 24 photographs of his best paintings. I also have gotten from him some of the originals of his new poems which are creating among the crowd of modernists a real sensation. He is doing in poetry what Picasso is doing in painting. He uses actual forms made up with letters. All these show a tendency towards the fusion of the so called arts. I am sure that this mode of expression will interest you.

I am working hard in making these people understand the convenience of a commerce of ideas with America. And I want to observe the spirit of what they are doing to bring it to "291." We need a closer contact with Paris, there is no question about it.

The "Soirées de Paris" is going to publish four of my caricatures in the next number: Vollard's, Apollinaire's, Picabia's, and yours.[44] They asked for them and I thought it good for all of us to really get in with this crowd.

Tell Haviland I bought another dandy negro head for him. It is really a peach[,] possibly the biggest in size I have ever seen.

I saw Mrs. Meyer before she went to London. We went around the galleries and as a result she bought a little Picasso quite characteristic of his latest style. I believe she has also some negro things.

I haven't seen Steichen but once. He doesn't come to Paris and to go to his place takes a whole day. Besides I believe he is not quite well yet and I am sure that my visits will only fatigue him.

I will go back to London next week. I have a plan with Muir to make some interviews in the style in which he made yours to try to place them in some of the big magazines in New York.

I have to do yet an awful lot of work and in a very short time for I intend to leave for N.Y. on the 1st of August much to my regret.

With best regards,

Yours,

de Zayas

De Zayas to Stieglitz, August 24, 1914
[ALS, Stieglitz Papers, YCAL]

August 24

Dear Stieglitz:

The broker to whom the negro things were sent wants to have a letter from you in order to transfer the paper to Masters. They have received the consular invoice only. The letter must be more or less in this tenor.

Kindly transfer all papers concerning the case sent to me by steamer "La Touraine" to my broker Mr. Masters, etc.

Masters says that he doesn't need the [?] your power of attorney. You must send the letter to Masters and they will take care of the transfer. The name of the other broker is Vandergrift [?] and Masters' address is 17 State St.

With best regards,

de Zayas

De Zayas to Stieglitz, September 13, 1914
[ALS, Stieglitz Papers, YCAL]

New York Sunday 13

My dear Stieglitz:

We arrived here yesterday night, not flying but retreating, and with all the honors of the war, for I brought with myself the pictures of Picasso, Braque and Picabia that I had promised you for the exhibition at 291. Also fifteen of the best negro things that has ever been brought to the civilized races (?).

I had all prepared for a Rousseau exhibition but it was beyond my forces to carry any more bundles.

I am more than sorry not to find you in town but hope to see you soon.

I left France and specially Paris in a very bad condition. Since the war started it seemed that all intellectuality had been wiped out. I believe that this war will kill many modern artists and unquestionably modern art. It was time otherwise modern art would have killed humanity. But what satisfies me is that at least we will be able to say the last word.

Personally I am well and so are the other members of the family. I probably will begin tomorrow my work for the World, going back to perform my stupid duties and I am only too glad to do it.

I left the Picabias in a very bad fix, he, serving in the army as automotivist, and she in the red cross. We tried very hard to have a permit to go with the general staff to make sketches, but it was impossible to get it. Anyhow I had the pleasure of hearing the sound of the German bombs and the French guns in Paris. I would have liked to see something more substansial but my resources didn't allow me to do it and so here I am loaded with bundles of art and hoping to see you soon.

> *Yours,*
> *de Zayas*

De Zayas to Stieglitz, August 16, 1915
[ALS, Stieglitz Papers, YCAL]

August 16—.

Dear Stieglitz:

I received your letter of the 13th. I had already written to Guillaume asking him to send the consular invoice and the affidavit. My letter left last Saturday. I went this morning to see Masters. Though Foinet charges in his bill an amount paid for a consular invoice it never came. He sent somebody to find out in the custom House whether they had it there. They didn't have it. Masters said he was going to try to give two bonds: one for the invoice and another for the affidavit, and that you have to sign the papers, or give him or me a power of attorney in order to do so.

They are now printing the deluxe of the Picabia number. We saw the proof and OKed it. Picabia has chosen a darker blue.

We sent to Paris 60 copies of the two last numbers, to people who have a real interest in modern art.[45]

Tomorrow I will send you a letter that I have been writing to you for the last three days. I beg of you to read it carefully, to consider it impartially and to give me a definite answer. Now that you are away from 291 you will be able perhaps to see things from a more accurate angle than being right in it. From your answer will depend in a good deal not only my attitude towards 291 but my entire future.

We must absolutely know where we are at, what we are going to do, and with what elements and persons. We are wasting an awful lot of work, energy and money that we have no right to waste, unless we concentrate our efforts to make that work, that energy and that money to some definite use we will fatally end by being absolutely disgusted with ourselves.

I haven't sent yet Haviland's article and mine to be set. Mrs. Meyer wants to write something for your number and I will wait until she sends her contribution which must be here in a couple of days. I will send it to you before taking it to the printers.

I will ask Picabia about the Picasso etching. I expect to see him today, and I will let you know immediately.

With best regards,

Yours

de Zayas

De Zayas to Stieglitz, August 23, 1915
[ALS, Stieglitz Papers, YCAL]

August 23–1915

Dear Stieglitz:

I am sending you a letter that Mrs. M. sent to me first before I went to see you. It is the result of the conversation I had with her and of which I spoke you of. It will give you clearly her attitude in the matter. She hasn't yet her article for the Steerage number, but she is working at it.

We have (Picabia and myself) been working at the idea. We have find an ideal place for a gallery, especially from the point of view of the business. It is located in 42nd St and 5th Ave. in the first floor and with windows that will allow [us] to exhibit pictures. The rent was $1800 a year but they will make it 1200 for the first year and 1500 for the second if one makes a contract for two years. We have seen other places outside of 5th Ave. But we think that of we are going to try to get at the public and we are going to spend money, work and time we might just as well do it so as to make the best we possibly can. A badly understood economy comes at the end very expensive. We will give you all particulars about this Gallery and about the means to keep it after my next interview with Mrs. Meyer which will probably be next Thursday.

At any rate we keep on working now that we have all the time to do so.

We have also another idea about announcing the opening of the new Gallery. That is instead of printing circulars that most of the people do not read and which cost quite a good deal of money to make a number of "291" with a drawing by Picasso, another by Braque and the two we make about "Elle" and put an insert in the form of the dummy I enclose.[46] The number in question is a very interesting one for it shows two subjects treated by four minds. We have chosen the drawings by Picasso and Braque which are both of the same subject as are the two that Picabia and I made. That in itself makes a very interesting point for our paper. In the insert we are going to print in one side under the heading of 291, notes as we used to do, and on the other two ads one of 291 Galleries, announcing the opening of the exhibition of the evolution of 291—and of the new galleries. We believe that in doing this we give more to the public than an explanation of what we are going to do, and instead of making promises we tell them what we are doing, showing at the same time the relationship of the two galleries.

If you agree with this idea we will make this number, number 9 and have it almost at the same time as the one of the Steerage. Tho' I am of the opinion that this number ought to come before the Steerage and make an announcement, telling all the value of the number in which the photogravure is to appear.[47] Think of this and let us know. We must think also about the way to get a good circulation for 291. We absolutely must make this paper support itself. And I believe it can be done if we only give it a good push. I will treat all this matters with Mrs. Meyer, as well as the financial end of the new gallery which as she said in her letter "should be carefully discussed." I think that after my interview with her you must come to a general meeting so that we should know exactly our respective positions in order to go ahead without losing time, for I believe we must both [—] 291 and the new gallery [—] open our works in October before any of the other galleries.

We got safely home last Friday, we made the trip without losing our way and in eleven hours all together. But in the city Picabia was arrested for speeding and had to pay a fine of $25.

He begs of you, if it is convenient to do so, to send him the check for the Picasso etching.

With our best regards to your family and in particular your mother.

Yours,

de Zayas

They will send the Japan paper that was left for the last number either today or tomorrow. The Picabia edition de luxe is here. It hasn't been opened.

Stieglitz to de Zayas, August 26, 1915
[ALS, de Zayas Archives, Seville]

Aug 26–1915

Dear De Zayas:

It is very difficult to decide things—serious ones—by letter. As for the new gallery the vital question to be considered is first, second & third—How much will it cost & where will the money come from.—

In the expenses there are to be reckoned: Rent—Insurance—Freight, etc., from Europe—Light—Fixing Up Place—& cost of possibly having some one there (this cost might be eliminated in the original estimate).

Besides there is printing—I figure out the cost for the first year to be close to $5000 (a minimum of $4000). Now there ought to be enough money in sight to pay this cost in case the total is a loss! That's the only way to begin. All else is idle speculation & will lead to misunderstanding & personal disappointments.

II. Unless we can get Picasso's support I feel the underlying thing we are intending to work for would be nullified. So how can we announce anything or do anything definite as far as printing goes or hiring a gallery until we hear from Picasso.—I don't believe in rushing into anything involving so much cash blindly.— Of course if you can raise the cash that's a different matter. That's the real issue at first. Until that's settled all else is of no importance.—As you know I believe in the idea—but where is the cash to come from?—That's been the hitch for the last few *years as you know.—My load is still too heavy as far as cash is concerned. I can assume no more risks in that line. I must pay my debts which I have incurred for 291. Until then I won't feel free.—As for the publication No's 7–8–9 could be brought out simultaneously if necessary.—I'll write to Mrs. Meyer tomorrow.—I hope you get my points—Greetings to you & Picabia. I'll send him money in a few days.*

St.

Stieglitz to de Zayas, August 26, 1915
[ALS, De Zayas Archives, Seville]

Aug 26–1915

Dear De Zayas:

I have just mailed you a hasty note & I hasten to supplement it. Of course if the money—capital (we must have capital, it's absurd to start a business without any & what is to be started is a business no matter what name it be given or what its aim (secondary) may be)—be forthcoming all your suggestions for 291 (the publication) are great. And meet with my approval. I repeat the whole matter, the main issue, depends upon the available cash. Cash in sight. Mrs. Meyer says the business should be self-supporting of course—But can it be the first year?—Even a gold mine is not self-supporting the first year or two 99 cases out of a hundred. **As you know I have no money.** *What little I may have will be eaten up by 291 proper in paying debts incurred. I harp on this matter as it is essential not to fool myself or anyone else. I don't know what Picabia can do.—I know what he is willing to do.— I do know what the Meyers can do—but I do not know what they are willing to do. Mrs. Meyer's letter was of interest but I don't agree with much of it. But that is of no importance.—291 to me has a greater angle of vision than she realizes.—of course I'm heart & soul for the Gallery, for the Idea, but I say again—it takes Capital. And secondarily it will take Picasso's undivided support to give it that standing we all wish it to have.—as for Guillaume as far as I'm concerned he is a means to an end—but to rely on him solely would be stupidity on our parts.—The location of new gallery is great. If we can connect.—The agent has asked for references for Picabia. I have told him what I know. The truth as I see it.—It would be great if the idea could be put into concrete form.—No one would be more delighted than I would. A great work could be done. I do hope we'll be able to do it.*

It is glorious up here. Rather autumn like.—The leaves are beginning to fall. It makes one feel that the end of summer is in sight. I wonder how 291 will seem to me when I get back this year.—I sometimes feel as if everything was less real—Is it my age?—Am I becoming old?—Really old?—

So Picabia had to pay a fine. What a waste & yet what a lark!—It was fine to have you both surprise me as you did. It was one of the finest surprises I ever had. With greetings to all.

As ever your old,

St.

De Zayas to Stieglitz, August 27, 1915
[ALS, Stieglitz Papers, YCAL (handwritten draft: De Zayas Archives, Seville)]

August 27–1915

Dear Stieglitz:

I just received your two letters of the 26: all the points you mention in your letters have been carefully considered by Mrs. Meyer, Picabia and myself. We realize perfectly what we are up against and all the trouble, work and expense we have to meet.

I saw Mrs. Meyer yesterday and we had a long talk on the practical side as well as on the moral side of the idea we want to realize.

First of all, Mrs. Meyer, Picabia and myself understand clearly that we must not expect any financial aid from you. Our aim is just the contrary, we want as far as possible to take away from you all load of this character. That is why we want to have the commercial point of view in the new gallery. This is perfectly understood.

In one of your letters you say that "the vital question to be considered is first, second and third How much will it cost and where will the money come from."

According to our estimates (Picabia's and mine) we will cover our necessary expenses for two years with $6,000. And the money will come from Picabia, Mrs. Meyer and Haviland, and in case that by unexpected circumstances the three of them would be unable to provide the money, Picabia is sure to be able to interest some of his friends to help us carry on our plans.

Our idea in making this new gallery is frankly and openly to make business. We want to make it not only self-supporting but the support of all the artists connected with it. You say that "even a gold mine is not self-supporting the first year or two 99 cases out of a hundred." We are aware of the fact, but in preparing ourselves to be one of the 99 cases we will try our best to be the one hundred.

You also say in one of your letters that "unless we can get Picasso's support I feel the underlying thing we are intending to work for would be nullified." and in the other that "it will take Picasso's undivided support to give it that standing we all wish it to have." I have talked over this point with Mrs. Meyer and with Picabia. We do not admit, and we cannot admit that a work we thoroughly believe in should be dependent from the wish or will of any man. We all agree that the support of Picasso would be of great importance but in no way indispensable. If Picasso should die today we would not change at all our plans. If he has already a contract with an art dealer and would not be able to give us directly his work, we would go on just the same; and at any rate we cannot have his undivided support because we cannot guarantee him any amount of money regularly. Picasso does not work for an idea. He works for his ideas and for money, in order to be able to keep on having ideas. Picasso is a very practical man, and we could not have his work exclusively unless we would make a contract with him. That we cannot do. And if we could I am of the opinion that we should not do it, for that would mean that we were following the same methods of the art dealers. You can though be sure that we will have all the Picasso paintings that we would need, and that is, after all the important thing.

As for Guillaume, our connections with him will be as they have been: **purely commercial.** To choose paintings and to deal with artists one of the best men that we could ever have. A man who is a painter himself, who has followed all the evolution of modern art, who knows everything there is to be known of this movement, who works for his own pleasures, who is well known for his honesty and rectitude and respected by all the different bands of the modern artists in Paris. A friend of Picabia whom I met several times in Paris, and who will try to connect us with Vollard and Mme Sagot[?] in case that we should need their assistance. We are trying to do things rightly by every possible way, and to be absolutely sure of what we are doing, with whom we are doing them, and for what we are doing them. You know very well that I have always been very particular about my associations, you can be sure that I will be still more particular in the future. By no means we will give cause to fall into "idle speculations that will lead to misunderstandings and personal disappointments." We will avoid that, in the financial as well as in the intellectual and artistic side of the gallery.

In short: our object in opening a new gallery is to do **business** not only to fight against dishonest commercialism but in order to support ourselves and make others be able to support themselves; in order to be able to live and make others live, and make them be able to continue the evolution of modern art. Also to make of New York a center of modern art, commercially and intellectually. We are convinced that between 291 and the new gallery we will be able to accomplish that.

Practically, we are not going to start a new enterprise, we are only going to continue your work with two different methods which complete each other: one purely intellectual at 291 and the other purely commercial at the new gallery.

We know that we are going to have a great deal of opposition, not only from outsiders but from the insiders of 291. We know that our task is not an easy one. But we have an absolute confidence in ourselves and in the idea we want to put into practice and we are very willing and determined to work it out.

We are going to put on sale in the gallery—drawings, paintings and sculptures of the very best of the modern movement—African and mexican art—photographs of the paintings of the modern artists from Cézanne to the most recent ones—also photographs of African and mexican art—Books on modern art.

With what we have and with what we expect Mrs. Picabia to bring we will have stuff worth for over $15,000: more than half remaining as security for any capital invested in the gallery.

I do not believe there could be a total loss nor that the total of the case could be a loss. Work of this kind always benefits somebody, at any rate, intellectually.

I believe that I have given you now our explicit account of what we have so far done, and I hope it will be approved by you in every point, and that you would find our attitude to be perfectly clear.

As Mrs. Meyer said in her letter to you, we have you as our leader, and I have to add, that as our leader you must have absolute confidence yourself and absolute confidence in every one of us. And when I say us I mean Mrs. Meyer, Haviland, Picabia and myself, for otherwise we will not be able to carry our plans to success.

*I had cuts made of the drawings of Picasso, Braque, Picabia and mine for num-
ber 9 of 291. I will send the proofs with the reading matter so as to be able to
work at the announcements of the two galleries. I have been thinking about the
retrospective exhibition of 291 and I believe it should be done as soon as possible. I
ask Picabia to have his Cézanne watercolors sent here and also the photographic
prints of his grandfather. I am sure you will be interested in considering them for
an exhibition.*

*We must also consider how to sell photographic prints at the new gallery. That
is entirely up to you. We hope you will carefully consider this point and will let us
know as soon as possible what kind of photography and what prints would be good
to put before the public.*

I will keep on telling you all our moves.

*If you have any suggestions to make do it without losing time. We want to open
in October. As soon as we have the gallery ready, I think it will be indispensable for
you to come to New York when we will have our general meeting.*

> *Yours,*
> *de Zayas*

Stieglitz to de Zayas, August 29, 1915.
[ALS, de Zayas Archives, Seville]

Aug 29–1915

Dear De Zayas:

*Thanks for your letter. It is clear & to the point. And I agree with everything
in it. Even the Picasso matter. As for the dissatisfaction that some "insiders" may
express—they have the liberty to express whatever they please—they may even become "outsiders." Such things don't affect me except perhaps in a personal way—
and that only for a short time. I'm glad you see the way clear ahead & that you are
actively at work. I am with you as you know. I have fullest faith in you & Picabia—&
Mrs. Meyer too when she understands clearly—As she seems to. I wrote as I did as
I wanted to be clearly understood as to my own position & feeling. You know me well
enough to realize that I'm heart & soul in the development of the idea—from the
practical as well as the theoretical point of view. I am convinced that if properly run
the business end will be a success. It will mean work—concentration—the desire to
do. I know you have that—And so has Picabia. As for Haviland I know how he
feels & what his desires & hopes are—but I also realize that his position may not
be what it was owing to the War & the state of Haviland & Co. And I am eager to
protect him as I am to protect you & Picabia. And Mrs. Meyer. Perhaps I'm the
Conservative in the venture—intentionally so perhaps. If it is necessary for me to
come to New York for a meeting I'm ready. As for opening up—I agree October will
be the month. How are you going to print the Braque & Picasso? On Halftone paper? We'll have to come to that finally, I suppose much as I hate it.*

*It's very cold up here. I am getting into fine physical condition so as to be ready
for the campaign. Greetings to Picabia & yourself.*

> *Stieglitz*

De Zayas to Stieglitz, August 30, 1915
[ALS, Stieglitz Papers, YCAL]

August 30–1915

Dear Stieglitz:

I have your letter of the 29. It confirms my expectation of your agreeing with every point of my letter of 27. We are going to enter into an affair which if it is not very, very solid in its foundation it will be ridiculous to undertake.

I am trying to get at a perfect understanding between those who are going to work for this idea. Your two letters of the 26 and mine to you of the 27 were shown to Mrs. Meyer and to Picabia. They both got your point and agree with my explanation of the situation. The final agreement about the financial side of our undertak[ing] is not yet settled. Tomorrow we are going to meet at 291, Mrs. Meyer, Picabia and myself to decide finally what is to be done and how it is to be done.

In the meantime, we had, Picabia and myself, a good talk with Kerfoot.[48] We explain in every detail what our idea is, and what we have done up to the present to realize it. He was very much interested in it. I also spoke to him about 291, the paper. I asked him his advice about how to make it self-supporting and we came to a very interesting conclusion and he promised to help us both in the idea of the gallery and of 291. We will speak with you about it. It will be too long to explain in a letter.

About 291, the paper, no. 7–8 will only have Haviland's article and mine. I am going to have them set tomorrow. For number 9 which we will publish as you suggested simultaneously with the Steerage number, we have already the cuts made, I am sending the proof to you. They came out in my estimations very well and we don't have to use halftone paper, of what I also am very glad. We want to use number 9 as a circular for announcing the new gallery and the opening of 291 (the gallery). We ought to print at least 2000 copies of this number, and I think the extra thousand will come cheeper than to have a special circular printed at the same time we will again try to get more subscribers for 291. In this number also we will start Kerfoot's idea for interesting the public in our publication.

I will write you tomorrow the result of our meeting. Perhaps, if we completely finish our agreement it would be necessary for you to come back and start working. We are seeing, every day, more clearly what we can do and the importance of it, and if we are together and have no obstructive elements we will undoubtedly succeed.

Yours,

de Zayas

Stieglitz to de Zayas, August 31, 1915.
Written on stationery that reads "Lake George, New York" [ALS, de Zayas Archives, Seville]

Aug. 31–1915

Dear De Zayas:

Your letter was very welcome. I'm glad you had the chance to speak with Kerfoot. I had hoped you would. He can be of great help if he is interested. And his being interested is proof that we are dealing with a living issue. Kerfoot is one of the few people I know who is always frank—though not brutally so when not necessary to be brutal. Of course print 2000 of that no. 9 if you think it advisable. It's in color, isn't it? I have never feared for the circulation of 291—it was better to hold pushing it for the autumn than to push it during the summer when it would have been ineffective. As for myself getting into harness before Sept. 25 don't count on that. It will be impossible for me to make arrangements to get back before—except for a day if necessary. In a way I feel it's a good thing that things are happening with me away. Why I'll explain some day. You'll agree with me. Of course I'm delighted with the course of events. I do hope we'll make a go of the new undertaking. We must, that's all. How about fixing up the new place? Remember we can get material through Lawrence at cost. The place ought to be severely simple but have some character. But undoubtedly you have ideas & so has Picabia. And Kerfoot has some. And how about A. E. M.? She has some too. The weather is very cold here & it makes me feel like getting into harness at once. But that is out of the question as I stated in the beginning of this letter. 291—the old place—can open up about October 15–20th. Before that the people we're after do not return to N.Y. We usually begin in November. But I agree this year it ought to be earlier. The season ought to be a full one. Remember me to Picabia. With heartiest greetings,
    Stieglitz

I had a very interesting letter from Hartley. He is to have a one-man show in Berlin in September & expects to be in N.Y. end of November.

De Zayas to Stieglitz, September 1, 1915
[ALS, Stieglitz Papers, YCAL]

Set. 1st-1915

Dear Stieglitz:

We had a meeting yesterday at 291, Mrs. Meyer, Picabia and myself. We practically settled the business end of our affair, and we are going to finish it up with Mr. Meyer today. He most likely will be the one to take charge of the money and of our idea. We are trying to work on absolutely solid basis and have with us a very practical man who understands both our idea and the way to do business. I am sure you will agree also with this point.

I take your mentioning the frankness of Kerfoot as not being brutal as a hint. Yes, my frankness in this affair has been ultra brutal. I have been all the time perfectly conscious of it. I felt all the time that the only way to come to a conclusion was first to destroy the untrustfullness that reigned among us. That every one should know what they were at 291 what was expected of them and for them to realize what they could really do. We cannot anymore have different groups talking about each other. That you often said was the cause of many of the misunderstandings of 291. My policy had brought good results. Every one has taken my frankness in the right way. I have to be exceedingly brutal with Mrs. Meyer about Picabia. She had some doubts about him, which fortunately through my intimacy with him I have been able to show that those doubts were unfounded.

You will have a phone or graphic report, when we will see each other about all our talks. And you will see how many of our misunderstandings have been understood. There cannot be any politics among us.

With all our conversations, I feel that we all have become stronger in out own ideas. We feel that we can really depend upon each other. Without this feeling it would have been impossible to do anything.

About your coming to New York, I believe that if you could be with us one or two days we will be able to actually finish up all out affairs.

I will write to you again tonight after having seen Mrs. Meyer. I expect to have today everything settled.

As for your being glad that all this should have been done without you, I think I understand your point, but you must not over do it, that is why I have taken care to tell you everything we have done. Of course there are yet many things about our program that I have not been able to tell you, considering them as of second importance for the present, and which are yet to be discussed with you.

With our best regards to your family,
> *Yours,*
> *de Zayas*

De Zayas to Stieglitz, September 1, 1915
[TLS, with handwritten postscript, Stieglitz Papers, YCAL (retained carbon: De Zayas Archives, Seville)]

Sept. 1, 1915

Dear Stieglitz:

I saw Mr. Meyer as I announced you in my letter this morning. He is willing to finance the new gallery and sign the lease for two years. The rent has been paid for the first and last month of the lease. He is going to the country for a few days and promised to think about our affair and give us next week a plan for the business side of it. This part of our undertake is quite settled *and we don't have to worry about it. It was up to us to build the foundation for the new undertake. The foundation has been built and is more solid than we ever expected it to be.*

Now comes a very important point to decide: Which will be the exact relation between "291" and the "Modern Gallery"?

We have already agreed on principle about a general program that is to say that "291" will be a place for experiments, where the evolution of modern art will be continued or at least will be tried to be continued and that the "Modern Gallery" will be the business side of 291.

Of course it is understood that not by going into business *we are going to neglect in any way our collective or personal development.*

Mrs. Meyer, Picabia and myself will work in the "Modern Gallery" for the development of the interest of the public in modern art from the commercial point of view, and in the selection of the work with which we are going to create that interest. Picabia will take care of Europe and Mrs. Meyer and myself of America. But none of us will ever do anything or take any step without the full agreement of those who compose our society: *Mrs. Meyer, Mr. Meyer, you, Picabia and myself. I don't count Haviland yet because I am* not *quite* sure *whether he will like to be with us under the present conditions.*

It is clearly understood that in the "Modern Gallery" the work of Picabia and my work will be conspicuous for their absence. We will eliminate it principally in order to have a greater freedom of action and also to avoid people thinking that we open the "Modern Gallery" for our personal advantage. Of course whenever it will be necessary to bring out Picabia's work or my own we will do so, but only under exceptional circumstances. In no way we will try to make a display of our work.

It is at 291 the place and the paper where we will bring all our intellectual efforts.

You know now what we have accomplished and what are our ideas and our plans. In order to be able to go ahead we must know what are your ideas and your plans.

We have to a great extent worked in this affair independently from you. The time has come where we all have to meet and define a policy or at least the order of ideas that we are going to follow, and also enter into the details for carrying on our undertake.

I will try to arrange a meeting with Mrs. Meyer for next week. I suppose it is immaterial to you whether it will be in New York or at her farm, and also that any day she might choose for the meeting will be convenient for you.

Yours,

de Zayas

P.S. I had this letter copied by Mario because I wanted to send a copy to Mrs. Meyer.—The Japan exhibition of "the Steerage" has come. We haven't open[ed] the package.

Mrs. Meyer has written an announcement for the new gallery it is very good. I met Kerfoot and showed it to him. He had some suggestions to make. He will have it ready tonight and I will send it to you tomorrow. It is to appear in "291" number 9. I have ordered the paper for numbers 7–8 and 9. It will take at least three weeks before we would have the numbers printed. We have talked over some ideas with Kerfoot about work to be done for both 291 and the new place that I am sure will please you greatly.—I have never written as much in my life.

de Z.

Stieglitz to de Zayas, September 2, 1915

Written on stationery that reads "Lake George, New York"
[ALS, De Zayas Archives, Seville]

Sept. 2–1915

My dear De Zayas:

Fine. Your letter in hand.—When I spoke about brutal frankness I really had no one in mind. But you seemed to feel that I meant you. I didn't. As I said, I meant no one. I simply was thinking of Kerfoot. By "brutal" frankness I meant direct frankness. And frankness should always be direct, otherwise it is not frankness. And frankness is quite unAmerican—as American is indirect. You were frank—have been frank—thank heavens!—Brutally frank too I suppose now that you say it. But I don't know when brutal. You have been very direct of late.—And no one was more grateful for it than myself. If it had not been for your taking that stand I would have given up in sheer disgust. Disgust at the blindness & lack of initiative of those closest to me.—For years every one seemed to rely on me—I suppose it was my fault that it was so—& during the past year or so I tried to make it clear that that attitude of waiting for me to do something was not fair to 291—to me—nor to the individuals themselves.—Fortunately you saw—understood—took the initiative. You & also Haviland to a certain degree. My own position had become disgusting to myself. And not entirely through my own doings.—But we won't go into the past.—The present is too full for that. I'm glad you straightened Mrs. Meyer out about Picabia.—It is essential that there is no distrust amongst the few working together. Absolute, brutal, frankness I believe in. Temperamentally few can stand it—though more can "give" it.—Of course I'm curious to hear about your interview with Eugene Meyer.—He can help the business end tremendously, not only in a financial way, but as to advice.—I'm absolutely no good in that direction. I'm enclosing check for Picabia. Will you give it to him & tell him how thankful I am that he has let me have that print. With greetings to you both & to Mrs. Meyer, when you see her,

Stieglitz

De Zayas to Stieglitz, September 4, 1915
[ALS, Stieglitz Papers, YCAL]

Sep. 4–1915

Dear Stieglitz:

Here is the announcement that Mrs. Meyer wrote and to which Kerfoot added some ideas. I believe it covers all we want to say.

Give us your opinion of it and suggestions if any.

Rogers ought to have sent the proof of the reading matter of the Steerage number. He hasn't. We are forced for the french to have the accents drawn and have a plate made. There has been no other way to do it.

Thanks for the corrections of my page. Even two frenchmen have seen it and they didn't discover any faults.

I believe it will be very good if you could come for our general meeting. Personally I consider your coming as indispensable, and so does Mrs. Meyer and Picabia. The meeting is fixed for Friday afternoon in New York.

Picabia wishes to thank you for the check.

Yours,
de Zayas

De Zayas to Stieglitz, September 8, 1915
[ALS, Stieglitz Papers, YCAL]

New York Sept. 8–1915

Dear Stieglitz:

Here are the english proofs of the two articles for the Steerage number. The french will be ready tomorrow.

I expected today a letter from you telling whether you will be able to come to New York Friday. I hope you will. There are many important things that cannot be settled unless you are here.

There are no further developments. What did you think of the announcement?

With best regards from Picabia and myself

Yours,
de Zayas

De Zayas to Stieglitz, September 8, 1915
[ALS, Stieglitz Papers, 1915]

                                                    Sept 8–1915
Dear Stieglitz:

    I wrote to you this morning. Your letter of the 7 has just arrived. Our meeting will be at Mr. Meyer's office 14 Wall St. at 2 or 3 o'clock in the afternoon. There will be there Mr. Meyer, Mrs. Meyer, Picabia, Kerfoot, you and I.[49]

    I hope you will manage to come. There are many things that have to be talked over in order to proceed work. Many of them depend from you.

    In case that you could not come let me know by telegraph at my house. 598 W. 177. For Friday morning I will be busy until possibly 12 o'clock. There are yet many things to do. We are now trying to arrange the place. It is impossible to get hold of Lawrence, as we have to go ahead without him.

        Yours,
        de Zayas

De Zayas to Stieglitz, September 14, 1915
[ALS, Stieglitz Papers, YCAL]

                                            New York Sept. 14–1915
Dear Stieglitz:

    I am sending the announcement for the Modern Gallery. I hope you will find it suitable.

    I believe that by saying that "291" will devote the Modern Gallery etc etc we will show plainly enough that it is the people of "291" who make the M.G. and that it is part of 291.

    The announcement has been O.K. by Mrs. Meyer and by Kerfoot, it only remains to be accepted by you to take it to the printer.[50]

    If you have some suggestions to make do it as soon as possible so we will be able to have the number of 291 before the end of the month.

    Everything otherwise is going on all right. I am pretty sure that the gallery will be ready by the day you will come back.

    With best regards,
        Yours,
        de Zayas

De Zayas to Stieglitz, December 17, 1915
[TL, Stieglitz Papers, YCAL (handwritten draft: De Zayas Papers, Seville)]

December 17, 1915

My dear Stieglitz:

Apropos of our conversation on my article on Photograph which appeared in Number 9 of "291," I don't see how my meaning could be misunderstood. When I say "Stieglitz represente l'histoire de la photographie aux Etats Unis. 'Camera Work' en est le temoignage." (I copy the French text because I wrote it originally in French and I am not responsible for the translation.)[51] By that phrase I meant that the work you have done for Photography represents the history of Photography in the United States. That "Camera Work" bears witness of all you have done for Photography; and as you personally are the one who has been the impelling force of all that has been done in that publication, and being in Camera Work all that could be considered the important phases of the development of Photography in the United States, I don't believe I was wrong in saying that you represent or comprise the history of photography in the United States. I did not refer to your photographs, or your work as a photographer, which are but one part of all you have done for photography.[52]

Cordially yours,

Stieglitz to de Zayas, January 20, 1916
[TL (retained carbon), Stieglitz Papers, YCAL]

291 Fifth Ave., New York.
January 20, 1916.

My dear De Zayas:

Miss Defries has written a lecture on machinery and art. She has requested me to send her to the following address—Box 87, Nassau, Bahamas—a photograph of Picabia and also some photographs of his work. I am going to send her a photograph of him, but haven't any of his work.

Have you any? Do you want to send her some? Or do you want to send them to me and have me send them to her?

Greetings.

De Zayas to Stieglitz, March 19, 1916
Written on stationery that reads "MODERN GALLERY / 500 Fifth Avenue / New York"
[ALS, Stieglitz Papers, YCAL]

March 19, 1916

Dear Stieglitz

I am sending you the dummy for the last number of '291.' It has been revised and accepted by Mrs. Meyer.

The article by Jacob "La Vie Artistique" has not been paid.[53]

Should you have any suggestions to make, please let me know it. If you find the material O.K. return it to me as soon as possible so I would be able to take it to the printer.

M de Zayas

Stieglitz to de Zayas, March 20, 1916
[TL (retained carbon), Stieglitz Papers, YCAL]

291 Fifth Ave., New York
March 20, 1916

My dear De Zayas:

I hasten to return to you dummy and matter for the "291," last number. It is A-1. But don't have the halftone made from the platinum print on page one. I shall try to get a good print for reproduction purposes done within a couple of days. I am simply rushed to the limit, but must manage to do this, so as to have the half tone as sharp and as clear as possible. The paper to be used for this number should be different from the paper used on the last. The one shortcoming of the last number, which by the way from a certain point of view was the best of the whole series; was not agreeable to me and spoils an otherwise perfect piece of work. This is my fault as I should have gone down to see Fleming personally about the paper. When ready this time I shall pick out a paper myself if you don't object.

As for paying Max Jacobs [sic], I will do so as soon as I get a little money. Some of the guarantee fund for 291 has not been forthcoming, and "291," the publication, has also tied me up as I have been forced to pay temporarily at least, a great deal more than my one-third. I have disputed the last bill of Rogers as it was unreasonably high. The charges for half tone were ridiculous. It should be understood that the plates in this Number Twelve should not cost more than eighteen cents a square inch. For this A-1 work can be done. As a matter of fact they can be done for a great deal less.

De Zayas to Stieglitz, April 24, 1916
Written on stationery that reads "MODERN GALLERY / 500 Fifth Avenue / New York"
[TLS, Stieglitz Papers, YCAL]

April 24, 1916

Mr. Alfred Stieglitz
291 Fifth Avenue
New York City

Dear Stieglitz:

This morning I received the enclosed letter from Picasso in answer to the proposition you suggested about the "Portrait d'Homme." The letter says:

> "Frinde de Zayas,
> I have just seen your brother and we have spoken about the matter of the painting I lent you, no. 1 of the list. If you want to do business and you promise to send me the money immediately I would leave it to you at the price of 4500 francs, and this is all I can do. Answer me immediately in order to know your decision."

Kindly let me know whether you are still interested in this painting. If you accept Picasso's price and conditions, it would be understood that the Gallery will charge you a commission of 10%.

Cordially,
M de Zayas

P.s. Do me the favor to return Picasso's letter.

Stieglitz to de Zayas, April 25, 1916
[TL (retained carbon), Stieglitz Papers, YCAL]

291 Fifth Ave., New York
April 25, 1916

Modern Gallery,
500 Fifth Avenue, New York.

My dear De Zayas:

Thanks very much for your kind trouble in making the inquiry from Picasso. Unfortunately it is not possible for me to accept the offer. It is way beyond my means. I had hopes that he might let me have the painting for 3000F. and I paying the Modern Gallery the ten percent commission on that. Of course I would like to have the painting as it means a great deal to me. But you know my circumstances. Of course I will have to go without the picture unless perhaps Picasso might listen to the following proposition. To accept 3000F. and in case the picture is ever sold, that one-half the premium above the $500.00 would go to him. Of course selling would not be in my mind unless I were forced to. Should he accept any such offer of course the Modern Gallery would receive its ten percent commission on the 3000Fs.

Have you heard anything from Fleming in connection with "291," or do you want me to phone to him? I do not like to interfere unnecessarily.

Once more thanks for the trouble you have taken in regard to the Picasso and hoping that Picabia is on the mend,

Yours etc.,

N. B. Enclosed I return the Picasso note to you as per your request.

De Zayas to Stieglitz, July 20, 1916
Written on stationery that reads "MODERN GALLERY / 500 Fifth Avenue / New York"
[ALS, Stieglitz Papers, YCAL]

July 20th 1916

Dear Stieglitz:

I received yesterday your check for $117. I am sending you the painting by Rivera "La Terrace du Café" and the receipt that Max Jacob gave me.[54]

With best regards,
M de Zayas

De Zayas to Stieglitz, August 21, 1916
Written on stationery that reads "MODERN GALLERY / 500 Fifth Avenue / New York"
[ALS, Stieglitz Papers, YCAL]

August 21, 1916

Alfred Stieglitz, Esq.
Lake George
New York

Dear Stieglitz:

Under separate cover I am sending you some photographs of Severini's work. They were brought to me by Pach, who is a friend of Severini and who received a letter from this artist asking him to see if it would be possible to have an exhibition of his work in New York. Pach says he has no interest whatever in exhibiting Severini's paintings outside of doing a favor to a friend.

I personally do not think that I ought to mix futurism with the work I will exhibit.

Perhaps you might be interested in showing this kind of work which nobody really knows in New York. Should you see any advantage for "291" to hold this exhibition and would like to have the pictures, I believe it would be advisable to write a letter to Pach saying what the object of "291" is and on what conditions you would have the exhibition, so it could be forwarded to Severini.[55]

Pach says that a very interesting article by Severini explaining his point of view on painting appeared in the Mercure de France on February first, and that he surely will write some introduction to his work if he should have an exhibition in New York.[56]

With best regards to your family,
     Cordially yours,
     M de Zayas

De Zayas to Stieglitz, September 11, 1916

Written on stationery that reads "MODERN GALLERY / 500 Fifth Avenue / New York"
[ALS, Stieglitz Papers, YCAL]

     September 11–1916

Dear Stieglitz

I send a copy of your letter, (that which concerned the Severini exhibition) to Pach, who is now in the country. He answered that he will write to Severini telling him exactly what you said. I am pretty sure he (Severini) will accept your conditions.

I believe it will be a very good thing to show the futuristic tendencies, so the people at least will not take every manifestation of modern art as Futurism.

I received today a letter from Brancusi telling me that if the bronze you have has been spoiled he would like to make another patine that will be good "for all time" and that being for his own benefit to do it he will not admit any remuneration.

We opened today our first exhibition. Every Gallery here seems to be busy rather early. But I think you are wiser to stay away from New York as long as you can. This town certainly is hell in Summer. I have been working hard and I think I have to keep on.

With best regards
     Yours,
     M de Zayas

Pack [sic] address is
     33 Beekman Place

Stieglitz to de Zayas, October 27, 1916
[TL (retained carbon), Stieglitz Papers, YCAL]

291 Fifth Ave., New York
October 27, 1916

My dear De Zayas:

Thanks for sending down the different pictures. It's funny how differently things look at 291 than elsewhere; to me at least. The Rivera, the large one, somehow-or-other does not seem to fit into the place down here. I don't know whether it is the size or what. It is mighty good, but it does not look anything as fine as it did on the wall in your little office. Somehow-or-other it doesn't seem in place here, and so I am going to take the liberty of sending it back, as there would be no use of having it flying around here, especially as you ought to be able to sell it at a fair price. It is a good picture.

As for the little Derain, I will keep that down here and show it with [the] other one, which I don't like as well. I won't buy the Derain for myself as I think it would be more advisable to take that money as well as the other, and later on get something which will give me more lasting pleasure. I am sure you feel the same way for me.

I cannot tell you how glad I am that the skies seem much clearer than in a long while.

Hoping to see you early next week,
Your old friend,

N.B. I will have Of deliver the Rivera as soon as he can.[57]

Stieglitz to de Zayas, April 11, 1917
[TL (retained carbon), Stieglitz Papers, YCAL]

291 Fifth Ave., New York.
April 11, 1917.

Dear De Zayas:

Enclosed has just been received. I cannot make out whether it is intended for you and me, or for you only. I therefore send it to you to open.

De Zayas to Stieglitz, April 12, 1917
Written on stationery that reads "MODERN GALLERY / 500 Fifth Avenue / New York"
[TLS, Stieglitz Papers, YCAL]

April 12, 1917

Mr. Alfred Stieglitz
291 Fifth Avenue
New York City

Dear Stieglitz:
    Enclosed please find the envelope addressed to both of us, which contained only two announcements of Jacob's book.
    M de Zayas

Stieglitz to de Zayas, May 17, 1917
[TL (retained carbon), Stieglitz Papers, YCAL]

291 Fifth Ave., New York
May 17, 1917

My dear De Zayas:
    I am giving instructions to Of to call for the Picabias and your things, together with the Derains to take up to the Modern Gallery, as radical changes are being made in my life.

De Zayas to Stieglitz, May 9, 1919
Written on stationery that reads "M. de Zayas / 500 Fifth Ave. / New York"
[ALS, Stieglitz Papers, YCAL]

Dear Stieglitz:
    I receive[d] your letter with considerable delay on account of being wrongly addressed. I am very glad to hear from you and it will certainly interest me to see your work of which Sheeler has spoken to me several times most enthusiastically.
    I am very busy these days, and I could only spend a few minutes with you, but after monday I will have more time to myself. If Tuesday afternoon would be convenient to you I will go to your studio in the afternoon at three.
    If I don't hear from you it will mean that I will [be] expected. If it is inconvenient, please let me know.
    With best regards
        Sincerely yours,
        M de Zayas

De Zayas to Stieglitz, August 27, 1920
Written on stationery that reads "M. de Zayas / 500 Fifth Ave. / New York"
[ALS, Stieglitz Papers, YCAL]

August 27 1920

My dear Stieglitz:

This just to let you know that I am still alive. I returned about 5 weeks ago and have been dreadfully busy.

I am sailing back tomorrow and will return early in October.

Things begin to clear up. But you know how it is here, one has to keep it up all the time.

I have been thinking of your exhibition and I believe it is greatly needed. It is the only way I can see to give to photography the resurrection it wants. I hope we will be able to do it this time.

With best wishes

Yours,

de Zayas

De Zayas to Stieglitz, February 25, 1921
Written on stationery that reads "M. de Zayas / 500 Fifth Ave. / New York" [ALS, Stieglitz Papers, YCAL]

Feb 25 1921

Dear Stieglitz:

Your exhibition has given me the idea that the time is most favorable to follow it with an exhibition of Photographs.

The work of your predecessors—Your own work—the work of your contemporaries of the days of the Photo Secession, when your acting was responsible for bringing them to the attention of the public—And finally the work of some of the men who have appeared subsequently.

I see as an advantage of much importance to give the public an opportunity to make a comparative study.

I would like to speak to you further about this idea and give you all the reasons for doing it.

I believe there is the best thing to do now. Please let me know when can I see you and talk things over.

Yours,

de Zayas

De Zayas to Stieglitz, August 3, 1922[58]
[ALS, Stieglitz Papers, YCAL]

August 3 1922

Dear Stieglitz:

I received your invitation to write something about photography. Because you asked me, I would have liked to do something, but it would have been against my wish. I dislike the idea of "getting in contact with the public." Neither the public nor I care a damn about each other.

Just the same I have been thinking a lot about photography on account of the false success that Man Rae [sic] has made here among the "intellectuals." It is amusing to see that in the matter of Judgement here [they] are on the same level than over there, if one could call that a level.

Coming back to photography I must say that I have come to the conclusion that it does not exist as yet. I mean the photography that will represent the object without the interference of man, who always has prejudices, points of view, selections etc. etc. Photography as it is done up till the present is nothing else than a means of expression of man—therefore it is Art. And I must also say that outside of what you and Sheeler have done in photography I find the rest quite stupid. Therefore if I would write on photography I would be compelled to make the eulogy of your work and of Sheeler's and neither of you need any eulogy.

I am glad to let you know that there is some one interested in having a set of Camera Work. The amateur is Doucet, who is no longer a dress maker but a collector of manuscripts and rare works of art including painting.[59] If there is a complete set to be had please let me know what would be the price. Also if you have two sets of 291.

Art in Paris seems to be more than dead. Only once in a while it comes back in the form of a chlorotic ghost. I really believe that Europe is getting the wisdom of decrepitude.

America is too young and Europe is too old to produce art, and there you are . . . and here I am . . .

I read in the paper that the Brooklyn Bridge is going to be closed because it needs repairing. That is America. They walk so much over a good thing until they make it useless. The same happened to their Constitution. And the Statue of Liberty remains intact!

My best wishes to you, and I mean it.

> *Yours*
> *de Zayas*

De Zayas to Stieglitz, February 15, 1924
[ALS, Stieglitz Papers, YCAL]

New York Feb. 15 1924

My dear Stieglitz:

Here I am at it again. I hope you will be able to come to the exhibition of paintings by Rousseau which will be opened next Monday at the Whitney Studio.[60]

I will be very happy to see you.

Yours,

de Zayas

De Zayas to Stieglitz, February 19, 1924
[ALS, Stieglitz Papers, YCAL]

February 19 1924

My dear Stieglitz:

The Whitney Studio Club is going to make an exhibition of "Abstract Art" with Picasso, Duchamp and Braque.[61] *They want to include some of my caricatures, although I am out of it entirely it would be pedantic of me to refuse. Will you lend the caricature I made of you and the one of Miss Rhodes and perhaps another one, if you have any other suitable?*

Also if you care to do it and have it handy, will you lend one of the Picasso drawings? I believe it would do good to show some of the old pictures that have not been surpassed as yet. I don't speak about my work.

Don't feel compelled to lend anything but do not fail to come to the Rousseau exhibition as you are one of the few that will enjoy it.

I am very much under the N.Y. weather and you know what this means.

Please let me know whether or not you will be able to lend those pictures as a catalogue is to be sent to the printers next Thursday.

Sorry to have to ask you this when you are in a N.Y. rush, but I had to.

Best wishes.

Yours,

de Zayas

De Zayas to Stieglitz, January 19, 1926
Written on stationery of "The Commodore / Forty-Second Street and Lexington Avenue / Grand Central Terminal / Pershing Square / New York" [ALS, Stieglitz Papers, YCAL]

Jan. 19 1926

Dear Stieglitz:

*According to your letter of Jan. 19 I will insure the paintings that you are lending for exhibition at the Wildenstein Galleries at the full price you marked in the list enclosed in your letter and against **all risks** during the time of the exhibition.*

For greatest safety I think it would be better that you should do as you suggested: to have them delivered at the Galleries and taken back when the exhibition is over. That will save also possible delay in the return.

You can be sure that all works under my care receive equal care irrespective of names, owners, etc.

We are insuring through Davies, Turner & Co.

We will be ready for hanging the exhibition next monday as we return to open the 27.

I hope these arrangements will be satisfactory to you. As the exhibition is to last three weeks I am insuring the paintings for one month.

Yours
M de Zayas

De Zayas to Stieglitz, no date
Written on stationery that reads "M. de Zayas / 630 Fifth Avenue / New York City" [ALS, Stieglitz Papers, YCAL]

Dear Stieglitz:

The enclosed is not free verse it is only prose, but I mean it.[62]

I don't know whether is good enough for you to use it and I want you to feel perfectly at liberty and not take my feelings into consideration. I have no feeling about publicity.

This does not mean that I am non-sensitive and therefore efficient bringing results.

Yours,
de Zayas

M. DE ZAYAS
630 FIFTH AVENUE
NEW YORK CITY
CLOUDS.
Photographs by Stieglitz.

A wheel is made of thirty sensitive spokes
but it is on account of the non-sensitive
central void of the hub that it turns.

Pottery is made of sensitive argil but it is
the non-sensitive hollow that is useful.

It is from the non-sensitive that efficiency
and results come.

Also:

An impetuous wind does not last long, a torrential
rain does not last a day. Nevertheless those effects
are produced by Heaven and Earth. If
Heaven and Earth cannot maintain a forced action,
how much less man could.

Many believe but little, others not at all.

So said the Sage.

Photography can be made not to be art if only
the non-sensitive camera is left to be efficient
and show results.

A forced action, art, cannot and does not live for
ever. Nature does. Let the non-sensitive
show us the eternal.

Photography begins to be photography. Until now
it has only been art.
Marius de Zayas

APPENDIX C
DE ZAYAS AND PICASSO

It was while attending the Salon d'Automne in 1910 that de Zayas first learned about Picasso and his work (see the introduction). Within weeks, he met the artist himself, introduced by Frank Burty Haviland (brother of Paul Haviland) and Edward Steichen. In November or December 1910, de Zayas, Burty, and Steichen paid a visit to Picasso in his studio on the boulevard de Clichy, the three serving as emissaries for Stieglitz to select recent drawings for an exhibition that was planned for "291."[1] Shortly thereafter, de Zayas recalled the event in a series of eight caricature studies, drawings that show the features of Frank Burty and his immediate surroundings becoming increasingly "cubified" as he and his colleagues approach the ambiance of Picasso's studio (figures 131–138). Curiously, Picasso himself is rendered in a relatively straightforward caricature style, seemingly uninfluenced by the environment of his own studio (which is filled with African carvings). Burty, in contrast, takes on a gradually more pronounced geometric appearance, until, in the last image, he is transformed—body and soul—into a monumental Cubist sculpture.

There can be little doubt that this series of caricatures was designed to illustrate—in a humorous way—the power of Cubism to influence all young artists who came into contact with it. Frank Burty, for example, was a twenty-five-year-old painter who befriended Picasso and Braque and consciously emulated the Cubist style they pioneered. But after having seen more examples of Picasso's work, and after having conducted a series of interviews with the artist in his studio, de Zayas soon came to the conclusion that Picasso and Cubism were among the most serious and vital forces in the progression of modern art.

De Zayas's conversations with Picasso took place in the early months of 1911. On the basis of this exchange, de Zayas wrote an article on Picasso in Spanish and arranged for its publication in the May 1911 issue of his father's magazine, *América: Revista mensual illustrada* (figures 139–141), an article that included, on its last page, a small caricature study of Picasso by de Zayas. Even before this essay appeared, de Zayas prepared an abridged English translation of the manuscript and sent it off to Stieglitz, who published it as a pamphlet and distributed it during the time of the Picasso exhibition at "291" in the spring of 1911 (and the same text was later reprinted in an issue of *Camera Work*).[2] It appears here in its most complete form (based on the text published by Stieglitz, with phrases omitted from the Spanish article restored in bold print).[3]

Pablo Picasso

Let me say at the beginning that I do not believe in art criticism, and the more especially when it is concerned with painting.

I grant that every one has the right to express their opinion in art matters, to applaud, or disapprove according to their own personal way of seeing and feeling; but I hold that they should do so without assuming any authority, and without pretending to possess the absolute truth, or even a relative one; and also that they should not base their judgements on established rules, upon pretense that they are consecrated by use, and by the criterion of high authority.

Between a civil or a penal judge, and a critic, there is no great difference. The judge judges according to the law, but does not make the law. He has to submit himself to the letter and the spirit of the law, though it might conflict with his personal opinions, because the law is an absolute rule of conduct, dictated by society, to which all have to submit. But art is free, it has never had, it has not, and will never have a legislature, in spite of the Academies; and every artist has the right to interpret nature as he pleases, or as he can, leaving to the public the liberty to applaud or condemn theoretically.

Every critic is a priest of dogma, of a system; and condemns implacably what he finds to be out of his faith, a faith not reasoned but imposed. He never stops to consider the personality of the artist whose work he is judging, to investigate what his tendencies are, what his purpose is, or what efforts he made to attain his object, and to what point he has realized his program.

I have devoted my life to the study of art, principally painting and sculpture. I believe I have seen all that is worth seeing, and I have never dared pass sentence on a work declaring it good, even if signed by the most renowned artist; nor declared it bad, though it bears the name of a person totally unknown. At the most, I dare say that it pleases or displeases me, and to express the personal motives of my impressions. **Sometimes, prompted by my good-humored spirit, I may have joked upon considering a painting or a statue, the same way that I joke with a pencil when I make a caricature. But, let it be kept in mind that when I make a caricature, I don't say to the public: "this is how so-and-so is," but this is how I see so-and-so through my lens of a caricaturist.**

Scholastic criticism has never profited anyone; on the contrary, it has always restrained the spirit of a creator, it has always discouraged, humiliated, and killed, those who have had the weakness to take it into consideration.

[There is] nothing more absurd than [to conclude] that because Phideas sculpted in a certain way, one ought to sculpt in that way now and in the future, until the end of time; that because Raphael painted in a certain way, Horace wrote poetry in a certain way, poets ought to continue singing in this way. If this extremely narrow criterion had always been followed, our museum would be full of Jupiter, Holy Families, and Madonnas, and our libraries of "Beatus ille . . ." *Michelangelo would never have sculpted his Horned Moses, Rembrandt and Frans Hals would never have produced their beautiful canvases,*

I.

131

II.

132

V.

135

VI.

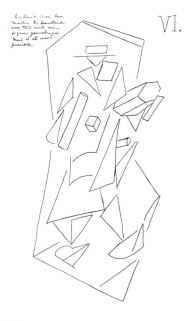

136

À l'Avenue d'Alma Mr Haviland était tout-à-fait en guitare

Au Boulevard du Chilly Mr Haviland n'était pas seulement en guitare, mais il avait déjà quelques triangles et un quadrilatère

133

134

137

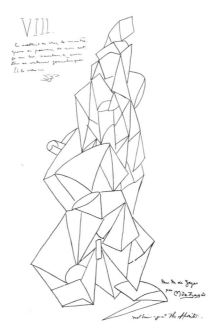

138

Shakespeare would never have written Hamlet and Victor Hugo would not have filled the entire XIXth century with the grandiose reverberations of his lyre.

Each epoch has had its artists, and must have its art, as each also has its men of science and its science; and anyone who intends to oppose a dike to the flood-tide of human genius, is a perverse or a fool.

This love for the dogma, the tendency of the academy to enchain, to suffocate and to vilify, has greatly damaged the countries in which it has prevailed. This has been the cause of delay in the progress in the art of Spain; and on account of this system we see the Spanish artists, those of personal inspiration and haughty spirit, perish there, or emigrate to Paris, looking for a better atmosphere. For though it is true that there is in Paris also an academic sect that suffocates, one which proclaims that outside of itself there is no salvation, nevertheless art has succeeded in conquering an independence which permits all sorts of attempts at new expression,[4] all kinds of tentative [actions] and [which] fights openly and without traps against scholasticism, without worrying about its high-sounding shouts, and its inoffensive anathemas.

Art has not died in Spain, or not at least among Spaniards. What is beginning to die is the old tradition, or rather the intransigent traditionalism. And the best proof of it is the notable number of Spanish painters living in Paris, who prosper there, gaining enviable fame, and who, at the end will figure among the French glories, instead of adding illustrious names to the already extensive Spanish catalogue.

I intend to make these artists known to the American world, describing the work of each one of them, not as I see, feel, and understand it, but as each one of them has conceived it. My task is not anti-Spanish [for] I love Spain too much to embark upon so disagreeable a crusade. On the contrary, I judge it [the crusade] imminently Spanish, because with it I re-vindicate for our race the place which corresponds to it, to which it has legitimate claim, by courage of ingenuity of its sons, who today carry throughout the world the artistic pavilion of Spain with as much glory as, in former times, the Spanish military regiments carried it through the camps of battle.

I want to tell at present of Pablo Picasso, from Malaga, who finds himself in the first rank among innovators, a man who knows what he wants, and wants what he knows, who has broken with all school prejudices, has opened for himself a wide path, and has already acquired that notoriety which is the first step towards glory.

I do not know if he is known in Spain, and if he is, whether they appreciate his efforts and study his works. What I know is that he is a Parisian personality, which constitutes a glorious achievement.

I have studied Picasso, both the artist and his work, which was not difficult, for he is a sincere and spontaneous man, who makes no mystery of his ideals nor the method he employs to realize them.

Picasso tries to produce with his work an impression, not with the subject but the manner in which he expresses it. He receives a direct impression from external nature, he analyzes, develops, and translates it, and afterwards executes it in his own particular style, with the intention that the picture should be the pictorial equivalent of the emotion produced by nature. In presenting his work he wants the spectator to look for the emotion or idea generated from the spectacle and not the spectacle itself.

From this to the psychology of form there is but one step, and the artist has given it resolutely and deliberately. Instead of the physical manifestation he seeks in form the psychic one, and on account of his peculiar temperament, his physical manifestations inspire him with geometrical sensations.

When he paints he does not limit himself to taking from an object only those planes which the eye perceives, but deals with all those which according to him constitute the individuality of form; and with his peculiar fantasy he develops and trans-

me sonreirá usted, á fin de que sus amigas supongan mucha cosas halagadoras para una mujer que ha ganado su apuesto. Nadie puede imaginarse que la deliciosa Mme. Decoeur ha sido rechazada por el loco de Meuzel, piense usted en eso, amiga mía . . . Y ahora, no

habiendo atentado ni en contra de sus días ni de su virtud, me despido de usted. No tema usted nada, estamos en la Plaza de la Estrella, á donde dije que nos condujeran después de un espacio de tiempo bastante para una aventura galante.

El auto se detuvo súbitamente. Mme. Decoeur saltó á la banqueta y se alejó huyendo precipitadamente. Su delicada silhueta desapareció rápidamente en la sombra, perdiéndose á los ojos de Meuzel, quien con amarga sonrisa murmuró:
—¡Hice bien!——

PABLO PICASSO
Por M. DE ZAYAS
(Fotografías de Kahnweiler)

Y O no creo en la crítica de arte, y menos cuando se refiere á la pintura.
Concedo á todo el mundo el derecho de expresar sus opiniones en materia de arte, de aplaudir ó de censurar, fundándose en su modo personal de ver y de sentir; pero sin erigirse en autoridad, sin pretender que es el poseedor de la verdad absoluta, ni aun siquiera de la relativa, y siempre que no cimente sus juicios en reglas establecidas, so pretexto de que están consagradas por el uso y por el fallo de altas autoridades.
Entre un juez civil, ó del ramo penal, y un crítico, hay gran diferencia. El juez juzga con la ley, y no de la ley; tiene que someterse á la letra y al espíritu de ésta, por más que se en-

cuentren en pugna con sus opiniones propias; porque esa ley es una regla de conducta imprescindible, dictada por la sociedad y á la que todos tenemos que someternos; mientras que el arte es libre, no ha tenido, no tiene, y jamás tendrá legislador, mal que pese á las academias, y cada artista está en su perfecto derecho para interpretar la naturaleza como le place, ó como le es posible, dejando, por supuesto, al público en libertad para aplaudir y para reprobar teóricamente.
Todo crítico es el sacerdote de un dogma, de un sistema, y condena implacable lo que se encuentra fuera de su fe; fe no razonada, sino impuesta. Jamás se detiene á considerar la personalidad del artista de cuya obra juzga, á averi-

guar cuál es su tendencia, cuál es su propósito, cuáles son los esfuerzos que ha hecho para lograr su objeto, ni hasta qué punto la realizado su programa.
He dedicado mi vida al estudio de las artes, principalmente de la pintura y de la escultura; creo haber visto detenidamente cuanto merece ser visto, cuanto hay que ver, y jamás me he atrevido á fallar que una obra es buena, así esté firmada por el artista de más fama, ni á declarar que es mala, así lleve el nombre de una persona completamente desconocida. A lo más que me atrevo es á decir que me agrada ó no me agrada, y á exponer los motivos personales de mi impresión. Algunas veces, llevado por mi espíritu de buen humor, habré bromeado al considerar un cuadro ó una

"La Hogaza de Pan"

139–141 Marius de Zayas, "Pablo Picasso," from the magazine *América: Revista mensual illustrada* (May 1911), pp. 363–365. This photograph: first page (p. 363) of the article.

estatua, lo mismo que bromeo con el lápiz al hacer una caricatura. Pero téngase presente que cuando hago una caricatura no digo al público: "así es fulano," sino así es como veo á fulano á través de mi lente de caricaturista.

Voy más lejos aún: la crítica escolástica no ha aprovechado á nadie. Por el contrario, siempre ha servido para poner plomo en las alas del espíritu creador, para desanimar, para humillar, para matar á quienes han tenido la debilidad de hacerle caso.

Nada más absurdo que porque así esculpió Fidias, así se debe esculpir hoy y en lo futuro, hasta la consumación de los siglos; que porque así pintó Rafael, así versificó Horacio, así deben seguir cantando los poetas. Si se hubiese seguido siempre ese estrechísimo criterio, estarían nuestros museos llenos de Júpiter, de Sacras familias y de Madonas, y nuestras bibliotecas de "Beatus ille." Ni Miguel Angel habría esculpido su Moisés Cornuto, ni Rembrandt ni Franz Hals no habrían legado sus preciosas telas, ni Shakespeare hubiese escrito el Hamlet, ni Víctor Hugo hubiese llenado todo el siglo XIX con las grandiosas resonancias de su lira.

Cada época tiene sus artistas y tiene su arte, lo mismo que tiene sus hombres científicos y tiene su ciencia, y todo el que intenta oponer dique á la marea montante del ingenio humano, es un perverso ó es un mentecato.

Ese apasionamiento por el dogma artístico, esa tendencia de la academia á encadenar y á sofocar, á envilecer, para decirlo de una vez, causa grandes perjuicios en los países en que existen. Esa ha sido una rémora para el progreso del arte en España, y á causa de tal sistema vemos que los artistas españoles de inspiración propia, de espíritu levantisco, que es el que conviene tener á un verdadero artista, ó perecen ó emigran á París, buscando una atmósfera más propicia, pues si es cierto que aquí también hay la secta académica que sofoca, que proclama que fuera de ella no hay salvación, el arte ha logrado conquistar una independencia notable que le permite toda clase de atrevimientos, toda especie de tentativas, y ríñe abiertamente y sin trabas contra el escolasticismo, sin preocuparse de su vocear rimbombante y de sus anatemas inofensivos.

Dígase lo que se quiera, el arte no ha muerto en España, al menos no ha muerto entre los españoles. Lo que va desapareciendo es la tradición, mejor dicho el tradicionalismo intransigente, y la mejor prueba de ello es el mayor número de pintores españoles que viven en París que prosperan y ganan envidiable fama, y que acabarán por figurar entre las glorias francesas, en vez de añadir nuevos nombres ilustres al extenso catálogo español.

Me propongo dar á conocer en el mundo americano á esos artistas, describiendo la obra de cada uno de ellos, no tal como la veo, como la siento y la comprendo; sino como cada uno de ellos la ha ideado. Mi labor no es antiespañola, que mucho amo á España para emprender en cruzada tan poco simpática. Por el contrario, la juzgo eminentemente española, como que con ella reivindico para nuestra raza el puesto que le corresponde, al que tiene legítimo derecho, por los bríos del ingenio de sus hijos, quienes llevan hoy por el orbe el pabellón artístico de España con tanta

gloria como, en otro tiempo, lo llevaron los tercios castellanos por los campos de batalla.

Hoy quiero hablar de PABLO PICASSO, un malagueño, que se encuentra en primera fila entre los innovadores, hombre que sabe lo que quiere y que quiere lo que sabe, que ha roto con todos los prejuicios de la escuela, que se ha abierto un amplio sendero y que ha alcanzado ya la notoriedad, primer escalón de la gloria.

¿Lo conocen en España? Si lo conocen, ¿aprecian sus esfuerzos y estudian su labor? Lo ignoro. Lo único que sé es que constituye una personalidad parisiense, lo que es ya un timbre de gloria.

He estudiado los cuadros de Picasso y he estudiado al artista, lo que nada tiene de difícil, pues es un hombre sincero y espontáneo, que no hace ningún misterio de sus ideales ni de los procedimientos que sigue para realizarlos.

Picasso procura producir en sus obras una impresión, más bien que por el arte mismo, por la manera en que estos han sido interpretados por él. Recibe una impresión directamente de la naturaleza

"El Pozo" Acosta de Ebrio, 1909

exterior, la analiza, la desarrolla, la traduce, por decirlo así, y después la ejecuta en su estilo particular, con el propósito de que el cuadro resulte el equivalente pictórico de la emoción que le produjo la naturaleza; entiéndase bien *de la emoción*. Al presentar su obra, quiere que el espectador busque y encuentre en ella únicamente la emoción ó la idea engendrada por el espectáculo, y no el mismo espectáculo.

De allí á la sicología de la forma no hay más que un paso, y el pintor lo ha dado resuelta y deliberadamente, al buscar en la forma, en vez de las manifestaciones físicas, las manifestaciones síquicas, y, en virtud de su temperamento especial, estas le inspiran sensaciones geométricas.

Cuando pinta no se limita á tomar de un cuerpo solamente aquellos planos que el ojo percibe, sino todos los que él cree que constituyen la individualidad de su forma, y en su peculiar fantasía' los desarrolla y transforma á medida que estos le van sugiriendo nuevas impresiones, las que manifiesta con nuevas

formas, pues la idea de la representación de un sér hace nacer otro sér, quizás distinto del primero, y que resulta el representado.

Cada uno de sus cuadros es el coeficiente de las impresiones que en el espíritu del artista ha causado la forma, y en ese cuadro debe ver el público la realización de un ideal artístico, juzgándolo por la sensación abstracta, sin pretender buscar los factores que entraron en la composición de esa suma.

Como su propósito no ha sido perpetuar en el lienzo un aspecto de la naturaleza exterior, para producir una impresión artística, sino representar por medio del pincel la impresión que él ha recibido directamente de la naturaleza, sintetizada por su fantasía, no fija en la tela el recuerdo de una sensación presente.

Es posible que alguien crea que mis explicaciones pecan por alambicadas. Pero no hay alambicamiento, sino que más bien peco por exceso de claridad, procurando hacer tangible lo intangible.

Picasso tiene un concepto de la perspectiva muy distinto del que es de uso corriente entre los tradicionalistas. Según su modo de pensar y de pintar, la forma debe ser representada en su valor intrínseco, y no como una relatividad con otros cuerpos. Mal le parece que un niño aparezca con un tamaño excesivamente mayor que el de un hombre, por el solo hecho de hallarse el niño en primer término y quererse indicar que el hombre se encuentra á cierta distancia. La pintura de la *distancia*, á la que se subordina todo en la escuela académica, parece á nuestro pintor un elemento que podrá tener gran importancia en un plano topográfico ó en un mapa geográfico, pero que resulta completamente falso é inútil en un cuadro artístico.

En sus cuadros, pues, no existe la perspectiva; no hay más que armonías sugeridas por la forma, y registros que se suceden para componer un acorde general dominante, que llena el rectángulo constituido por el cuadro.

Siguiendo el mismo sistema filosófico en cuanto se refiere á la luz, como lo siguió en cuanto á lo relativo á la forma, para él no hay colores, sino efectos de luz. Esta produce en los cuerpos ciertas vibraciones, y estas producen en el individuo ciertas impresiones. De aquí resulta que el cuadro de Picasso nos presenta la evolución que lo mismo la luz que la forma han operado al desarrollarse en su cerebro para producir la idea, y, por lo tanto, su composición, no es, al fin de cuentas, más que la expresión sintética de sus emociones.

Aquellos de mis lectores que hayan estudiado con detenimiento y sin prejuicios greco-romanos, el arte egipcio, sabrán que los hijos del Nilo y del Desierto buscaban en sus obras la realización de un ideal concebido de meditaciones ante el río misterioso y de éxtasis ante la soledad imponente, y por eso convertían la materia en substancia y daban á la substancia el reflejo de lo que es sólo esencia. Algo por el estilo pasa en la obra de Picasso: una representación artística de la sicología de la forma.

140   Second page (p. 364) of the de Zayas article on Picasso.

"La Mandolinista"

"Retrato del Sr. Kahnweiler"

tratando de representar en esencia lo que parec existir, cuando más, en substancia.

Y así como cuando contemplamos una parte de una catedral gótica, nos sentimos poseídos de una sensación abstracta, producida por un conjunto de figuras geométricas, cuya significación no percibimos y cuya forma real no comprendemos de pronto, así las pinturas de Picasso tienden á producir un efecto análogo, que obliga á hacer abstracción de los seres y de los objetos que son la base del cuadro, y cuya representación es el sumum á que su fantasía ha podido llevarlos por medio de una evolución geométrica.

Según su juicio, todos los pueblos, en sus comienzos artísticos, han procurado representar la forma bajo un aspecto fantástico, modificándola para adptarla á la idea que han querido expresar por medio de ella, de modo que, en el fondo, todos esos pueblos han venido persiguiendo el mismo ideal artístico con parecida tendencia técnica que constituyen su yo intelectual.

¿Qué valor tienen estas teorías? El mismo que el que posea cualquiera otra, y no es de mi incumbencia ni entra en mi propósito calificarla. Me contento con llamar la atención de aquellos á quienes interesa el movimiento artístico actual, enseñándoles la parte más visible de esta evolución, y poniendo de manifiesto las tendencias que se van afirmando en el

espíritu del público observador y de buena fe. No hay, por otro lado, ni lo ha habido nunca, un crítico de arte capaz de considerar y de aquilatar el valor de la obra contemporánea. Están dentro de la evolución sin darse cuenta de ello, como los que van en un tren á todo vapor, no se dan cuenta de la distancia que van recorriendo; les parece que el tren está fijo en un lugar y que es el paisaje el que huye ante sus ojos.

Y, lo repito, no soy un crítico de arte, sino un expositor del movimiento artístico que estoy observando. Presento los hechos, dejando que cada cual saque las deducciones que mejor le parezcan.

Picasso no se preocupa en lo más mínimo tampoco de la opinión del público. Como todo verdadero artista, piensa y ejecuta primero para sí, para corres-

ponder á sus deseos íntimos, para satisfacer una necesidad ingente de su espíritu. Si la mayoría del público pretende no comprender sus cuadros, será porque esa mayoría no ve en el arte más que lo que le han enseñado á ver, y no puede gozar más que con aquellas obras en las que encuentra los elementos que de antemano espera encontrar, y que corresponden á los moldes á que está acostumbrado. Otra parte del público, justamente la que se da por más ilustrada, se niega á ver en la obra del artista lo que éste ha sentido y lo que ha querido expresar, buscando únicamente aquello que los que lo forman están acostumbrados á sentir y quieren que les expresen de la manera que tienen preconcebida, ó en la que están educados.

Unos y otros, al verse contrariados, se creen defraudados, y en vez de achacarlo á su falta de intelectualidad artística, á su carencia del sentido de análisis, condenan al artista, porque comete el imperdonable pecado de ver con sus propios ojos, de sentir con su propia alma, de pensar con su propio cerebro, de perseguir un nuevo ideal, de abrir nuevos senderos, de amar á su modo y de expresar su amor en rimas, en ritmos y en vibraciones especiales, emanaciones de un alma atrevida que necesita de lo infinito para hacer su espacio, y de la eternidad para hacer su tiempo.

141 Third page (p. 365) of the de Zayas article on Picasso.

forms them. And this suggests to him new impressions, which he manifests with new forms, because from the idea of the representation of a being, a new being is born, perhaps different from the first one, and this becomes the represented being.

Each one of his paintings is the coefficient of the impressions that form has performed in his spirit, and in these paintings the public must see the realization of an artistic ideal, and must judge them by the abstract sensation they produce, without trying to look for the factors that entered into the composition of the final result. As it is not his purpose to perpetuate on the canvas an aspect of the external nature, by which to produce an artistic impression, but to represent with the brush the impression he has directly received from nature, synthesized by his fantasy, he does not put on the canvas the remembrance of a past sensation, but describes a present sensation.

It is possible that someone might believe that my explanations sin by [being] over-subtle. But there is no over-subtlety, on the contrary, I sin more by excess of clarity, endeavoring to make the intangible tangible.

Picasso has a different conception of perspective from that in use by the traditionalists. According to his way of thinking and painting, form must be represented in its intrinsic value, and not in relation to other objects. He does not think it right to paint a child in size far larger than that of a man, just because the child is in the foreground and one wants to indicate that the man is some distance away from it. The painting of distance, to which the academic school subordinates everything, seems to him an element which might be of great importance in a topographical plan or in a geographical map, but false and useless in a work of art.

In his paintings, perspective does not exist: in them there are nothing but harmonies suggested by form, and registers which succeed themselves, to compose a general harmony which fills the rectangle that constitutes the picture.

Following the same philosophical system in dealing with light, as the one he follows in regard to form, to him color does not exist, but only the effects of light. This produces in matter certain vibrations, which produce in the individual certain impressions. From this it results, that Picasso's painting presents to us the evolution by which light and form have operated in developing themselves in his brain to produce the idea, and his composition is nothing but the synthetic expression of his emotions.

Those who have studied Egyptian art without Greco-Roman prejudices, know that the sons of the Nile and the desert sought in their works the realization of an ideal conceived by meditation before the mysterious river and by ecstasy before the imposing solitude, and that is why they transformed matter into form and gave to substance the reflection of that which exists only in essence. Something of this sort happens in Picasso's work, which is the artistic representation of a psychology of form in which he tries to represent in essence what seems to exist only in substance.

And likewise, just as when we contemplate part of a Gothic Cathedral we feel an abstract sensation, produced by an ensemble of geometrical figures, whose significance we do not perceive and whose real form we do not understand immediately, so the paintings of Picasso have the tendency to produce a similar effect, they compel the spectator to forget the beings and objects which are the base of the picture, and whose representation is the highest state to which his fantasy has been able to carry them through a geometric evolution.

According to his judgement, all the races as represented in their artistic exponents have tried to represent form through a fantastic aspect, modifying it to adapt to the idea they wanted to express.

And at the bottom, all of them have pursued the same artistic ideal, with a tendency similar to his own technique.

What worth do these theories have? The same as that which poses any other, and it is not my concern, nor does it enter into my intent to qualify it. I

am satisfied to call to the attention of those who are interested in present artistic movements, showing them the most visible part of this evolution, and putting forth as a manifesto the tendencies which are being affirmed in the spirit of the observant public of good faith. There is not, on the other hand, and never has there been an art critic capable of considering and perceiving the worth of contemporary work. They are within the evolution without being aware of it, like those who ride a train at full speed, they do not realize the distance they are covering; it seems to them that the train is fixed in one place and that it is the landscape that speeds before their eyes.

And, I repeat, I am not an art critic, but an exponent of the artistic movement which I am observing. I present the facts, allowing each to draw what deductions he sees fit.

Picasso does not preoccupy himself in the least either with public opinion. Like every true artist, he thinks and creates first for himself, to correspond to his intimate desires, to satisfy an inherent need of his spirit. If the majority of the public pretends not to understand his paintings, it must be because that majority does not see in art more than it has been taught to see, and cannot enjoy it except through those works in which they find the elements which they beforehand expected to find, and which correspond to the models to which they are accustomed. Another part of the public, precisely that which passes itself off as the more enlightened, refuses to see in the work of the artist what this one has felt and what he has wanted to express, seeking only that which those who have taught them are used to feeling, and [that which] they want expressed to them in the manner they have preconceived, or in which they have been educated.

The ones and the others, upon seeing themselves crossed, believe they have been cheated, and instead of chalking it up to their lack of artistic intellect, to their lack of analytical sense, they condemn the artist, because he commits the unforgivable sin of seeing with his own eyes, of feeling with his own soul, of thinking with his own brain, of being consistent with himself, of pursuing a new ideal, of opening new paths, of loving in his own manner, and of expressing his love in rhymes, rhythms and special vibrations, emanations of a daring soul which needs of the infinite to create its space, and of eternity to create its time.

Marius de Zayas
Photo-Secession Gallery.
March Twenty-eighth, 1911.
(From advance proof, "Camera Work," No. 34.)

Stieglitz was certainly pleased with de Zayas's text. About a week after the Picasso exhibition opened at "291," he sent de Zayas a copy of the catalogue (actually an advance proof of the article from the forthcoming issue of *Camera Work*), on which he wrote, "This little pamphlet is doing its work beautifully."[5] As for de Zayas, he continued to remain in close contact with Picasso. During his next trip to Europe in 1914, de Zayas visited Picasso again in his Paris studio and, as he reported to Stieglitz, they "had a very interesting and intimate talk on art and on his latest manner of expression." They also talked about photography, a field into which, as he told Stieglitz, Picasso "confesses that he has absolutely enter[ed]."[6]

When de Zayas returned to New York and opened his own gallery in 1915, he continued to make caricatures, and in one of the last issues of *291*

142 Marius de Zayas, *Portrait of Picasso,* 1915, charcoal.

he reproduced his charcoal *Portrait of Picasso* (figure 142). If this drawing is any indication of de Zayas's evolving style, he was headed toward the hermetic. One author, who reads the diagonal shape in the center of the composition as the horns of a bull, has interpreted this image as an illustration of the "dialogue between beauty and power," for, as he sees it, the horned figure and rose on the left "refer to Picasso's Spanish origins, symbolized by the bullfight." This same author has also suggested that these elements might also have been intended to represent "the delicate sensibility of his [Picasso's] Rose Period with the brutality of his Cubist phase."[7] This caricature, whatever its meaning, was the last de Zayas was to publish, for, from this point onward, he would increasingly devote his time and energy to the demands of his business.

When de Zayas's new gallery opened, he was anxious to feature the work of Picasso. Not only did he include examples of Picasso's work in the first exhibition, but in a show that was held in December 1915 (which also included African Negro sculpture) he proudly exhibited eleven paintings by the artist, two of which, as noted in the catalogue, were "Picasso's latest works." Although the catalogue was little more than a checklist of the works shown, de Zayas apparently planned to include an introduction, for a typewritten draft is preserved in the De Zayas Archives:

> *Picasso's works have been, according to the general view, the initiative to the expressionistic, cubistic and futuristic movement. Picasso has nothing to do with it but that he has made the first artistic move, and he does not want to have anything to do with it. The difference between him and the movement is noticeable in the fact that he has never made similar utterances, that he never tried to explain the reason for the inconsistency in his art of painting, psychic or physically, but that he simply was painting.*
>
> *Quietly he stood in his studio and created his pictures, smiling at the others who in the meantime got hot heads while discussing in the street the necessity of a renovation of the art of painting, etc. If anyone asked him why he painted like this, he did not know what else to say but that he had to paint this way. While one could see exhibitions by the younger artists of the various countries, France, Germany, Italy, Russia, Norway, etc., which all had more or less the characteristic of Picasso's artistic personality, the young Spaniard never sent a picture of his to the exhibition, and only a few dealers and private collectors, or sent by them to an exhibition, one would here and there find some works from his hand.*
>
> *So it is the first time that an opportunity is offered at the Modern Art Gallery, to see a collection of the whole course of his evolution, and if someone who is not satisfied with a superficial observation leaves the exhibition with the conviction to have had before him the outlet of an artistic will, of an unique artistic character and that of a real man, then it has not missed its aim.*

As de Zayas became more involved in the operation of his gallery, it was inevitable that his relationship with Picasso should take on a more businesslike character. Their exchange dealt primarily with details pertaining to the transport, pricing, sales, and methods of payment for his work. Research has revealed that Picasso took a great deal of interest in the commercial presentation of his work and often dealt directly with prospective buyers. The following letter from Picasso (written in Spanish but here presented in translation) is characteristic of their exchange.[8]

[Written on stationery of Les soirées de Paris*]*

Paris, 14 September 1916
5 bis R. Schoelcher
Paris 14 e

My friend Marius,

Yesterday your brother came to see me[9] so that we could talk, on your behalf, about the paintings that you still have in your possession and which I loaned to you. You already know what the prices are that I gave you, but nevertheless I will copy the list for you.

Small paintings.

no. 5	*still life—francs*			*500*
no. 6	"	"	"	*500*
no. 7	"	"	"	*500*
no. 8	"	"	"	*500*
no. 9	"	"	"	*500*

Drawings

no. 1	*———————francs*	*300*
no. 2	*———————"*	*200*
no. 3	*———————"*	*200*
no. 4	*———————"*	*500*
no. 5	*———————*	*300*
no. 6	*———————"*	*500*

so that the paintings amount to 2500 francs and the drawings to 2000, the sum being 4500. You tell me that I ought to give you a reduction of some of the prices, and that perhaps that way you could keep them yourself. I will make this [reduction] and if you are agreeable, please tell me by return mail, since I would like to settle this business as soon as possible. If you want, I will give you the lot for the price of 3700 francs which you would then send me right away. If this is not suitable for you, I would like you to send them (the paintings) to me because it is better that I have them here.

I sold the portrait here that I had in America, of a woman in front of a chimney seated in an armchair with a feather boa, and for the price that I was asking.[10]

A hearty handshake from your friend who loves you,

Picasso

If we carry out this deal and if you send me a check, make it out to my full name like this: Pablo Ruiz Picasso[11]

143 Marius de Zayas, *Portrait of Picasso,* ca. 1919–1921. Pencil on paper, 11 × 8 1/2 in.

A few days after the Picasso exhibition opened at the Modern Gallery, de Zayas wrote a letter in Spanish to the artist, telling him about the exhibition and, in particular, about an offer he had received for one of the paintings in the show.[12]

[written on stationery of The Modern Gallery]

December 16, 1915

My dear friend,

Under separate cover I am sending you the invitations to the show of your paintings, which began in this gallery last Monday.

I am sorry to tell you that because of a mistake on the shipper's part, the five small paintings did not arrive together with the larger ones and won't be in this city until next week.

In the four days of your show, we have had an offer for the purchase of painting no. 1, "Portrait d'Homme."[13] The price that we have had to assign to this painting seems a bit high, since to the six thousand Francs which you are asking, we have had to add expenses and our commission. Nevertheless, I think surely something will be done and at the end of the show we will be able to give you a satisfactory account of it. Your paintings of the period of the "Portrait d'Homme" I think are the ones that can be sold most easily here. On selling this one, I would be grateful if you would be kind enough to send us another of the same period or tell us the price that you could offer the "Modern Gallery" in case the painting were to be bought at retail.

The intelligent public here is pleased to see that the rumor that you have abandoned your art completely to return to totally objective [representational] painting is false.

I would also be grateful if you could kindly tell me whether you would be willing to do a drawing especially for "291." In this case, please tell me also when we would be able to expect it.

From all appearances, so far we expect to do well with the show, so that we will be able to do business with you in a more solid manner. It is important to take into account that the only way to be able to do something serious is by having some time. Therefore, I would be grateful, if it is convenient, if you would leave your paintings that you can with us for the entire winter season. The gallery cannot buy paintings at prices excessively reduced and that is perhaps not best for you. But in the case that you prefer to sell at retail, with some concessions on the painting discussed [Portrait d'Homme], please get in touch with my brother, Jorge de Zayas, 1 rue Jacques Offenbach, giving him the prices and letting him know which paintings he can photograph, of those you are willing to let us have.

"291" will reproduce "Dans un Jardin" on the first page.[14] The reproduction has come out very well and I hope that you will be pleased this time.

With my greetings to Rivera, I remain your affectionate friend
M. de Zayas

Before abandoning the art of caricature altogether, de Zayas made one last *Portrait of Picasso* (figure 143), a drawing made on the verso of stationery for the De Zayas Gallery. Here the artist is rendered in a more traditional style of caricature, an image that seems to have been based on a photograph of Picasso in his studio taken a few years earlier by George de Zayas (figure 144). Only the upper portion of Picasso's features are visible, for he is de-

144 *Picasso,* ca. 1914. Photograph by George de Zayas.

picted peering at the viewer from behind a square opening, meant to represent either a window or—more provocatively—a canvas. The artist's famous black eyes are timelessly locked with those of the viewer, while the rest of his body is strategically masked from sight, as if to suggest that Picasso's eyes are the vehicle to his artistic genius, which, in turn, is made visible to us—as viewers—through the canvases he produces.

On a trip to Paris during the spring of 1919, de Zayas again contacted Picasso, this time with the idea of writing a book about him and his work. "I am very interested in seeing you," he wrote in a note, "first to settle pending accounts, and secondly, to discuss a book project about your work in painting, showing the evolution of your career until the present."[15] It is not known whether de Zayas ever managed to settle his accounts with Picasso, but for one reason or another, the book he proposed never materialized.

After de Zayas closed his gallery in 1921 and relocated to Europe, he resumed his friendship with Picasso and likely engaged in new discussions with the artist in his Paris studio. In 1923 Forbes Watson, editor of *The Arts,* wrote de Zayas and asked if he could secure articles about well-known Parisian artists written by other artists. He was especially interested in "any article that Matisse or Picasso would want [to write]," and he specifically asked "if you could get Derain or Braque or Matisse to write about Picasso." De Zayas liked Watson's idea, but he did not think it would be easy to realize. "Those fellows [the artists] do not like to express opinions," he confided in a letter to Sheeler, "nor ever mention others in the business." Nevertheless, he was willing to try. "I will be satisfied if I can make them write about themselves," he told Sheeler.[16] Apparently, de Zayas tried and succeeded, for two months later *The Arts* published a long and informative statement by Picasso (although because the magazine failed to credit its source, it is still unknown whether de Zayas conducted the interview from which the statement was derived).[17]

De Zayas continued to include Picasso's work in every group show he organized, including all the "Tri-National" and "Multi-National" exhibitions that toured through various European capitals during the 1920s. As with many artists disposed toward modernism, his brief encounter with Picasso and an exposure to his work changed his life. In the 1940s—just about the time when he was working on "How, When, and Why Modern Art Came to New York"—he composed three short handwritten texts on Cézanne, Matisse, and Picasso. The Picasso text, which has not been previously published, demonstrates the degree to which de Zayas believed that Cubism was a success, for as he saw it, its influence stretched far beyond the realm of the visual arts.

Picasso

The "cubistic" painting of Picasso and Braque was not of spontaneous generation. The non-representative forms in their pictures was arrived at by successive steps and by a methodic process of transformation. In the work of these two artists prior to their cubistic period, they recapitulated all the steps done by others from the realist representation to the forms that have a meaning all their own and are not images of any preexistent object. The evolution of cubism is very well defined and all its precedents can be accounted for. That is why Picasso affirms with the assurance of experience that form in art is only a means of expression and whether it is identical to the visual images of the outer world or that it might be totally different, it is none the less a form and it is none the less expressive. In all forms there is a plastic principle which is the base of its expression and that is its geometrical elements. When in a work of art those geometrical elements are in perfect equilibrium, in a logic and precise correlation, it is of little importance, from the point of view of pure plastics, that those forms expressed by its geometrical elements, should take the shape of a virgin, or a tree, of an apple—or that they should constitute an entirely new form. The plastic expression of the work remains the same. If one eliminates from the form in a work of art all element of representation of the visual image of things, one arrives, when one can do it, to the Socratic idea of pure beauty. When he says that "by the beauty of figures I do not have in mind those figures that most people can imagine, for example, beautiful bodies or beautiful paintings; I speak of that which is straight and round and of works of that kind, planes and solids and works done in the round and by the square, if you can understand my thought. For I withheld that those figures are not as the others beautiful by comparison, but that they are always beautiful for themselves and by their own nature."

When cubism attained its most "non representative" forms it became an art of pure creation and invention—offering the artist a new field of freedom for all sorts of new conceptions of form. The followers of cubism turned it into a purely mental art and it is yet to be determined whether or not the many tendencies drawn out of cubism have produced works worthy of being called works of art, the fact remains that cubism, such as it is understood and practiced by Picasso and Braque, has had a great influence in the other branches of art including literature, music, sculpture, architecture, and subsequently interior decoration and furniture.

The influence of cubism on the other arts produced a great fecundity of invention in all sorts of directions. With the freedom to chose one's own subject, the freedom to express in any chosen way what the artist wanted to say, the mind of both the artist and the public has undergone a strenuous exercise in which the optic sense has been developed to see and understand the plastic value of practically everything that surrounds us. The poster and the advertisement of today is manifestly influenced by cubism, and there is scarcely any branch of the graphic and plastic arts in its varied manifestations from the purely artistic to the purely commercial and even the utilitarian objects that have not been to a greater or lesser degree influenced by cubism, that art which was met in its beginnings with the greatest demonstration of horror and protest.

De Zayas held Picasso and his work in high regard throughout his life, at a time when many critics still failed to recognize the artist's talent and importance. It was for this reason that in 1947, when Leo Stein—the former collector who had known Picasso personally but who, many years earlier, had rejected modern art—published a book that contained a bitter attack on Picasso's intellect,[18] de Zayas felt compelled to respond.

Leo Stein is indeed a very amateurish amateur, the kind that only see themselves when they look at a work of art, and all depends on the mood they see at the moment. See what he says about Picasso in "Appreciation": a powerful imagination if you will, but intellect never, and "with Picasso as a man, and an artist, well and good, but with Picasso as a thinker there is nothing doing." Leo thinks that to be a thinker one must think in terms of words, and from that point of view he is right. Picasso does not think in words, he thinks in plastic terms, he is a very poor theoretician. Picasso is certainly intellectual when he paints, and it is possible that he is emotional when he thinks. He has intellectualized all forms of art from the art of the cave man to that of the African negro, as if saying in each one of his pictures inspired by the others: "See, this is what they really mean," but he says it in plastic terms, in his own language, not in words.

When de Zayas wrote these words, he was sixty-seven years old. Although he had stated at the close of "How, When and Why Modern Art Came to New York" that "the war was over," he still considered it his personal responsibility to defend Picasso and all expressions of modern art, for until the end of his life, he remained one of its most dedicated propagandists.

NOTES

INTRODUCTION

[1]"Cubism," *Arts and Decoration* (April 1916), p. 284.

[2]The most complete study of de Zayas's art and life is the exhibition catalogue by Douglas Hyland, *Marius de Zayas: Conjurer of Souls,* Spencer Museum of Art, Lawrence, Kansas, September 27, 1981. Before this publication, two master's theses were the only monographic studies on de Zayas: Eva Epp Raun, "Marius de Zayas: The New York Years," University of Delaware, May 1973; and Leslie Cohen, "Marius de Zayas and the Modern Movement in New York," Queens College of the City University of New York; October 1973. De Zayas's contribution to American art is also discussed in William Innes Homer, *Alfred Stieglitz and the American Avant Garde* (Boston: New York Graphic Society, 1977), pp. 52–56, 190–196. For additional references to studies devoted to de Zayas's caricatures see notes 6 and 12.

[3]Biographical details regarding de Zayas's activities before and after his years in New York were obtained through interviews with Mrs. Virginia Harrison–de Zayas and Rodrigo de Zayas, Seville, Spain, February 1979.

[4]De Zayas described his first meeting with Stieglitz to Dorothy Norman, who published it in her book *Alfred Stieglitz: An American Seer* (New York: Aperture, 1973), p. 107.

[5]"Caricature and New York," *Camera Work* (April 1909), pp. 17–18.

[6]Anonymous review, "Why Cartoonist De Zayas Is Drawing Crowded Houses," source unknown (this and numerous other reviews of this exhibition are preserved in the De Zayas Archives, Seville). See also Acton Davies, "News of the Theatres," *Evening Sun,* May 5, 1910; "Society in Distortion," *New York Daily Tribune,* April 27, 1910; "De Zayas Applies Parisian Novelty to Fifth Avenue," *Evening World,* April 27, 1910; "'Boulevardiers' of New York Shown in Caricature," *New York Times,* May 1, 1910; "Seen in the World of Art, *New York Sun,* May 1, 1910; "Along Fifth Avenue, *New York American,* May 2, 1910; "Up and Down Fifth Avenue," *New York World,* May 22, 1910; Guy Pène du Bois, "Caricatures Are Difficult to Draw, Because They Must Be Devoid of All Malice," *New York American,* August 8, 1910; *Metropolitan Magazine* 32, no. 4 (July 1910). For a discussion of this exhibition and other de Zayas caricatures see Craig R. Bailey, "The Art of Marius de Zayas," *Arts* (September 1978), pp. 136–144.

[7] For the complete text of this and all extant letters in the de Zayas–Stieglitz exchange see appendix B.

[8] "The New Art in Paris," *Camera Work* (April–July 1911), pp. 29–34.

[9] For more on de Zayas's relationship with Picasso see appendix C. William I. Homer traced the interchange of avant-garde activities between Paris and New York—stressing de Zayas's crucial role—in a paper entitled "Picasso, Stieglitz, and the 291 Circle: New Light on the Paris-New York Axis," which was presented at the 1978 annual meeting of the College Art Association. Professor Homer is currently preparing this paper for publication.

[10] Letter dated April 21, 1911 (see appendix B).

[11] It would be easy to condemn this book today for the racist theories it contains, but in an attempt to explain the reasons why African art exhibited certain primitive characteristics, de Zayas only repeated theories that were widely accepted in the scientific community of his day.

[12] The most detailed analysis of these caricatures is presented in an article by Willard Bohn entitled "The Abstract Vision of Marius de Zayas," *Art Bulletin* 62, no. 3 (September 1980), pp. 434–452.

[13] Letter from de Zayas to Stieglitz, January 25, 1911 (see appendix B).

[14] Homer, *Alfred Stieglitz,* p. 55.

[15] Letter dated June 30 and July 1, 1914 (see appendix B). On the theories of Simultanism in Paris during this period see Virginia Spate, *Orphism: The Evolution of Non-Figurative Painting in Paris, 1910–1914* (New York: Oxford, 1979), pp. 19–22.

[16] For a detailed analysis of this work see Willard Bohn, "Marius de Zayas and Visual Poetry: 'Mental Reactions,'" *Arts* 55, no. 10 (June 1981), pp. 114–117.

[17] See Francis M. Naumann, "The New York Dada Movement: Better Late Than Never," *Arts* 54, no. 6 (February 1980), p. 143. Figure 3 in this article is a reproduction of a photograph of Torres Palomar holding a group of mailing tubes for *291*. See also Francis M. Naumann, *New York Dada: 1915–1923* (New York: Harry N. Abrams, 1994), pp. 192–194.

[18] Although Wolff's collection of verse was later published in book form (*Songs of Rebellion, Songs of Life, Songs of Love* [New York: Albert and Charles Boni, 1914]), what he inscribed for de Zayas was a copy of *The Glebe,* Ridgefield (September 1913), where these poems first appeared. The inscription is not dated, but it was probably made in 1916, during the time when Wolff's sculpture was on display in a group exhibition at the Modern Gallery (see appendix A).

[19] Robert Motherwell, ed., *The Dada Painters and Poets: An Anthology* (New York: Wittenborn, 1951), bibliography no. 185b, p. 351.

[20] In a letter dated only "May 20" (which, on the basis of internal evidence, can be dated to 1933), Barr told de Zayas that he was "sure you have some interesting memories of 'pioneer' days in New York with Picabia, Stieglitz and the others." In a letter written three years later (on Museum of Modern Art stationery and dated

June 10, 1936), Barr told de Zayas, "I look forward to seeing the truth about the 'Origins of Modern Art in New York'—so help you God." Apparently, by the mid-1940s de Zayas had still not begun his account, for in a draft preserved in the De Zayas Archives in Seville, de Zayas wrote, "I have been asked by the editor of this magazine to write my impressions about Modern Art in New York after an absence of twenty years." Later, in this same manuscript, he notes that the year is 1947.

[21] I should like to thank Mrs. Virginia Harrison–de Zayas and her son, Rodrigo de Zayas, for having granted me generous access to archival material preserved in their home in Seville, Spain, and for having allowed the publication of this manuscript. My gratitude is also extended to Anne d'Harnoncourt and the late John Rewald, both of whom helped me to identify the location of many artworks reproduced in this book.

HOW, WHEN, AND WHY MODERN ART CAME TO NEW YORK

[1] The first Matisse exhibition was held at "291" from April 6 through March 11, 1908, and consisted of drawings, lithographs, watercolors, etchings, and one painting. Several reviews of this exhibition were reprinted in *Camera Work,* no. 23 (July 1908), pp. 10–12.

[2] For a full account of this exhibition and the reception of Cézanne in America see John Rewald, *Cézanne and America: Dealers, Collectors, Artists and Critics* (Princeton: Princeton University Press, 1989).

[3] De Zayas's article was published in *Camera Work* (April–July 1911), pp. 65–67, and an offprint of the essay served as a catalogue for the exhibition (see appendix C).

[4] For the full text of this article see appendix C.

[5] The list of paintings—as derived from the catalogue—is provided in appendix A.

[6] Albert C. Barnes, "Cubism: Requiescat in Pace," *Arts and Decoration* (January 1916), pp. 121–124.

[7] So far as we know, Picabia returned to New York in the spring of 1915.

[8] This primitive artifact—a "Soul Catcher" made by the natives of Danger Island—was identified in the collection of the British Museum, London, and published by Willard Bohn, "The Abstract Vision of Marius de Zayas," *Art Bulletin* 62, no. 3 (September 1980), fig. 4, p. 436.

[9] For a reproduction of this photograph see Edward Steichen, *A Life in Photography* (New York: Doubleday, 1963), fig. 31.

[10] Stieglitz dedicated this inscription to de Zayas, but in composing this account, de Zayas intentionally omitted his name.

[1] *The Evolution of French Art: From Ingres and Delacroix to the Latest Modern Manifestations,* exh. cat., Arden Gallery, New York, April 29–May 24, 1919.

[2] Letter dated December 17, 1919; the complete file of de Zayas–Vignier correspondence is preserved in the De Zayas Archives, Seville, Spain.

[3] A nine-page affidavit from the Patterson, Crawford, Miller & Arensberg law firm of Pittsburgh, Pennsylvania—verifying the terms of a financial agreement that had taken place between de Zayas and Arensberg on January 3, 1919—is preserved in the De Zayas Archives, Seville. In a "Statement of Assets & Liabilities" dated January 31, 1921, Arensberg's name is listed under the category of liabilities in the amount of $118,349 (copy on file in the Butler Library, Columbia University, New York).

[4] See the catalogue *Etching, Lithographs, Original Drawings by Zorn, Whistler, Corot, Daumier, Delacroix, Degas and Others: The Collection of Marius de Zayas with Additions,* Anderson Galleries, New York, sale no. 1509, held on May 28, 1920 (a price-marked copy of this catalogue is in the collection of the New York Public Library).

[5] Hamilton Easter Field, *Arts* (October 1921); quoted in Eva Epp Raun, "Marius de Zayas and the Modern Movement in New York," master's thesis, Queens College of the City University of New York, October 1973, p. 47.

[6] De Zayas to Stieglitz, August 3, 1922 (see appendix B).

[7] Sheeler to de Zayas, letters dated October 30, 1922, and November 20, 1922 (De Zayas Archives, Seville).

[8] A price-marked copy of this catalogue is preserved in the library of the Metropolitan Museum of Art, New York; see *Paintings, Etchings, Drawings, Sculpture: The Collection of Marius de Zayas of New York City,* Anderson Galleries, sale no. 1725, held on March 23 and 24, 1923. I am grateful to Susan Alyson Stein for having provided me with a photocopy of this catalogue.

[9] More on de Zayas's involvement with the Whitney Studio Club can be found in Avis Berman, *Rebels on Eighth Street: Juliana Force and the Whitney Museum of American Art* (New York: Atheneum, 1990), pp. 191, 198–200.

[10] Both the "Tri-National" and "Multi-National" exhibitions were accompanied by catalogues, copies of which are preserved in the De Zayas Archives, Seville. The De Zayas Archives also contains a scrapbook of press clippings for these exhibitions, which were favorably received in most of the countries where they were shown.

[1] The information contained in this appendix was compiled by Marie T. Keller, whose assistance I gratefully acknowledge.

[2] According to a review appearing in the *New York Globe* (January 11, 1916), the "Negro Sculpture Exhibition" was still on view during the "Picabia Exhibition."

[3] The catalogue included illustrations of *Le bouquet de fleurs* (see figure 16 above) and *Le château noir* (see figure 14).

[4] The catalogue contained illustrations of *Carved Wood*, which is known today by the title *Prodigal Son* (see figure 58) and *Portrait of Mme. P. D. K.*, known today as *Princess X* (see figure 54). The last page of the catalogue listed the following names, indicating that works by these artists could be found at the Modern Gallery: Daumier / Cézanne / Lautrec / Van Gogh / Picasso / Brancusi / Picabia / Derain / Marie Lorencin [*sic*] / Manolo / Burty / Vlaminck / Rivera / Braque / and Mexican Pre-Conquest Art / African Negro Sculpture.

[5] On the last page of the catalogue, de Zayas again listed the artists whose works could be found at the Modern Gallery, except that he here corrected the spelling of Marie Laurencin (see the previous note).

[6] On the last page of the catalogue, de Zayas again provided a list of the artists whose work could be found at the gallery (see notes 4 and 5), adding the name Constantin Guys.

[7] According to a review that appeared in *Arts and Decoration* (December 1916), several sculptures by Brancusi were also on view during the time of the Perdriat exhibition.

[8] During this exhibition, examples of African sculpture were also available for view; see "Weird Art from Darkest Africa," *World Magazine,* February 4, 1917.

[9] The cover of the catalogue is illustrated with *Le bel attelage* (see figure 111).

[10] De Zayas mistakenly dated this clipping "Oct. 15, 1917."

[11] De Zayas mistakenly dated this review "Jan. 20–1919."

[1] *Salon d'Automne,* 8me Exposition, Grand Palais, Paris, October 1–November 8, 1910. See Donald E. Gordon, ed., *Modern Art Exhibitions, 1900–1916* (Munich: Prestel, 1974), vol. 2, pp. 426–29.

[2] *Salon d'Automne,* cat. no. 849. The present location of this nude is unknown, but it was discussed in Roger Allard, "Au Salon d'Automne de Paris," *L'art libre* (November 1910), p. 442 (for a reproduction, see Joann Moser, *Jean Metzinger in Retrospect,* exh. cat., University of Iowa Museum of Art, Iowa City, August 31–October 13, 1985, fig. 23, p. 49).

[3] The "real article" is, of course, Picasso (on de Zayas's relationship with Picasso, see appendix C). Paul Burty Haviland (1880–1950) was the son of Charles Haviland and Madeleine Burty. His father was owner of the Haviland china manufacturing company in Limoges, France. The young Haviland met Stieglitz around 1907 and became an important participant in the activities of "291," acting as the gallery's secretary and contributing articles to *Camera Work*. His brother, Frank Burty Haviland (1886–1971), was a painter who lived in Paris and helped provide introductions to a number of artists de Zayas and Stieglitz wanted to meet.

[4] Alfred Maurer (1868–1932) was an American painter who had already shown several times at "291" and who would go on to exhibit at the Armory Show (see Elizabeth McCausland, *A. H. Maurer: A Biography of America's First Modern Painter* [New York: A. A. Wyn, 1951]; and Sheldon Reich, *Alfred H. Maurer, 1868–1932,* exh. cat., National Collection of Fine Arts, Smithsonian Institution, February 23–May 13, 1973). In the 1910 Salon d'Automne, he exhibited a landscape and a still life (cat. nos. 843 and 844; see Gordon, *Modern Art Exhibitions,* p. 428).

[5] Edward Steichen (1879–1973) is best known today for the important contribution he made to the art and history of photography, although in this period he was also known as a painter. In 1905, it was his studio at 291 Fifth Avenue in New York that was turned into the Little Gallery of the Photo-Secession. Before the war he traveled frequently to Paris but corresponded often with Stieglitz, drawing his attention to artists whose work he thought should be shown at "291," including Rodin, Matisse, Cézanne, Brancusi, and Picasso. Although he exhibited his work frequently in this period, he is curiously not listed in the catalogue of the 1910 Salon d'Automne (see Gordon, *Modern Art Exhibitions,* p. 429).

[6] Max Weber (1881–1961) was a painter and sculptor who, from 1905 through 1908, had lived in Paris, where he had studied with Matisse, befriended Henri Rousseau, and frequently visited the apartment of Gertrude and Leo Stein. His work was brought to Stieglitz's attention by Steichen. In the spring of 1910, he was shown at "291" in the exhibition of younger American painters. But Weber steadfastly refused to recognize any quality in Steichen's photographic work and vocally condemned it, which eventually led to his rupture from Stieglitz and the entire orbit of artists who frequented "291" (see William Innes Homer, *Alfred Stieglitz and the American Avant-Garde* [Boston: New York Graphic Society, 1977], p. 135).

[7] John Marin (1870–1953) made repeated trips to Europe from 1905 through 1910, residing primarily in Paris, where he became part of the New Society of Younger American Painters, which included D. Putnam Brinley, Arthur B. Carles, Maurer, Steichen, and Weber.

[8] De Zayas is here referring to "The International Exhibition of Pictorial Photography," organized by Stieglitz and the Photo-Secession Gallery for the Buffalo Fine Arts Academy, Albright Art Gallery, Buffalo, New York, November 3–December 1, 1910.

[9] Alvin Langdon Coburn (1882–1966) was born in Boston but lived most of his life in England. He was a founding member of the Photo-Secession, and by 1910 he had already been featured in two exhibitions at "291" (the first from March 11 to April 10, 1907, and the second from January 18 to February 1, 1909).

[10] De Zayas's caricature accompanied an article by William R. Hereford, "Five O'Clock Tea in Paris," *World Magazine,* December 18, 1910.

[11] This last word is written somewhat illegibly; de Zayas might have meant to write the French word *gemme,* meaning "gem" or "precious stone."

[12] J. Nilsen Laurvik (d. New York, 1953) was a Norwegian-born critic who lived in New York and wrote articles on modern art for a number of different magazines, including *Century* and *International Studio.* He is also author of *Is It Art? Post-Impressionism, Futurism, Cubism* (New York: International Press, 1913), copies of which were on sale at the Armory Show.

[13] See appendix C.

[14] Mitchell Kennerley (1878–1950) was publisher of *The Reader* and *The Forum,* the latter of which ran de Zayas's article in its February 1911 issue ("The New Art in Paris," pp. 180–88; this article was later reprinted in *Camera Work* 34–35 [April–July 1911], pp. 29–34). On Kennerley see the biography by Matthew J. Bruccoli, *The Fortunes of Mitchell Kennerley: Bookman* (New York: Harcourt Brace Jovanovich, 1986).

[15] The book de Zayas sent must have been the small book by Julius Meier-Graefe, *Paul Cézanne* (Munich, 1910), the first monograph on the artist.

[16] For the text of this article see appendix C.

[17] The exhibition consisted of eighty-three drawings and watercolors by Pablo Picasso and was held at "291" from March 28 through April 25, 1911. For more on de Zayas and Picasso see appendix C.

[18] Stieglitz made what was to be his last trip to Europe from May through November 1911 (he visited Munich, Stuttgart, Paris, and Lucerne).

[19] John Nilsen Laurvik, "Alfred Stieglitz, Pictorial Photographer," *International Studio* 44 (August 1911), pp. xxi–xxvii.

[20] It was probably at this time that de Zayas made a caricature of Dr. Berg, which was later published in *Camera Work* 46 (dated April 1914; published October 1914), p. [31]. Albert Ashton Berg (1872–1950) was a gastroenterologist and a surgeon at Mount Sinai Hospital (see Douglas Hyland, *Marius de Zayas: Conjurer of Souls,* exh. cat., Spencer Museum of Art, Lawrence, Kansas, September 27–November 8, 1981, p. 100).

[21] De Zayas mistakenly dated this letter "1903," when he clearly meant to write "1913."

[22] Guillaume Apollinaire (1880–1918) was editor of *Les soirées de Paris;* de Zayas's caricature of the poet appeared in the July–August issue of the magazine (p. 378).

23 Daniel-Henry Kahnweiler (1884–1979) was the principal dealer of modern art in Paris, handling the work of Picasso, Braque, Gris, Léger, Derain, Klee, and Masson (see Pierre Assouline, *An Artful Life: A Biography of D. H. Kahnweiler, 1884–1979,* trans. Charles Ruas [New York: Grove Weidenfeld, 1990]). In the original letter, de Zayas spelled the name "Kanweiller."

24 De Zayas is here referring to the painter Abraham Walkowitz (1880–1965), as confirmed in the next letter.

25 Paul Guillaume (1891–1934) was a Parisian dealer of modern and African art, with whom de Zayas would go on to establish an important working relationship (see his account, page 55 above). On Guillaume's activities see the publications of Colette Giraudon, *Paul Guillaume et les peintres du XXe siècle: De l'Art Nègre à l'avant-garde* (Paris: La Bibliothèque des Arts, 1993), and *Les arts à Paris chez Paul Guillaume, 1918–1935,* exh. cat., Musée de l'Orangerie, Paris, September 14, 1993–January 3, 1994.

26 De Zayas is here referring to the Washington Square Gallery, which was founded by Robert Coady and the sculptor Michael Brenner, and which opened in December 1914 (see Judith Zilczer, "Robert J. Coady, Man of *The Soil,*" in *New York Dada,* ed. Rudolf E. Kuenzli, [New York: Willis Locker & Owens, 1986], pp. 31–43).

27 The photograph was by Eduard Steichen and appeared in the issue of *Camera Work* dated April–July 1913 and published November 1913 (vol. 42–43, p. [31]).

28 Ambroise Vollard (1868–1939) gave Cézanne his first solo exhibition in 1895 and remained the painter's dealer until his death in 1906. His book on the artist, *Paul Cézanne, His Life and Art,* appeared in both French and English editions in 1914.

29 Marie Rapp Boursault (Mrs. George K. Boursault) was Stieglitz's secretary at "291."

30 For more on Coady see the references provided in note 26.

31 One of the pictures Stieglitz took at this gathering is preserved in the Papers of John Marin, Archives of American Art, Smithsonian Institution, Washington, D.C. (for a reproduction see Douglas K. S. Hyland, "Agnes Ernst Meyer, Patron of American Modernism," *Archives of American Art Journal* 12, no. 1 [Winter 1980], fig. 1, p. 64).

32 Charles Daniel (1856–1971?) opened his gallery at 2 West 47th Street in December 1913, and, over the years, showed many of the same artists as Stieglitz (see *Charles Daniel and the Daniel Gallery, 1913–1932,* exh. cat., Zabriskie Gallery, New York, December 22, 1993–February 12, 1994).

33 R. Child Bayley (1869–19??) was a British critic and magazine editor. From 1892 through 1898 he served as assistant secretary to the Royal Photographic Society and later became editor of the *Amateur Photographer.* His best-known book was *The Complete Photographer* (London, 1906). He was one of many who paid tribute to Stieglitz in the book edited by Waldo Frank and others, *America and Alfred Stieglitz* (New York: Literary Guild, 1934), pp. 89–104.

[34] This is, of course, the English dramatist and literary critic George Bernard Shaw (1856–1950), and Muir is probably the distinguished Scottish poet Edwin Muir (1887–1959). On Bayley, see note 33.

[35] Roger Fry (1877–1934), the English painter and critic, organized the seminal exhibition of Post-Impressionist painting at the Grafton Gallery in London in 1910 (from which the Armory Show drew its inspiration). See the biography by Frances Spalding, *Roger Fry: Art and Life* (Berkeley: University of California Press, 1980).

[36] See note 9.

[37] John Weichsel (1870–1946) was a tireless promoter and defender of modern art, and he wrote occasional articles for *Camera Work* (see Gail Stavitsky, "John Weichsel and the People's Art Guild," *Archives of American Art Journal* 31, no. 4 (1991), pp. 12–19.

[38] The painting de Zayas describes is probably *I See Again in Memory My Dear Udnie,* 1914 (Museum of Modern Art, New York), and the show he proposed, consisting of only three paintings—entitled "An Exhibition of Recent Paintings—Never Before Exhibited Anywhere—by Francis Picabia"—opened at "291" on January 12, 1915.

[39] The work of Marie Laurencin (1885–1956) was never exhibited at "291" but was shown later by de Zayas at the Modern Gallery (see appendix A).

[40] Marsden Hartley (1877–1943) was given his second solo show at "291" from January 12 through February 14, 1914. Shortly after this exhibition he left for Paris, but by the time this letter was written (summer 1914), he had already moved to Berlin (where he would remain until December 1915).

[41] On June 25, 1914, Agnes Meyer wrote to Stieglitz from the Hôtel Crillon, Paris: "De Zayas took me to Kahnweiler's to see Picasso's latest things and I not only admired but purchased. A sweet little still-life with saw-dust grapes and wallpaper background but a thing that belongs to me, that wanted to come to me as old Kümmel." (Stieglitz Papers, YCAL).

[42] The de Zayas issue did not appear until October 1914 (no. 46, dated April 1914).

[43] This undated text is placed here in sequence, for it follows the request made by Stieglitz in the previous letter.

[44] These caricatures appeared in the July–August 1914 issue of *Les soirées de Paris.*

[45] This special number is the one that contained Picabia's mechanical portraits of his friends in New York (*291,* nos. 5–6 [July–August 1915]). A snapshot taken in this period (Archives of Rodrigo de Zayas, Seville) shows the artist Torres Palomar holding mailing tubes for *291* (reproduced in Francis M. Naumann, "The New

York Dada Movement: Better Late than Never," *Arts* 54, no. 6 [February 1980], fig. 3, p. 144).

46 The issue de Zayas describes is no. 9 (November 1915), which closely approximates the format he outlines in the sketches that accompany this letter (not illustrated here), although the page of notes he planned did not appear in the final printing.

47 The special issue containing a print of *The Steerage* was published as nos. 7–8 (September–October 1915).

48 John Barrett Kerfoot (1865–1927) wrote humorous articles for *Camera Work* and served as its associate editor from 1905 to 1917.

49 Apparently, during this meeting the Meyers disagreed with Stieglitz's idea of how "291" and the Modern Gallery should differ. After the session they fired off a letter to de Zayas, making their opinions clear: "After carefully considering Stieglitz's false version of the separation of 291 and the Modern Gallery, we both decided that the most dignified thing to do is to ignore it altogether. At first Eugene was going to send him a hot letter and then he decided that it would dignify S. too much to send him a letter at all. He always claims that Camera Work is a record. It is more of a record of himself with all his virtues and all his pitiful weaknesses than anything else. And after all who reads Camera Work? The Modern Gallery can stand on its own feet and needs not fear a Stieglitz. . . . My advice to you is: Have nothing more to do with Stieglitz. Never see him, never think of him. That chapter should be closed for all of us. To have known S. is very beneficial, to let him hang on is sure destruction. A[gnes] E[rnst] M[eyer] (undated letter, De Zayas Archives, Seville; a copy of this letter is on file at the Butler Library, Columbia University, New York).

50 The announcement appeared as an insert to issue no. 9 of *291,* but Stieglitz objected that it had been abbreviated from a text he apparently approved; he later published the full text of the original announcement in *Camera Work* (see " '291' and the Modern Gallery," no. 48 [October 1916], pp. 63–64).

51 The text as published in English reads, "Stieglitz comprises the history of photography in the United States. 'Camera Work' bears witness to this." (*291,* nos. 7–8 [September–October 1915].

52 In spite of this apparent misunderstanding, Stieglitz remained on good terms with de Zayas. Approximately two weeks after this letter was received, he provided the following report about de Zayas and his gallery in a letter to Paul Haviland: "De Zayas is well under way with the Modern Gallery and although it is turning out to be something entirely different than he originally intended, it is an interesting experiment. I hope he succeeds. Above all I hope he will get some material benefit out of it. It is high time that he should get some money for his work. I keep dinning this into his ears for I always feel De Zayas is no business man even though he may have gone into business. And by businessman I mean that he protects his own interest as well as the interest of others. Well, we will see." (Stieglitz Papers, YCAL.) In a letter dated November 1, 1916, Stieglitz told Haviland, "De Zayas and I see each other frequently." (Stieglitz Papers, YCAL.)

[53] This article appeared in *291,* nos. 10–11 (December 1915–January 1916).

[54] *La terrace du café* is a painting by Diego Rivera (see figure 108).

[55] Stieglitz showed twenty-five paintings, drawings, and pastels by Severini at his gallery from March 6 through March 17, 1917.

[56] See Gino Severini, "Symbolisme plastique et symbolisme littéraire," *Le mercure de France,* February 1, 1916 (reprinted in *Futurisme: Manifestes, documents, proclamations,* ed. Giovanni Lista [Paris: L'Age d'Homme, 1973], pp. 210–15).

[57] George Of (1876–1954) was a painter and collector who earned his living as a framer.

[58] This letter was published in a special issue of the magazine *MSS* devoted to answering the question, "Can a Photograph Have the Significance of Art?" (no. 4 [December 1922], p. 18).

[59] Jacques Doucet (1854–1929) was a fashionable Parisian clothier who collected modern art and important literary manuscripts. His art collection was dispersed after his death, but his manuscripts are preserved in the Bibliothèque Littéraire Jacques Doucet, Universités de Paris (on Doucet and his collection see François Chapon, *Mystère et splendeurs de Jacques Doucet* [Paris: Jean-Claude Lattès, 1984]).

[60] No catalogue for this exhibition survives, but we do know that the show consisted of at least eight paintings by Rousseau, several of which can be identified (see Avis Berman, *Rebels on Eighth Street: Juliana Force and the Whitney Museum of American Art* [New York: Atheneum, 1990], pp. 199–200).

[61] This show was selected by Charles Sheeler and was held at the Whitney Studio Club in March 1924. It featured works by Picasso, Braque, de Zayas, and Duchamp, as well as African sculpture (see Berman, *Rebels on Eighth Street,* pp. 202–203).

[62] De Zayas likely wrote this poem in response to his first viewing of Stieglitz's cloud photographs, called "Equivalents," which the photographer began in 1923 and continued to produce until 1932 (see Rosalind Krauss, "Equivalents," *Arts* 54, no. 6 [February 1980], pp. 134–137).

APPENDIX C

[1] In his memoirs, Steichen later recalled that "the actual selection of Picasso's contributions for the exhibition in New York was made by the Mexican caricaturist Marius de Zayas and the sculptor Manolo, a compatriot and friend of Picasso's" (Edward Steichen, "Introducing Modern Art to America," chap. 4 in *A Life in Photography* [Garden City: Doubleday, 1963], n.p.). As early as 1912, however, Paul Havi-

land had already reported that it was de Zayas, Frank Haviland, and Steichen who "cooperated with Picasso in choosing the limited number of drawings which could be accommodated in the Little Galleries" ("Photo-Session Notes: Sculptures by Henri Matisse," *Camera Work,* no. 38 [April 1912], p. 36). Paul Haviland provides much the same information in an open letter to Stieglitz, dated January 25, 1913, which was also published in *Camera Work* (no. 41 [January 1913], p. 43).

2 See Marius de Zayas, "Pablo Picasso," *America: Revista mensual illustrada,* New York, vol. 6 (May 1911), pp. 363–365. A copy of the pamphlet is preserved in the De Zayas Archives, Seville, and is reprinted in *Camera Work* 34–35 (April–July 1911), pp. 65–67.

3 These portions of the article were translated by Maria Troncoso, whom I should like to take this opportunity to thank for her generous assistance.

4 The words *new expression* do not actually appear in the Spanish text. The word de Zayas used was *atrevimiento,* which is usually translated as "insolence" or "audacity."

5 See appendix B, letter dated April 4, 1911.

6 See appendix B, letter dated June 11, 1914. On the subject of Picasso and photography see Paul Hayes Tucker, "Picasso, Photography, and the Development of Cubism," *Art Bulletin* 44, no. 2 (June 1982), pp. 288–299 (and a response to this article by Edward F. Fry, "Letters," *Art Bulletin* 45, no. 1 [March 1983], pp. 145–146). See also Anne Baldassari, *Picasso photographe, 1901–1916,* exh. cat., Musée National Picasso, Paris, 1994.

7 Willard Bohn, "The Abstract Vision of Marius de Zayas," *Art Bulletin* 62, no. 3 (September 1980), p. 439.

8 We can assume that there must have been other letters, for another is quoted by de Zayas in an earlier exchange with Stieglitz (see appendix B, letter dated April 24, 1916). For more on Picasso's involvement with the commercialization of his work see Michael C. FitzGerald, *Making Modernism: Picasso and the Creation of the Market for Twentieth-Century Art* (New York: Farrar, Straus and Giroux, 1995).

9 De Zayas's brother was Jorge (or George), who lived in Paris and had established close contacts with many of the artists living there. Like his brother, George de Zayas was an artist who specialized in the making of caricatures. In 1919, eleven of his lithographs depicting the modern artists of Paris accompanied the publication of a book by Curnonsky entitled *Huit peintres, deux sculptures et un musicien très modernes.*

10 The painting Picasso refers to can be securely identified as *Portrait of a Girl* (see figure 40), which was acquired by Eugenia Errazuriz, a Chilean from a wealthy family, who purchased a number of important Cubist pictures directly from Picasso (for more on this remarkable woman see John Richardson, "Tastemakers: Eugenia Errazuriz," *House & Garden* [April 1987], pp. 76–84). Mr. Richardson identified this painting for me and kindly provided me with a copy of his article.

[11] This translation was prepared by Maria Troncoso. It should be noted that although Picasso refers to de Zayas as his "amigo," throughout the letter he addresses de Zayas with formal pronouns.

[12] This letter—and four others from de Zayas to Picasso—are preserved in the Archives, Musée Picasso, Paris. I am grateful to Colette Giraudon for having provided me with access to these documents, and to Cristina Sanmartin, who prepared translations of the letters for me.

[13] This "Portrait d'Homme" is likely Picasso's *Head of a Man*, ca. 1910 (see fig. 34), which, apparently, Stieglitz had expressed an interest in purchasing (see appendix B; letters dated April 24, 1916, and April 25, 1916). Eventually, the painting was purchased from the Modern Gallery by John Quinn (see Judith Zilczer, *"The Noble Buyer": John Quinn, Patron of the Avant-Garde*, exh. cat., Hirshhorn Museum and Sculpture Garden, Smithsonian Institution, Washington, D.C., 1978, p. 177).

[14] The only work by Picasso to be reproduced on the cover of *291* is the still life *Glass, Pipe, Dice and Playing Card*, 1914 (see fig. 41), which appeared on the first page of the December 1915–January 1916 issue (nos. 10–11).

[15] De Zayas to Picasso, letter dated only "Sabado," but postmarked March 3, 1919 (Picasso Archives, Musée Picasso, Paris). I am grateful to Thomas Girst for confirming the date of this postmark on a visit to the Picasso Museum, and to Cristina Sanmartin for providing a translation of this letter.

[16] Forbes Watson's letter to de Zayas is undated, but de Zayas's letter to Sheeler is dated February 15, 1923 (both in the De Zayas Archives, Seville).

[17] The article by Picasso was entitled "Picasso Speaks: A Statement by the Artist" and appeared in the May 1923 issue of *The Arts* (7, no. 5, pp. 315–329). An editorial note preceding the article states that "Picasso gave his interview to *The Arts* in Spanish, and subsequently authenticated the Spanish text which we herewith translate." De Zayas's name is not mentioned anywhere in the article, although, as was later reported by Alfred H. Barr, Jr. (see *Picasso: Fifty Years of his Art,* exh. cat., Museum of Modern Art, New York, 1946, bibliography, item no. 1, p. 286), in 1939 Forbes Watson identified de Zayas as the person who conducted the interview. In spite of this information, because of the article's similarity to an interview later published by the French writer Florent Fels, William S. Rubin has suggested that it was probably Fels rather than de Zayas who conducted the original interview (Rubin, "Picasso," in *"Primitivism" in 20th Century Art,* ed. William S. Rubin, exh. cat., Museum of Modern Art, New York, 1984, pp. 260, 366, nn. 63 and 64).

[18] Leo Stein, *Appreciation: Painting, Poetry & Prose* (New York: Crown, 1947); the portion of Stein's text that de Zayas quotes is from p. 182.

LIST OF ILLUSTRATIONS

If the location of a work is not provided, it can be assumed that its present where-abouts are unknown.

INTRODUCTION

RODIN

Exhibited at the Photo-Secession, 1908

Exhibited at the Photo-Secession, 1910

MATISSE

Exhibited at the Photo-Secession, 1910

Exhibited at the Photo-Secession, 1912

CEZANNE

Exhibited at the Modern Gallery, 1916

ROUSSEAU

Exhibited at the Photo-Secession, 1910 (all works formerly Collection Max Weber)

MANOLO

Exhibited at the Photo-Secession, 1911

Exhibited at the Modern Gallery, 1916

PICASSO

Exhibited at the Photo-Secession, 1911, and at the Armory Show, 1913

Exhibited at the Photo-Secession, 1914–1915

Exhibited at the Photo-Secession, 1915, and at the Modern Gallery, 1916

30 Pablo Picasso, *Violin and Guitar,* 1913. Philadelphia Museum of Art, Walter and Louise Arensberg Collection. Page 25.

Exhibited at the Modern Gallery, 1915–1916

31 Pablo Picasso, *Les pauvres,* 1905. Etching. Page 25.

32 Pablo Picasso, *Man Rowing,* 1910. Museum of Fine Arts, Houston, Texas. Page 25.

33 Pablo Picasso, *Two Women.* Page 25.

34 Pablo Picasso, *Head of a Man,* c. 1910. Private collection, London. Page 29.

35 Pablo Picasso, *Female Nude,* 1910. Philadelphia Museum of Art, Walter and Louise Arensberg Collection. Page 30.

36 Pablo Picasso, *Woman Seated in an Armchair,* 1910. Musée National d'Art Moderne, Paris. Page 30.

37 Pablo Picasso, *Man in a Bowler Hat, Seated in an Armchair,* 1915. Art Institute of Chicago. Page 30.

38 Pablo Picasso, *Guitar Player,* 1916. Moderna Museet, Stockholm. Page 30.

39 Pablo Picasso, *Bar-Table with Musical Instruments and Fruit Bowl,* 1913. Page 32.

40 Pablo Picasso, *Portrait of a Girl,* 1914. Musée National d'Art Moderne, Paris. Page 36.

41 Pablo Picasso, *Glass, Pipe, Dice and Playing Card,* 1914. Picasso estate. Page 36.

42 Pablo Picasso, *Studies of Apples.* Page 36.

43 *Picasso,* c. 1914. Photograph by George de Zayas. Page 38.

BRAQUE

Exhibited at the Photo-Secession, 1914–1915

44 Georges Braque, *Still Life (Violin),* 1913. Philadelphia Museum of Art, Walter and Louise Arensberg Collection. Page 40.

Exhibited at the Modern Gallery, 1916

45 Georges Braque, *Still Life,* 1913. Private collection. Page 40.

46 Georges Braque, *Musical Forms,* 1913. Philadelphia Museum of Art, Walter and Louise Arensberg Collection. Page 40.

291—THE MAGAZINE

STIEGLITZ

MARIN

THE MODERN GALLERY

VAN GOGH AT THE MODERN GALLERY
Exhibited at the Modern Gallery, 1915

MODERN SCULPTURE AT THE MODERN GALLERY
Exhibited at the Modern Gallery, 1916

DIEGO RIVERA AT THE MODERN GALLERY

Exhibited at the Modern Gallery, 1916

107 Diego Rivera, *Portrait of Mariewone (Madame Marcoussis)*, c. 1915. Art Institute of Chicago. Page 103.

108 Diego Rivera, *La terrace du café*. Metropolitan Museum of Art, New York, Alfred Stieglitz Collection. Page 103.

109 *Diego Rivera,* 1915. Photograph. Page 107.

DAUMIER, GUYS, AND TOULOUSE-LAUTREC AT THE MODERN GALLERY

110 Honoré Daumier (?), *Third Class Carriage*. Page 108.

111 Constantin Guys, *Le bel attelage*. Page 108.

112 Henri de Toulouse-Lautrec, *Aristide Bruant*. Lithograph. Page 111.

113 Henri de Toulouse-Lautrec, *The Red Divan*. Museu de Arte Moderna, São Paulo. Page 111.

ANDRE DERAIN AT THE MODERN GALLERY

Exhibited at the Modern Gallery, 1917

114 André Derain, *Alice in a Green Dress,* 1907. Museum of Modern Art, New York. Page 117.

115 André Derain, *Woman,* c. 1914. Philadelphia Museum of Art, Walter and Louise Arensberg Collection. Page 117.

116 André Derain, *Head of a Woman*. Page 117.

117 André Derain, *Head of a Woman with Shawl*. Page 117.

118 André Derain, *Italian Woman,* 1913. Museum of Modern Art, New York, gift of Dr. Alfred Gold. Page 118.

119 André Derain, *Still Life*. Page 118.

120 André Derain, *Still Life*. Page 118.

121 André Derain, *Woman*. Page 118.

122 André Derain, *Still Life [after Cézanne]*. Private collection, New York. Page 121.

123 André Derain, *Head of a Woman*. Page 121.

Exhibited at the Modern Gallery, 1918

124 Maurice Vlaminck, *Flowers*. Page 123.

125 Maurice Vlaminck, *The Port*. Page 123.

126 Maurice Vlaminck, *Still Life*. Page 123.

127 *At the Terrace of the Café du Dome,* Paris, ca. 1908. Photograph: Lucien Lefebvre with a group of American artists. Page 127.

AFTERWORD

APPENDIX A

No illustrations

APPENDIX B

No illustrations

APPENDIX C (PICASSO AND DE ZAYAS)

139–141   Marius de Zayas, "Pablo Picasso," from the magazine *América: Revista mensual illustrada* (May 1911), pp. 363–365. Pages 217–219.

142   Marius de Zayas, *Portrait of Picasso,* 1915, charcoal. Original drawing lost; reproduced in *291,* nos. 10–11 (December 1915–January 1916). Page 222.

143   Marius de Zayas, *Portrait of Picasso,* ca. 1919–1921. Pencil on paper, 11 × 8 1/2 in. Collection Rodrigo de Zayas, Seville. Page 225.

144   *Picasso,* ca. 1914. Photograph by George de Zayas. De Zayas Archives, Seville. Page 227.

INDEX OF NAMES

Cézanne, Paul, 11–17, 39, 44, 68, 70, 102, 105, 106, 120, 137–138, 161, 171, 175, 182, 191, 192
exhibitions, 11–17, 20, 44, 87, 96, 122, 124, 125, 126, 137–138, 140, 141, 154, 155, 182, 192
Chamberlain, J. Edgar, 20, 46, 61
Chase, William Merritt, x
Coady, Robert, 174
Coburn, Alvin Langdon, xiii, 159, 176–177, 178
Cortissoz, Royal, 6, 10–11, 41
Courbet, Gustave, 154
Covert, John, 131, 155
Crowninshield, Frank, 44

Daniel, Charles, 175
Daniel, Mell, 149
Daumier, Honoré, 37, 49, 106–113, 122, 124, 147
Davies, Arthur B., 41, 44, 94, 131, 154, 155, 181 (?)
De Casseres, Benjamin, vii, x
De Zayas, George, 181, 202, 226, 227
De Zayas, Marius. *See also* Modern Gallery
biography, vii, 131–133
caricatures, vii–x, xii, xvi, 75, 78, 79, 80, 88, 170, 171, 176, 184, 210, 212, 214–215, 221–223, 225, 226
De Zayas Gallery, 131–132
mentioned in reviews, 16, 49, 59, 62, 63, 64, 66, 68, 73, 98, 109, 122, 125
writings, xi, xiii–xiv, 23, 28–34, 57–59, 63–67, 85–87, 110, 115–116, 162, 183, 211, 212–221, 223, 228–229
De Zayas, Rafael, vii, 165, 166, 167, 212
de Meyer (artist), 176
Defries, Amelia Dorothy, 200
Degas, Edgar, 67, 112, 154, 155
DeKay, Charles, 2
Derain, André, 31, 57, 115, 116–120, 121, 122, 124, 125–126, 141, 143, 150–151, 152, 153, 205, 206, 226
Desseignes, Ribemont, 139
Dodge, Mabel, 182
Doucet, Jacques, 208
Dougherty, P., 127
Dove, Arthur, 93
Du Bois, Guy Pène, 8, 28, 62, 82
Duchamp, Marcel, 51, 113, 209

Eddy, Frederick W., 64, 106, 125

Fénéon, Félix, 13
Ferat, Serge, 152
Field, Hamilton Easter, 132
Flagg, James Montgomery, x
Foinet, Lucien Lefebvre, 126, 127, 179, 186
Friseke, F., 127
Frueh, Alfred J., 80
Fry, Roger, xiii, 10, 120, 176

Gauguin, Paul, 95, 155
Glackens, William, 7
Glason (American artist in Paris), 127
Gleizes, Albert, 113
Goya, Francisco de, 112, 163
Gris, Juan, 152
Guillaume, Paul, 56, 106, 120, 170, 171, 172, 174, 179, 186, 189, 191
Guys, Constantin, 37, 106–113, 124, 147, 149–150
Gwozdecki, Gustave de, 153

Hapgood, Hutchins, 42
Hare, Meredith, 44
Harriman, Mrs. E. H., 132
Harrington (art critic), 7
Hartley, Marsden, 181, 194
Haviland, Frank. *See* Burty (Haviland), Frank.
Haviland, Paul B., xi, 73, 80, 157, 162, 163, 164, 165, 169, 172, 174, 177, 182, 184, 186, 190, 191, 192, 196, 197
Hayashi, Tadasu (?), 109
Henri, Robert, 7, 16
Hessel (art dealer), 106
Hoeber, Arthur, 6, 10, 11
Homer, William, xi
Huneker, James, 8, 10, 20, 84

Ingres, Jean-Auguste-Dominique, 21, 31, 42

Jacob, Max, 56, 73, 75, 201, 203, 206
Johnson, Morton, 127

Kahnweiler, Daniel-Henry, 170, 171, 172, 174

Kandinsky, Wassily, 176

Karpel, Bernard, xiv

Kerfoot, John Barrett, 73, 75, 193, 194, 195, 197, 198, 199

Komroff, Manuel, 53

Kuhn, Walt, 16, 41, 42, 44, 131, 155

Laboureur, Jean-Emile, 148

Laurencin, Marie, xiii, 115–116, 124, 148, 153, 171, 174, 179, 181

Laurvik, John Nilsen, x, 2, 161, 164, 166, 167

Lawson, Ernest, x

Lawyer, Phil, 127

Lefebvre, Lucien. *See* Foinet, Lucien Lefebvre

Limantour, José Yves, 161

Luks, George Benjamin, 7

Man Ray, 82, 208

Manet, Edouard, 17, 20, 109, 154

Manolo (Manuel Martínez Hugue), 21, 22, 122, 124, 125, 141

Marin, John, 8, 72, 73, 80, 82–83, 87–90, 93, 158, 159, 173, 174, 175

Matisse, Henri, 2, 4–5, 7–10, 33, 44, 59, 62, 66, 70, 71, 154, 157, 164, 171, 174, 226

Maurer, Alfred, 8, 87, 157

McBride, Henry, 44, 49, 62, 82, 89, 106–112, 116, 119, 125–126, 128

McCormick, W. B., 6, 46

McPherson (American artist in Paris), 127

Metzinger, Jean, x, 157

Meyer, Agnes Ernst, 73, 75, 174, 175, 182, 184, 186, 187–199, 201

Meyer, Eugene, Jr., 94, 174, 175, 182, 195, 196, 198, 199

Millet, François, 109

Modern Gallery, xiii, 90–96, 126–128, 187–199

Modigliani, Amedeo, 99–102, 140

Montross Galleries, 126, 181

Morgan, J. P., 81

Muir, Edwin (?), 176, 178, 185

Of, George, 205, 206

Pach, Walter, 203–204

Pascin, Jules, 115

Perdriat, Hélène, 146, 152